ARCHITECTS' DRAWINGS

A Selection of Sketches by
World Famous Architects
Through History

KENDRA SCHANK SMITH

ELSEVIER

AMSTERDAM • BOSTON • HEIDELBERG • LONDON • NEW YORK • OXFORD
PARIS • SAN DIEGO • SAN FRANCISCO • SINGAPORE • SYDNEY • TOKYO
Architectural Press is an imprint of Elsevier

Architectural
Press

Architectural Press
An imprint of Elsevier
Linacre House, Jordan Hill, Oxford OX2 8DP
30 Corporate Drive, Burlington, MA 01803

First published 2005

British Library Cataloguing in Publication Data
A catalogue record for this book is available from the British Library

ISBN 0 7506 57197

For information about all Architectural Press publications
visit our website at http://books.elsevier.com/architecturalpress

Typeset by Charon Tec Pvt. Ltd, Chennai, India
www.charontec.com
Printed and bound in Great Britain

CONTENTS

ACKNOWLEDGEMENTS

This book was supported by a grant from the Graham Foundation for Advanced Studies in the Fine Arts. I would also like to thank the University of Utah for supporting this project through a University Faculty Research Grant and the approval of a sabbatical leave.

I would like to offer my appreciation to the many people who helped prepare this book for publication. This includes the many archivists who sent copies of the illustrations, helped arrange copyright permissions, and graciously accommodated my visits. My thanks goes to the numerous friends and colleagues who provided suggestions and helped me make initial contacts, I truly appreciate your interest in this project. Professor Uchida and the independent researcher So Hatano, of the Tokyo Institute of Technology, were especially helpful in locating images from the historic Japanese architects. To all the contemporary architects who graciously sent their sketches for inclusion in this volume, I offer my appreciation.

I would like to thank the students at the College of Architecture + Planning, University of Utah, who helped me translate correspondence. Ben Lawrence was particularly talented in editing the text for consistency and grammar, thanks for your candid questioning. I would like to recognize the Undergraduate Research Opportunities Program students, James Gosney and Antonia Vazquez, who helped begin the initial research of architects and archives.

My heartfelt thanks to my Graduate Assistant, Brenda Roberts, who catalogued research materials, scanned images, coordinated correspondence, reviewed the text, and generally helped in many ways for over a year. I appreciate your cheerful attitude. Thank you for your patience and incredibly charming correspondence.

I would like to thank Dr. Marco Frascari for his insightful advice throughout the years. To my family who always believed in this project, I appreciate your support. Most of all, I would like to thank my husband Albert C. Smith, for his encouragement and consistent faith that this book would happen.

ILLUSTRATIONS

Figure 1.1 / Bramante, Donato
Untitled. Uffizi, UFF 1714 A. Approx. 15.5 × 16.6 cm; ink on paper. ©Uffizi Gallery, Florence, Italy.

Figure 1.2 / da Vinci, Leonardo
Codex Atlanticus, studies for the tiburio of Milan Cathedral. Biblioteca Ambrosiana, f. 851 *recto*. 28.2 × 23.7 cm; ink; *c.* 1487. ©Biblioteca Ambrosiana, Milan, Italy.

Figure 1.3 / Peruzzi, Baldassare
Study of a sepulchre. Uffizi, UFF 159 A. 12 × 13 cm; brown ink and wash. ©Uffizi Gallery, Florence, Italy.

Figure 1.4 / da Sangallo, Antonio
Design for a freestanding tomb seen in elevation and plan. Uffizi, UFF 1153 A.v. 11.1 × 15.5 cm; Pen and brown ink, brush and brown wash, on tan laid paper; 1484–1546. ©Uffizi Gallery, Florence, Italy.

Figure 1.5 / Buonarroti, Michelangelo
Base/molding profile studies for San Lorenzo (Basi di pilastro per la Sagrestia Nuova, scritte autografe). Fondazione Casa Buonarroti, 10 A *recto*. 28.3 × 21.4 cm; red chalk, pen and ink; *c.* 1520–1525. ©Fondazione Casa Buonarroti, Florence, Italy.

Figure 1.6 / de L'Orme, Philibert
Heliocoidal staircase in perspective. Musée du Louvre, INV 11114, *recto* (ART157963). 38.2 × 24.3 cm; brown ink, black lead, feather pen; *c.* 1505–1568. ©Musée du Louvre, Départment des Arts & Graphiques. Photo credit: Réunion des Musées, Nationaux/Art Resources, NY.

Figure 1.7 / da Vignola, Giacomo Barozzi
Elevation, sections sketch page. Uffizi, UFF 96 A.v. 30 × 44.5 cm; ink and wash. ©Uffizi Gallery, Florence, Italy.

Figure 1.8 / Palladio, Andrea
Sketch page for the Baths of Agippa, and Hadrian's Villa, Tivoli. RIBA, VII/6R *verso*. Approx. 7 × 10 in; ink on paper. ©RIBA Library Drawings Collection, London, England.

Figure 1.9 / Scamozzi, Vincenzo
Study sketch of column capitals. Uffizi, UFF 1806 A.v. Ink, wash and graphite. ©Uffizi Gallery, Florence, Italy.

Figure 1.10 / Jones, Inigo
Studies of voussoired windows, after Serlio. RIBA, Jones & Webb 76, 77, 78. #76: 16.7 × 16.5 cm; #77: 8.2 × 19.8 cm; #78: 28 × 19.1 cm; graphite, pen and brown ink with brown wash over scorelines; 1618. ©RIBA Library Drawings Collection, London, England.

Figure 3.3 / Boullée, Etienne-Louis
Cenotaph, in the shape of a pyramid. Bibliothèque Nationale de France, Ha 57 FT 6, 4/237 IM.281 Plate 24. 39 × 61.3 cm; ink and wash; 1780–1790. ©Bibliothèque Nationale de France.

Figure 3.4 / Latrobe, Benjamin Henry
US Capitol under construction, seventh set. The Maryland Historical Society, 1960.108.1.9.12. August 1806. ©The Maryland Historical Society, Baltimore, Maryland.

Figure 3.5 / Jefferson, Thomas
Monticello: mountaintop layout (plan). Massachusetts Historical Society, N61; K34. 22.8 × 36.9 cm; ink, with a few additions, much later, in pencil; before May 1768. ©Courtesy of the Massachusetts Historical Society.

Figure 3.6 / Soane, Sir John
Sketch of a design for the south side of the Lothbury Court, Bank of England. Sir John Soane's Museum, Soane 10/3/6. 56.5 × 68.4 cm; pencil, pen and brown ink with pink, brown, and grey washes; November 9, 1799. ©By courtesy of the Trustees of Sir John Soane's Museum, London, England.

Figure 3.7 / Schinkel, Karl Friedrich
Sketches of a church at Grundriß Square. Staatliche Museen zu Berlin, SM 41d.220. 40.3 × 30.3 cm; black ink; 1828. ©Staatliche Museen zu Berlin-Kupferstichkabinett/bpk; photo Joerg P. Anders.

Figure 3.8 / Pugin, A.W.N.
Details on the Avignon travel sketches. The Metropolitan Museum of Art, 35.33.3, II 16, p.6 sketchbook. 15 × 10 in.; graphite and ink on sketchbook page. ©All rights reserved, The Metropolitan Museum of Art.

Figure 3.9 / Paxton, Joseph
Crystal Palace proposal end elevation and cross-section sketch. V&A Picture Library, CT 14412. Pen and ink on blotting paper; June 11, 1850. ©V&A Picture Library, London, England.

Figure 3.10 / Labrouste, Henri
Croquis de structures. Bibliothèque Nationale de France, Ha Mat 1 F18293. Ink and wash on paper. ©Bibliothèque Nationale de France.

Figure 4.1 / Richardson, Henry Hobson
Small sketch from west, preliminary sketch, All Saints Episcopal Cathedral (Albany, NY). Houghton Library, Harvard College Library, HH Richardson Papers, ASA F3. 10 × 13 cm; graphite on tracing paper; 1882–1883. ©Courtesy of the Department of Printing and Graphic Arts, Houghton Library, Harvard College Library.

Figure 4.2 / Hunt, Richard Morris
Sketch for the base of the Statue of Liberty. The Museum of the American Architectural Foundation, Box 1865. 11⅛ × 7⅝ in.; graphite, ink, wash on paper. ©Prints and Drawings

Collection, The Octagon, The Museum of the American Architectural Foundation, Washington, D.C.

Figure 4.3 / White, Stanford
Freehand sketches of large estates. Avery Architectural and Fine Arts Library, White DR 35, SW46:19. 4.74 × 7 in.; graphite on paper. ©Avery Architectural and Fine Arts Library, Columbia University in the City of New York.

Figure 4.4 / Sullivan, Louis
Study of ornamental frame for Richard Morris Hunt Memorial portrait for *Inland Architect*. Avery Architectural and Fine Arts Library, FLLW/LHS 123. 17 × 20.3 cm; pencil on paper; August 7, 1895. ©Avery Architectural and Fine Arts Library, Columbia University in the City of New York.

Figure 4.5 / Ferriss, Hugh
Crest of Boulder, Hoover Dam, The Power in Buildings series. Avery Architectural and Fine Arts Library, NYDA.1000.001.00010. 30.7 × 23.3 cm; charcoal on tracing paper on board; September 14 between [1943–1953]. ©Avery Architectural and Fine Arts Library, Columbia University in the City of New York.

Figure 5.1 / Olbrich, Josef Maria
Untitled. Staatliche Museen zu Berlin, Hdz 10092. Ink on paper. ©Staatliche Museen zu Berlin, Kunstbibliothek.

Figure 5.2 / Wagner, Otto
Perspective sketch. Inv. No. 96.021/30 *verso*. Museen der Stadt Wein, Inv. Nr. 20.003. 34.8 × 21 cm; ink on paper. ©Museen der Stadt Wein.

Figure 5.3 / Gaudí, Antonio
Colonia Güell church, study for the nave of the church drawn on an inverted photograph of the funicular model. Catedra Gaudi, Cat. 48.7. Ink on inverted photograph. ©Courtesy of Catedra Gaudi, Barcelona, Spain.

Figure 5.4 / Mackintosh, Charles Rennie
Sketch of doors for various palaces in Florence. (Contents: Florence, sketch u.l. shows door at the Palazzo della Zecca, Piazzale degli Uffizi, Florence. Sketch u.r. shows door of the Palazzo di Bianca Cappello, Via Maggio, Florence. Sketch l.l. shows the Palazzo Bartolini Salimbeni, Florence. Sketch l.r. shows trabeated forms of classical architecture.) National Library of Ireland, PD 2009 TX 64. 17.4 × 12.6 cm; pencil; 1891. ©Courtesy of the National Library of Ireland.

Figure 5.5 / Loos, Adolf
Modena park verbauung. Albertina, ALA 343 C4. Graphite on paper. ©Albertina, Wein.

Figure 5.6 / Guimard, Hector
Design for chimney (Cheminée et trumeau pour Castel-Beranger). Musée des Arts Décoratifs, INV.GP 508, Cl.11438. 7 × 9.5 in.; ink on paper; *c.* 1897. ©Musée des Arts Décoratifs, Paris. Photo Laurent Sully Jaulmes, Tous droits réservés.

Figure 5.7 / Lutyens, Edwin Landseer
Design for Viceroy's House. RIBA, Lutyens [58] 73. Graphite on paper. ©RIBA Library Drawings Collection, London, England.

Figure 5.8 / Horta, Victor
Sketch of the main concert hall. SOFAM, XVIII.15.24. 27.6 × 21.9 cm; graphite and pen on paper. ©2004 Victor Horta/SOFAM, Belgique.

Figure 5.9 / Ito, Chuta
Sketch of gate of Shrine Shinobazu Bentendo Tenryumon. Graphite on grid paper. 1914. © Graduate Research Engineering. The University of Tokyo.

Figure 5.10 / Hoffman, Josef
Synagoge in Galizien. Kupferstichkabinett der Akademie der bildenden Künste, Inv.-Nr. 26.315. 15 × 26 cm; pencil; 1914. ©Kupferstichkabinett der Akademie der bildenden Künste, Wein.

Figure 5.11 / Greene, Charles Summer & Greene, Henry Mather
Rough sketches of window details, G. Lawrence Stimson House. Avery Architectural and Fine Arts Library, NYDA.1960.001.03708. 12.4 × 10.2 cm; pencil on paper; 1907. ©Avery Architectural & Fine Arts Library, Columbia University in the City of New York.

Figure 6.1 / Sant'Elia, Antonio
Study for a power station. Musei Civici di Como. 21 × 28 cm; ink on paper; 1913. ©Proprieta dei Musei Civici di Como.

Figure 6.2 / de Klerk, Michel
Sketch of design for a water tower with service buildings in reinforced concrete. NAI, archive de Klerk 26.3/0321. 31.9 × 79.1 cm; pencil on tracing paper; 1912. ©Netherlands Architecture Institute, Rotterdam.

Figure 6.3 / Eiffel, Gustave
Eiffel Tower, detail of the opening of the arch. Réunion des Musées Nationaux/Art Resource; Musée d'Orsay, ARO 1981–1297 [53] (ART 177561). 27.5 × 42.5 cm; graphite, pen and ink. ©Réunion des Musées Nationaux/Art Resource, New York; Musée d'Orsay, Paris, France.

Figure 6.4 / Lissitzky, Lazar Markovich
Proun, study. VanAbbemuseum, Inv.nr.244. 40.3 × 39 cm; charcoal on paper; c. 1920–1923. ©Collection VanAbbemusuem, Eindhoven, The Netherlands.

Figure 6.5 / Tatlin, Vladimir Evgrafovich
Sketch of the Monument to the Third International. Moderna Museet. c. 1919. ©Moderna Museet, Stockholm, Sweden.

Figure 6.6 / Mendelsohn, Erich
Columbushaus exploratory sketches. Staatliche Museen zu Berlin, Hdz EM 192. 31.5 × 25.4 cm; ink on paper; 1931–1932. ©Staatliche Museen zu Berlin, Künstbibliothek.

Figure 6.7 / Morgan, Julia
Student rendering of a theater in a palace, Ecole des Beaux-Arts. Environmental Design Archives. 8.75 × 13 in.; graphite, ink, watercolor and gouache on yellow tracing paper, mounted on cream drawing paper; 1902. ©Julia Morgan Collection (1959–2) Environmental Design Archives, University of California, Berkeley.

Figure 6.8 / Reitveld, Gerrit Thomas
Rough draft variation of zigzag child's chair Jesse. RSA, 485 A 012. 20.5 × 15.7 cm; crayon, ink on paper; July 13, 1950. ©Reitveld Schroder Archive (RSA) Centraal Museum, Utrecht.

Figure 6.9 / Finsterlin, Hermann
Sketchbook page. Hamburger Kunsthalle/bpk, KH 11a. 31.9 × 25.8 cm; pencil and color pencil on transparent paper; c. 1920. ©Hamburger Kunsthalle/bpk, Berlin. Photo Christoph Irrgang.

Figure 7.1 / Asplund, Erik Gunnar
Architect Competition proposal 'Tallum'; 'Study of the Chapel Basin' sketch of the 'Toward the Crypt' series; The Swedish Museum of Architecture. 25 × 25 cm; thick paper; 1915. ©The Swedish Museum of Architecture, Stockholm.

Figure 7.2 / Terragni, Giuseppe
Monumento ai Caduit, Erba, preliminary perspective sketches. Centro Studi Giuseppe Terragni. Ink and graphite; 1928–1932. ©Per concessione del Centro Studi Giuseppe Terragni.

Figure 7.3 / Yasui, Takeo
Sketches of details for the special drawing room of the Nihonbashi Nomura building. Graphite on grid paper. ©Yasui Archives.

Figure 7.4 / Wright, Frank Lloyd
Annunciation Greek Orthodox Church, Wauwatosa, Wisconsin. The Frank Lloyd Wright Foundation, FLLW 5611.001. 37 × 30 in.; graphite pencil and color pencil on white tracing paper; 1956. The drawings of Frank Lloyd Wright are Copyright ©2004 The Frank Lloyd Wright Foundation, Scottsdale, AZ.

Figure 7.5 / Griffin, Marion Mahony
Federal Capital competition, left panel, view from summit of Mount Ainslie (Part A). National Archives of Australia, Series #41854 38, Accession #A710/1. 63.2 × 232.7 cm (A, B, and C); watercolor; 1911–1912. ©National Archives of Australia, A710, 48.

Figure 7.6 / Saarinen, Eero
David Ingalls Rink perspective study. Yale University Library Archives, #5081. 8.5 × 11 in.; dark pencil on yellow notebook paper; c. 1953. © Yale University Library Archives, New Haven, Connecticut.

Figure 7.7 / Le Corbusier
Plate #322, Sketchbook 18, Volume 2. Le Corbusier Foundation/ARS, Carnet E18. 15 ×
10 cm; Ink on sketchbook paper; February 1951. ©Le Corbusier Foundation ©2003 Artists
Rights Society (ARS), New York/ADAGP, Paris/FLC.

Figure 7.8 / Gropius, Walter
Lorant Residence, Arlington, VT; sketch of plan with circulation routes. Busch-Reisinger
Museum, Harvard University Art Museums, BRGA.95.2. 22.9 × 22.8 cm; graphite and
colored pencil on paper; 1942. ©Courtesy of the Busch-Reisinger Museum, Harvard
University Art Museums, Gift of Walter Gropius. Photo credit: Allan Macintyre. Image
copyright: ©2003 President and Fellows of Harvard College.

Figure 7.9 / Mies van der Rohe, Ludwig
Theater, project combined elevation and section. The Museum of Modern Art/SCALA/
ARS/Art Resource, #717.1963. 121.9 × 243.8 cm; graphite, ink, cut and pasted papers;
May 1909. Digital Image ©The Museum of Modern Art/Licensed by SCALA/ARS/Art
Resource, NY.

Figure 7.10 / Kahn, Louis
President's Estate, the first Capital of Pakistan. University of Pennsylvania and the
Pennsylvania Historical and Museum Commission, #675.108.23. 30.5 × 61 cm; graphite
and charcoal on white trace; March 23, 1965. ©Copyright 1977 Louis A. Kahn Collection,
University of Pennsylvania and the Pennsylvania Historical and Museum Commission.

Figure 7.11 / Villanueva, Carlos Raúl
Museo Soto sketch. Fundación Villanueva Caracas, #3219r. 21 × 18 cm; graphite on
sketch paper; c. 1969. ©Fundación Villanueva Caracas.

Figure 7.12 / Aalto, Alvar
Preliminary studies for Finlandia Hall, Helsinki. The Alvar Aalto Museum/Drawing
Collection. 30 × 75 cm; pencil on tracing paper; 1962/1967–1971, 1973–1975. ©The Alvar
Aalto Museum/Drawing Collection.

Figure 7.13 / Gray, Eileen
Plan, section, and elevation. V&A Picture Library, AAD/1980/9/16. 10 × 8 in.; pencil on
paper. ©V&A Picture Library, London, England.

Figure 7.14 / Barrágan, Luis
Lomas Verdes, Mexico City, 1964–1973, #212 color marker. ©2004 Barragan Foundation,
Switzerland/Artists Rights.

Figure 7.15 / Moore, Charles Willard
Elevation studies for campanile and arcade. The Charles Moore Center for the Study of
Place. 5 × 10 in.; ink on paper napkin; 1975–1978. ©The Charles Moore Center for the
Study of Place, Austin, Texas.

Figure 7.16 / Smithson, Alison
Sketch plans for two Snowball Appliance Houses. CCA, DR 1995:0052. 12 × 11.5 cm; pen and black ink on tracing paper; 1957. Collection Centre Canadien d'Architecture/Canadian Centre for Architecture, Montréal ©Alison and Peter Smithson.

Figure 7.17 / Candela, Felix
Paragnas en San Jerominio. Avery Architectural and Fine Arts Library, DR 69–12. Approximately 12 × 16 in.; marker sketch with shadows; 1960. ©Avery Architectural and Fine Arts Library, Columbia University in the City of New York.

Figure 7.18 / Rossi, Aldo
Perspective sketches, sketch plans, and detail sketches for the Centro Direzionale, Florence. CCA, DR 1987; 0152. 29.7 × 21 cm; blue ballpoint pen and black felt tip marker on glossy white paper; 1977. © Collection Centre Canadien d'Architecture/Canadian Centre for Architecture, Montréal.

Figure 8.1 / Agrest, Diana
Sport City, Design process: plan study, overall view. Sport City, Shanghai, China. Aerial view: 13 × 9.5 in., Plan: 13 × 10.5 in.; black ink on trace paper; October 18, 2003. ©Agrest and Gondelsonas.

Figure 8.2 / Ando, Tadao
Preliminary design sketch, light slit on the altar. Church of the Light, Ibaraki, Osaka, Japan. 11.7 × 8.5 in.; felt pen on Japanese paper (*washi*); 1987. ©Tadao Ando.

Figure 8.3 / Botta, Mario
Sketch studies for the ground floor plan and verifications of the building's volume and shape. The Cymbalista Synagogue and Jewish Heritage Center in Tel Aviv, Israel, 1998. 31 × 50 cm; pencil on white sketching paper; 1996. ©Mario Botta.

Figure 8.4 / Calatrava, Santiago
Sketch plan (05). Tenerife Concert Hall, Santa Cruz de Tenerife, Canary Islands, Spain. 30 × 40 cm; watercolour; 1999. ©Santiago Calatrava.

Figure 8.5 / Chen, Shi Min
Section sketch. Nan Hai Hotel, SheKou, ShenZhen, China. 8.3 × 11.7 in.; pencil on tracing paper; October 24, 1982. ©Chen Shi Min.

Figure 8.6 / COOP HIMMELB(L)AU
Prix, Wolf D. (1942) and **Swiczinsky, Helmut** (1944). Untitled sketch. BMW Welt, Munich, Germany. 29.7 × 21 cm.; black felt pen; 2001. ©COOP HIMMELB(L)AU.

Figure 8.7 / Correa, Charles
Housing sketch. 1999. ©Charles Correa.

Figure 8.8 / Diller, Elizabeth
Blur process sketch. Blur Building, Swiss Expo 2002. 7.5 × 7.5 in.; ink on napkin; December 28, 1998. ©Elizabeth Diller.

Figure 8.9 / Gehry, Frank
Process elevation sketches. Guggenheim Museum, Bilbao, Spain. 12.3 × 9.2 in.; October 1991. ©Gehry Partners, LLP.

Figure 8.10 / Hadid, Zaha
Preliminary sketch. Vitra Fire Station, Weil Am Rheim, Germany. 11.7 × 16.5 in.; acrylic and ink on tracing paper; 1991. ©Zaha Hadid.

Figure 8.11 / Hara, Hiroshi
Mid-Air City sketch. Umeda Sky Building, Kita-ku, Osaka, Japan, 1993. 3.6 × 2.1 in.; air brush, colored pencil; 1989. ©Hiroshi Hara.

Figure 8.12 / Hecker, Zvi
Spiral sketch. Spiral Apartment House, Ramat-Gan, Israel. 21 × 29 cm; black ink on white paper; 1986. ©Zvi Hecker.

Figure 8.13 / Hollein, Hans
Museum in der Rock of the Mönchsberg Competition 1989, 1st Prize which became: The Guggenheim Museum Salzburg 1990. Feasibility study and 2001 updating of project as Art Center Monchsberg. 75.5 × 55.5 cm; pencil, crayon on transparent paper; 1989. ©Hans Hollein.

Figure 8.14 / Krier, Rob
Spatial sequences sketch. Prager-platz, Berlin, Germany. 26 × 30 cm; oil chalk with pencil on canvas; 1978. ©Rob Krier.

Figure 8.15 / Larsen, Henning
Sketch featuring many of the studio's most important buildings. Various projects. 21 × 29.7 cm; fountain pen on paper. ©Henning Larsen Tegnestue A/S.

Figure 8.16 / Legorreta, Ricardo
Section sketch. UCSF Mission Bay Campus Community Center, San Francisco, California. Felt marker on paper. ©Ricardo Legorreta.

Figure 8.17 / Lynn, Greg
Preliminary exploratory museum sketches. Ark of the World Museum and Interpretive Center, San Juan, Costa Rica. 11 × 14 in.; ink on Bristol paper; March 3, 2002. ©Greg Lynn FORM.

Figure 8.18 / Miralles, Enric
Preliminary plan sketch. Mollet del Valles, Park and Civic Center, Barcelona, Spain. Graffiti and crayon on paper; 1992–1995. ©Enric Miralles-EMBT Enric Miralles Benedetta Tagliabue Arquitectes Associats.

Figure 8.19 / Murcutt, Glenn
Sketch plan. Glenn Murcutt Collection: Marika Banduk [Alderton] House, Yirrikala (PXD 728/Roll 230/A 135). 26 × 37 cm; pencil sketch on butter (trace) paper; 1992. ©The Glenn Murcutt Collection, Mitchell Library, State Library of New South Wales.

Figure 8.20 / Piano, Renzo

Elevation sketch. Cultural Center Jean-Marie Tjibaou, Nouméa, New Caledonia. 8.3 × 11.7 in.; felt pen on paper; 1991. ©Renzo Piano.

Figure 8.21 / Roche, Kevin

View of Central Administration Building. Headquarters of Banco Santander, outside Madrid, Spain. ©Kevin Roche.

Figure 8.22 / Safdie, Moshe

Exploration Place sketch. Exploration Place Science Museum, Wichita, Kansas. ©Moshe Safdie.

Figure 8.23 / Siza Vieira, Álvaro Joaquim Melo

Process sketch. Galician Center for Contemporary Art, Santiago de Compostela, Spain. ©Álvaro Siza.

Figure 8.24 / Soleri, Paolo

Drawing of an early concept of Arcosanti. (from the Paolo Soleri sketchbook #7, page 333). Arcosanti Foundation, Mayer, Arizona. April 1971. ©Paolo Soleri.

INTRODUCTION

Through history, architects have manipulated visual imagery to assist the design process. Such imagery has assumed the form of construction documents, design drawings, analysis and details, various forms of sketches, and images conceived in the mind's eye. The philosopher Richard Wollheim writes that representational seeing involves 'seeing as' (1971). It requires foresight and imagination to comprehend a two-dimensional visual image as a three-dimensional inhabitable structure. Since it is economically unfeasible to test a construction full scale, architects depend on substitute media to assist in their visual thinking. Humans are seldom able to imagine a fully formed impression of a complex configuration, such as a building, entirely in the mind. Through visual artifacts, architects can transform, manipulate, and develop architectural concepts in anticipation of future construction. It may, in fact, be through this alteration that architectural ideas find form.

The architectural theoretician Marco Frascari suggests that drawing can guide architects to an understanding of architecture as both constructed and construed, because drawings intrinsically convey theory: 'Real architectural drawings are not illustrations, but pure expression of architectural thinking.'[1] Wolfgang Meisenheimer also explored the role of drawing to examine architectural thinking when he wrote: 'And the question arises of whether a new, different understanding of architectural <u>drawing</u>, alludes to a new and different understanding of <u>architecture</u>!?' (1987, p. 119). Meisenheimer's assertion asks if media and method affect design thinking and, therefore, the structures architects create. It is important to consider the inherent potential of representational media to surpass mere communication. This is a vital issue for the study of architectural sketches, and will be contemplated throughout this book.

Images are ever present. Visual stimulus in the commercial realm eliminates the possibility of an 'innocent eye' in a contemporary phenomenon the philosopher Richard Kearney calls the 'culture of the image' (1988). This overindulgence of imagery suggests the continuous mirror play between imagination and reality in postmodern culture; the image is always in process, subjected to constant reinterpretation. The ambiguous and unfinished qualities of sketches epitomize this notion. Additionally, current interest in architectural design process stems from a belief that process, or sketches as indicative of process, can be viewed as a direct link to inspiration. Although research into *Genetic Criticism* finds that process may not be altogether linear, it is expressive of design thinking. Appropriately, the discussion of image, its text, and context can be investigated for its influence on the imagination and design process of architects. In this age of extensive computer use and the proliferation of visual stimulus, it is essential that architects question and interpret the media they utilize. By exploring the historical role of sketches as instruments of thinking, commonalities and differences will surface. From these, one may ascertain a definition of architectural sketches and expose their importance in the production of architecture.

This book examines a history of architectural sketches, exploring their physical technique, comparing them to architects' built work and speculating on how they convey architectural intention in design process. Sketches, inherently different than drawings, illustrate conceptual design thinking through architects' personal dialogue. Tracing the development and use of sketches by prominent architects reveals them to be instruments for recording, discovering, designing, communicating, visualizing, and evaluating architectural constructs. Such an exploration will provide insight into the role of sketches as mediators for the inception of architecture.

DEFINITION OF SKETCHES

The word 'drawing' presents a general term, whereas 'sketching' focuses on a specific technique. Both can take the form of an action or object, verb or noun, as each can imply movement. The Oxford English Dictionary defines a sketch as a brief description or outline 'to give the essential facts or points of, without going into details.' Sketches document the primary features of something or are considered 'as preliminary or preparatory to further development' (1985). Historically, the act of sketching or drawing on paper involves line. At its most basic level, the production of line constitutes making marks with a pointed tool, initiated by movement and force. In reverse, eyes follow a line and with that action the 'line's potential to suggest motion is basic' (Lauer, 1979, p. 151). A line, or mark, made with the bodily action of the hands, demonstrates its ability to cause reflective action, as it attracts the human eye to follow it. This cognition spurs associative thoughts, as the line suggests new forms (Lauer, 1979). Much of the 'motion' of a sketch comes from the physical action of the hand; in this way, the tool becomes an extension of the body and reflects the human body. James Gibson, the psychologist and philosopher, writes concerning human contact with a drawing and suggests that making marks is both viewed and felt (1979). The 'gesture' of this intimate participation with a sketch gives it meaning and individuality.

The control of a hand on the drawing tool yields not a consistent line, but one that is varied, thick or thin. The quality of the mark is important, since individual lines produce association in the minds of architects. Gibson believes, in company with philosophers such as Aristotle, that it is reasonable to suppose that humans can think in terms of images (1982). Conversely, but consistent with his theories of visual perception, there cannot be vision without the cognitive action of thought.

Sketches can be analogous for actions that do not involve a mark on paper. For example, a quick skit by a comedian may be deemed a 'sketch,' although it does not involve the mark on a surface. Thus, a sketch may be defined by its preliminary and essential qualities. Sketches may also comprise three-dimensional actions preliminary to architecture, such as the fast 'sketch' model, or be conceived of digitally as a wire-frame massing in the computer. In such ways, the intention takes precedence over the media. How sketches act to assist design thinking designates their value.

As these definitions imply, sketches are notoriously imprecise; valueless physically, and seen as a means to find something or communicate rather than as prized objects in and of themselves. They are usually, but not necessarily, loose and lacking in detail. Some architects make simple but precise diagrams, while others may use sketches purely for communication with other architects or the client. Whatever technical method an architect employs, they all touch, if ever so briefly, on a period of conception where the design is in its beginning stages, made up of tentative and incomplete thoughts.

The medium (pencil, clay, charcoal, computer, etc.) is not as important in defining a sketch, as its relative function in the design process. Many architects use charcoal or soft pencils to emphasize line, and make the drawing expressive yet vague enough to allow for allusions and analogies. Some architects employ inexpensive tracing paper to sketch quickly, still others draw preliminary studies slowly on expensive paper. Some diagram in the fashion of the *parti* and others carefully redraw a known building to deform or transform its image. The varied media and techniques used to sketch may complicate a definition of these images. It is more important to consider their use as conveyors of likeness.

As representations, sketches act as substitutes for mental impressions. This is important to architectural sketching as a creative endeavor, because not knowing how mental impressions originated leads creative people to proclaim that such impressions came from the imagination. Imagination represents objects that are absent from view, can be used to change or interpret that which has been observed, or can recognize and reuse items which are known (Warnock, 1976). The implication for architects when conceptualizing a potential design becomes evident. Creative inspiration may be credited to an expanded associative capacity of certain individuals, or it may be attributed to magic or divine intervention. Whatever the case, the imagination encourages speculation because the images in the mind and on paper can assume any possibility (Casey, 1976).

Architects contain within themselves the experiences and faculties necessary to interact with this visual stimulus, because the act of sketching is in some ways dependent upon memory. Thoughts, images, and experiences – all part of the architect's whole being – determine what the sketch will be. Body memory, interpretation, and even specific items that are retained in memory over other experiences, influence what the architect sketches. The architectural theoretician Robin Evans retells the mythological origins of drawing when he describes Diboutades tracing the shadow outline of her departing lover's profile on a wall (1986). For Diboutades the outline acted as a memory device to remind her of the absent person. Similarly, drawing and sketching for architects depends upon a relative amount of likeness, a visual imagery that conveys conceptual comparison. Such resemblance connotes an indication for associative memory, suggesting architectural sketches do not depend upon a 'faithful picture.' Both as a method for retaining information and thoughts, and as a medium for inspiration and transformation, sketches constitute a personal dialogue for each architect.

Sketches may acquire various physical shapes, but their similarities lie in how and why they are utilized and trusted by architects. Stemming from their relationship to function, it is necessary to expand their definition by treating them as illustrative of their use in the design process. Architects often employ sketches for conceptual design to discover or attain knowledge, to accompany brainstorming, and to find allusions or associations. The sketch can become the medium to express emotional or poetic concepts.

Architects also use sketches to record important events or ideas for later use. These notations may be travel companions to aid in visual recollection or to register an emotion or thought. Architects often employ sketches to visually test abstract conceptual forms. They may be used to 'try something out for fit' as a type of evaluation. Similarly, sketches may help to finalize the formation of a mental image as a method to visualize an undefined direction. Most architects draw to see and understand, whether it is an observation of perceptual stimulus or from a mental impression conjured up by imagination. The Italian architect Carlo Scarpa expresses this concept well: 'I want to see things, that's all I really trust. I want to see, and that's why I draw. I can see an image only if I draw it' (Dal Co, 1984, p. 242).

Since perception has little resemblance to a drawn image, it may be possible to ask if a drawn illusion can promote understanding. This suggests how sketching equates with the cognitive act of seeing. The sketch can portray a mode of comprehension as the philosopher Maurice Merleau-Ponty expresses when discussing Paul Klee and Henri Matisse: 'The line no longer imitates the visible; it "renders visible"; it is the blueprint of a genesis of things' (1964, p. 183). 'Rendering visible' implies an understanding deeper than an illusion. This may be a distinct feature of sketches that are often incomplete and vague. Again, this is evidence of the sketch's role in 'seeing' as understanding. The architect's mind must be able to immerse itself in the making (Gibson, 1982). The sketch facilitates a form of visualization; specifically making physical a conceptual impression. It cannot be denied that sketches are affected by the memories and imagination of each architect, as experiences and individual traits color the techniques and products of these actions.

The sketch, for an architect, may allow for the discovery of a concept at the beginning of a project; however, they can be employed in all stages of the design process, even as an observational recording long after the building is constructed. In early stages, an architect's imagination is open to many possibilities; no potentiality is ruled out (Casey, 1976). These options might be fragmented and vague, but they begin a thinking process, as this first sketch often must be drawn with great speed to capture the rapid flashes of mental stimulation. Werner Oechslin feels the sketch is the appropriate medium for design: 'The sketch is ideally suited for capturing the fleetingness of an idea' (1982, p. 103). If the sketch itself is a brief outline, then it may, in fact, reflect the brief thoughts of the mind.

Artists' and architects' sketches maintain some similarities but are intentionally very different. Displaying the physical qualities that convey observational likeness, artists use sketches as artistic expression, where they act as preliminary to two-dimensional finished drawings or paintings or represent a completed entity. Sculptors employ sketches as preliminary thoughts for three-dimensional artifacts. Conversely, architects very seldom consider sketches as a final product. They are primarily intended to envision a future building. Robin Evans succinctly states this function of architectural drawings when he writes that images 'precede the act of building' (Blau and Kaufman, 1989, p. 21). Like artists' sketches, they may function to sway public opinion or promote theoretical argument. In most cases, sketches are a personal exploration unlike the conventions of construction drawings, without precise meaning and often destroyed upon the completion of the building.

This study makes use of, but is not based in, iconology since architectural sketching is not strictly a symbolic art. The meanings acquired with combinations of lines often are distinctly personal to the architect. Although they may contain a few conventions of architectural communication, these sketches cannot be 'read' for specific universal meaning (Evans, 1986). They are not visual 'shorthand' and do not directly equate the visual with the verbal. Shorthand suggests a foundation in symbols that have acquired known and culturally accepted meanings. It is not necessary that these sketches be comprehended by anyone except the architect, and while they can be attractive, their beauty need not be questioned. As architectural representations their physical appearance is irrelevant. They are valued for qualities other than their beauty. Ambiguous and tentative, they easily carry emotions and subtleties of illusion and allusion. The look of the sketch is not as important as the role it plays in the design process.

Architects depend upon sketches as the medium for the creative process they employ to conceptualize architecture. Since they are easily transformable images, they play a major role in architectural thinking; they form and deform architectural ideas. This flexibility affects architectural understanding, and the comprehension requires reflection and translation. Sketches are the visual manifestation of character or attitude that allows the transformation of a physical object or concept into another dimension or media. Exploring the representational qualities of sketches discloses the tangible and intangible aspects that make them fundamental in any process of design. Illustrative of this sentiment Filarete, the Renaissance architect, describes their importance: 'Execution teaches many things and everything cannot be fully narrated here . . . everything that is done by the hand partakes of drawing . . . it is an unknown and little appreciated science. You would do very well to learn it, for it would acquaint you with a thousand delights' (1965, pp. 82 and 149).

APPROACH TO THE STUDY OF ARCHITECTURAL SKETCHES

It is appropriate now to present the method of approach to this collection of architects' sketches. The subject matter is visual; meaning, the observation and interpretation of marks on a page. Sketches are unique. They may have complex meanings and various techniques. They comprise a compilation of forms standing for an object or thought as a representation, which does not necessarily include a program or statement of intention. Translating these often cryptic marks can be difficult. James Smith Pierce suggests the problem of deciphering intent when examining drawings from the history of art and architecture: 'If he [the architect] has not set down his purpose in writing and his age has left no substantial body of theoretical writing or criticism to help us gauge his intent, we must follow the traces of his hand preserved in those drawings that are records of his mind and spirit' (1967, p. 119).

Although architects may write about their theories and philosophies, few can communicate verbally the complexities found in their sketches. They may not be able to translate their visual design experience into words. Important, then, in the interpretation of these sketches are the ideals of the various movements with which each architect is identified; the context, times, and location of their practice; their repertoire of built work; critics' assessment of their work; and any writings, manifestos, or treatises that reveal their beliefs. Once these materials have been collected and analyzed, meaning can be deduced by inspecting the sketch itself. By concentrating on 'the traces of the hand' as the primary text, it becomes possible to discuss issues observed in the physical sketch, and to speculate on both conscious and subconscious intention. Such analysis may contemplate various possibilities, yet may consider only a fragment of the numerous ideas embedded in the sketch. Although most of the sketches included here represent a multifaceted narrative, this discussion touches on one theme to elucidate an insight drawn from each sketch. For example, it is possible to compare a sketch to the corresponding architect's built work; in other cases, the commission or project is unknown. Generally, examining the repertoire of the architect's remaining sketches provides insight into their style, technique, and thought processes. This interpretation is speculative by drawing conclusions based on literary theories, art theory, and observations of the marks they make on a surface.

Each example in this book involves the following: a short biography of the architect, information pertinent to the sketch and the architect's body of work, a discussion of the physical techniques of the sketch, and an exploratory interpretation. It is hoped that the comparison to historical context and the architect's recorded theories will clarify and enrich the reader's understanding of the 'mind and spirit' of the physical tracings.

This book is meant to convey a history of architectural sketches. This tells a story of architects' design images from the Renaissance to contemporary architectural practice. History books and in fact the history of architecture can be relayed through the study of monumental buildings, by following thought as compared to cultural and social events, by comparing differences between regions, or by styles, to mention a few methods. This book can be read as a history of the times, culture, development, styles, and architectural thought manifest in the images architects use for design process. It has been envisioned as a story following a general timeline. As a narrative starting with the Renaissance, it will provide a survey highlighting work by prominent architects revealing developments and paradigm shifts. Compared to a necklace of pearls, the effect can be unified and cohesive. But to extend this analogy, the pearls (the chapters or architects) can also be appreciated individually as vignettes or snapshots of specific movements' or architects' influences and techniques.

HISTORY OF DRAWING AND SKETCHING

The history of representation is probably as old as civilization itself. Humans have always attempted to infuse meaning into the objects they observe in nature and the things constructed. The art historian E. H. Gombrich, when discussing the origins of art, writes that humans assembled structures to shelter themselves from elements of nature such as rain, as well as from the spirits that controlled the natural environment (1985). These spiritual forces were equally as potent as the environmental dangers. Gombrich concludes that for these early humans, 'there is no difference between building and image-making as far as usefulness is concerned' (1985, p. 20). He suggests that there exists a certain amount of magic involved in representation.

The paintings in the caves of Lascaux in France, or any other wall paintings by indigenous peoples, may have chronicled a successful hunt, told a story of heroism, or acted as a talisman to ensure an equally good hunt the following year. Much of what remains of ancient civilizations are the architectural monuments sturdy enough to stand the test of time. Similarly the temporary materials of most visual communication have been lost, one exception being paintings on the walls of Egyptian structures. As evidenced by these paintings, the Egyptian culture had a tremendous amount of graphic language. Created with pigment on stone and subsequently buried, these communications survived. But one may suppose that this productive culture also inscribed papyrus, wooden pallets and stone or clay tablets to communicate necessary information. The museum of Egyptian archaeology in Barcelona possesses a 'Representation of the god Imhotep' from approximately 600 BC. Imhotep, the first recorded architect, who also was deified, has been sculpted holding a roll of papyrus. Knowing he was responsible for the design of much Egyptian architecture, it would be reasonably safe to propose he was carrying architectural drawings. It may be equally rewarding to presume he was pictured with written documents concerning construction.

Some drawing instruments survive from this period. Maya Hambly, writing on the history of drawing tools, acknowledges that a scale rule, a drawing instrument and a form of plan have been located and dated from Babylon, approximately 2000 BC (1988). The architectural historian Spiro Kostof proposes that Egyptian architects used leather and papyrus for record drawings, where 'sketch-plans were incised on flat flakes of limestone' called *ostraka* being the communication on the job site (1977, p. 7). Egyptian builders employed plans and elevations that were obviously diagrammatic outlines and layered drawings indicating spatial relationships. Egyptian painting has displayed plans of gardens, but whether these images were intended as descriptions of a finished site, or as preparation for building, remains difficult to surmise.

Builders in China used silk and paper for architectural drawings (plan and elevation), and drawings cast or etched into bronze exist from the Warring States period (475–221 BC). The Chinese had developed techniques for making paper as early as 100 AD. Making its way to Europe (1100 AD in Morocco and 1151 AD in Spain), this technology arrived in Italy approximately 1256 AD, where linen rags provided the fiber necessary for production. Beginning in the fourteenth century, paper was available in abundance, but it was not until the mid-nineteenth century that wood pulping expanded its manufacture (Hutter, 1968; Dalley, 1980). Compasses used to construct circles had been employed by the early Egyptians, although they were constructed simply of two hinged metal legs. Mathematical instruments such as astrolabes were developed in the third to sixth century during the rise of Islamic civilization (Hambly, 1988). In the study of vision and light, the Chinese understood that light traveled in parallel and straight paths as early as the fifth century BC (Hammond, 1981). In anticipation of the *camera obscura*, Mo Ti documented the understanding of an inverted image projected through a pinhole. Comparatively, Arab physicists and mathematicians comprehended the linearity of light in the tenth century (Hammond, 1981). In the thirteenth and fourteenth centuries, lenses were common, but Roger Bacon has been erroneously credited with invention of the *camera obscura*. Although not completely documented, it is very possible they were commonly used to observe eclipses of the sun and subsequently transformed into an apparatus for copying.

Greek architects, some of whose names are known, designed temples heavily influenced by tradition. The temples served as templates, precedent models, for subsequent construction (Smith, 2004; Coulton, 1977; Porter, 1979). Additionally, these architects employed three-dimensional *paradigma* to describe details and *syngraphai*, written specifications (Hewitt, 1985). Examples of full-scale building details have been found inscribed on a wall of the Temple of Apollo at Didyma (Hambly, 1988). It may be surmised that, with the study of geometry by Euclid, Greek architects utilized geometrical instruments and that builders would have used scale rules and set squares to achieve precision construction (Hambly, 1988). Kostof mentions these *anagrapheis*/descriptions, but wonders how the refinements in temple design could have been accomplished without drawings. The role of the Roman architect was less immersed in precedent and had a relative amount of autonomy in construction (1977). Vitruvius advocated the implementation of *graphia* (plan), *orthographia* (elevation), and *scaenographia* (perspective) (1934). Hambly states that Romans utilized dividers, set squares, scale rulers and calipers. Although these items were primarily builders' instruments, ruling pens and styli have been found which may have a more direct relationship to architecture and engineering drawings (1988). Temporary notation involved inscribing a wax tablet with a stylus that could be easily erased with the blunt end of the tool. Working plans and sketches most likely were drawn on temporary materials such as clay tablets (Kostof, 1977).

Although paintings and various types of documents survive from the Middle Ages, very few drawings exist. It has been suggested by the historian Robert Scheller that this dearth of preparatory sketches may be due to the lack of value given to them. They were viewed only as process and consequently destroyed (1995). He also proposes that the media used for sketches and drawings may have been too scarce and expensive for common use. Most probably, artists and architects sketched on whatever materials were available, i.e., wood, stone, or parchment, and as process these have not endured. One example of a clearly architectural drawing dates from approximately 820 to 830 AD. The Plan of St. Gall was drawn on parchment and describes an ideal monastery. Measuring 113 cm vertically and 78 cm horizontally, this drawing indicates the spatial relationships of buildings within a compound. Substantially schematic, the plan has been arranged on a grid, drawn in both red and black ink, with single lines to represent doors and columns (Price, 1982).

Far more common were the model and pattern books of medieval architects. Guild books (or lodge books) recorded methods of construction and architectural theory for use by the building trades. Largely practical, they characterized Gothic building practices (Bucher, 1979). These books were organized into categories of theory, figure drawing, and carpentry. They served the lodge members, and the lodge itself was the repository for this inherited knowledge. A preserved sketchbook by Villard de Honnecourt displays the value these types of pattern books had for medieval architects. They accompanied the architects on journeys, retained visual notes and acted as professional licensure to prove the bearer's skills and represent their interests as they were searching for employment. De Honnecourt's sketchbook chronicled framing drawings, patterns for details and ornament, construction methods, elevations, plans, and patterns for tracery (Bucher, 1979). The sketches date from the early 1200s and are drawn on parchment in graphite, scored, and filled with ink. *The Dictionary of Architecture* from 1892 indicates that drawings on parchment delineating ground plans and elevations exist from the eleventh century, although these may not resemble the scale and articulation expected from contemporary architectural drawings. The architects of the Middle Ages were craftsmen, refining the cathedral image primarily without the use of visual representation. Large incisions have been found on many of the walls of these cathedrals, most likely functioning as templates for details such as tracery (Kostof, 1977). Architectural drawings prior to the Renaissance were not common, and architects/builders did not conceive of the building in its entirety before construction. Rather, buildings such as cathedrals were a process of experimentation on the site: 'Projecting the geometric physiognomy of a building or city was a prophetic act, a form of conjuring and divining, not merely the personal will of the author. Architectural drawings, therefore, could not be conceived as neutral artifacts that might be transcribed unambiguously into buildings' (Péréz-Gomez and Pelletier, 1997, p. 9).

Although few sketches with architectural themes have been retained from this period, one may speculate that proportions or geometries, as well as construction details, were sketched to communicate conceptual propositions. It would have been difficult to convey intention without some form of visual description. Drawings may not have been preserved, perhaps, because they were later reused for recording – such as the text on the back of the St. Gall plan. Possibly, they were destroyed when their usefulness was complete, or by the architectural guilds in an attempt to keep their building practices secret (Kostof, 1977). From the practice of hand-copying religious texts, sketches appear in the margins of illuminated manuscripts from medieval monasteries. Acting as illustrations to further elucidate biblical narrative, the margins allowed enough space for small decorations of ink and paint. These visual musings occasionally acted as rude commentary in contrast to the serious text. As decorative doodlings and caricatures, they were freehand sketches often in the genres of political satire or comic relief (Randall, 1966).

Artists of the thirteenth and fourteenth centuries were moving towards a sense of pictorial realism. These artists, refining religious icons, had little need for a theory of perspective. The Japanese painters and printmakers, attempting a three-dimensional view devised a language of perspective where objects further in the background were zigzagged higher onto the page. Similarly, medieval perspective indicated objects in the distance be rendered higher in the frame of the painting. Although without mathematical accuracy, these artists located the onlooker's position and used architectural elements such as niches to create an illusion of three-dimensional space (White, 1972).

Many inventions and developments in drawing and painting surfaced during the fifteenth century. Filippo Brunelleschi has been credited with the rediscovery of rules for 'constructed' perspective rendering in 1420 (White, 1972; Péréz-Gomez and Pelletier, 1997). These architects (primarily Brunelleschi and Leon Battista Alberti) became attracted to this study because they believed that in using architectural themes they were able to beguile the somewhat magical aspects of geometry and proportion into perspective depth in painting (Péréz-Gomez and Pelletier, 1997). Perspective aids such as simple frames divided into squares were employed in the early 1400s (Hambly, 1988). Alberti used a show or perspective box and invented an apparatus for constructing perspectives using strings. The *camera obscura*, possibly in common use, reflected an object through a lens onto a slanted mirror. Projected onto a drawing surface, and reduced in size, the image could then be traced (Hutter, 1968; Dalley, 1980; Hammond, 1981). Artists and painters used such tools and instruments to represent the world around them, but they were also able to use similar techniques to envision the future. For various reasons a history of architectural sketches really begins with the artists and architects of the Renaissance.

RENAISSANCE BEGINNINGS

There are several explanations as to why very few architectural sketches, and drawings in general, have been found that date from before the fifteenth century. There is not a simple answer to this question, but rather numerous factors that affected the proliferation and subsequent retention of sketches beginning with the Renaissance.

The political and economic climate of Italy in the cinquecento formed a stable and intellectual society. The region of Tuscany had experienced growth in population accompanied by economic prosperity. The government required literate representatives, and international trade fostered an educated and cultured populace. These wealthy patricians became patrons of the arts. The Catholic Church began a building program that continued to support artists and architects for centuries (Allsopp, 1959; Benevolo, 1978; Wittkower, 1980).

With this wealth came a refined worldview. Development in goods and services, some from around the world, encouraged expeditions between the continents, scientific exploration of the heavens, discoveries concerning instruments for navigation and astronomy, the printing press, and advancements in social reform. This period of relative enlightenment – of humanism – emerged primarily in Europe (Wittkower, 1949). It was reflected in the East with independent developments as well as reciprocal exchange of ideas.

In Italy, with a break from the perceived 'dark ages,' the emergence of humanism brought the development of rational thought, which did not rely on strict Christian traditions. Still deeply religious, these artists and architects interested in humanism viewed the sketch as a direct vehicle of inspiration (Gordon, 1975). Richard Kearney describes how this was a change from beliefs in the Middle Ages. He writes that medieval 'imagination was essentially interpreted as a mimetic activity – that is, as a secondhand reflection of some "original" source of meaning which resides beyond man' (1988, p. 115). Attitudes had changed celebrating the individual and the power of reason during this period of rediscovered classical civilization (Trachtenberg and Hyman, 1986). Leonardo da Vinci, for example, explored nature with an empirical approach, and his curious mind engaged in speculation. This creativity was human-inspired, rather than directed by God or a blatant imitation of nature. Significance was attached to a work of art by credit being given to the artist or architect. Independent of the communication of religion, the work of art could stand on its own – it was no longer merely an extension of magic or ritual (Kris and Kurz, 1979).

This time period also initiated the academic tradition and the workshops prompting the interdisciplinary practice of *designo* (Barasch, 1985). *Designo* can be described as the visual expression that gives shape to an artistic concept. A definition by Renaissance biographer and theoretician Giorgio Vasari from his 1568 *Lives of the Artists* describes the cognitive action of a sketch as the physical manifestation of thinking: '[T]he Idea of perfect form comes to the individual artist from experience and long practice; the ability to discern the Idea and then the skill to represent it accurately are both essential for *disegno*' (Currie, 1998, p. 138). The concept of *designo* as interpreted by Aristotle referred to the actions anticipating the work of art (Barzman, 2000). Vasari associated the concept with both drawing and theory, suggesting that it developed from the intellect. Karen-edis Barzman equates *disegno* to the figures of geometry, because it involves the abstraction of natural bodies revealing universal truths. In this way, the connection to theory surfaces and consequently, the artist understands the 'why' of their art. These developments helped initiate the activity of sketching during the Renaissance, but they represent only part of the story.

Discoveries and developments in science, the availability of paper and the desire to graphically calculate geometry and proportions encouraged the architect's hand pertaining to architectural sketches. An attitude about science and philosophy spurred questioning among learned people. Experiments such as those by Sir Isaac Newton in the fourteenth century required precise instrumentation, as did surveying and engineering construction. The earth was no longer at the center of the universe, and writings by Copernicus and other astronomers necessitated diagrams and various forms of recording. Machines, such as clocks, contributed to this interest in the philosophical and natural world. The visual calculations of algebra and geometry proliferated as knowledge was shared. This resulted in attitudes engaging visual speculation and exploration of the unknown or newly proposed. These occurrences invariably affected and enhanced the visual speculation of architectural sketches at the threshold of the profession.

The building techniques and the practice of architecture affected the development of sketches for Renaissance architects. When the writings by Vitruvius were rediscovered (he had been known in the Middle Ages but was rediscovered as interest was revived), architects of the Renaissance had a model for practice (Kostof, 1977). Vitruvius had paired theory with practice, the knowledge of building and the ability to understand why. He advocated the architect as scholar, understanding art and culture, and the activities necessary to architecture such as law, music/acoustics, astronomy, and philosophy (Vitruvius, 1934). As a person of science the architect could maintain theoretical knowledge of proportion and perspective (Kostof, 1977). Thus, these architects needed to acquire an education by sketching directly from antiquity. In Spiro Kostof's book *The Architect*, Leopold Ettlinger explains how the Renaissance architects engaged drawings (1977). They employed drawings to record the physical shapes of the artifacts, to measure and calculate proportions, to explore building construction and to represent these buildings in drawing form. The desire to record what they observed made the sketch invaluable as an extension of the pattern books of the Middle Ages. Although architects were not organized into guilds, the prestige of the architect was elevated. They were responsible for the work on the site and could choose the craftsmen. These architects clearly used drawing to conceive of the designs for their architecture. The early Renaissance architect Sanzio Rapheal advocated the use of two types of architectural projection: plans and elevations (Kostof, 1977). Drawings that remain from the Renaissance include plans, elevations, sections, perspectives, both conceptually describing early ideas and exploring a tremendous quantity of details. It is difficult, however, to trace drawings through the construction process which puts their use on the site or their role as construction documents into question. Ettlinger speculates that these drawings (especially of antique details) served to inform builders of a new paradigm for construction. The functions of sketches are more obvious as they act to show how these architects conceived and tested ideas. Depending less on traditions, having control over the construction process, and convincing their patron of the project before construction began encouraged architects to include sketches in their vocabulary.

Giorgio Vasari certainly had a role in the retention of architectural sketches during the Renaissance. Vasari believed in the relationship between the architectural inception and the sketch. The sketch, as the best example of architectural expression, became associated in value with the individual architect. Vasari, perceiving this relationship, began collecting architectural sketches. He gave mythological stature to these Renaissance architects with his publication *The Lives of the Artists*. Ernst Kris and Otto Kurz discuss the ascension of artists and architects to mythical status. They write that while the Middle Ages respected craftsmanship, the Renaissance viewed beauty in the unfinished remnants of inspiration: 'The Cinquecento no longer regarded the imitation of nature as the acme of artistic achievement, but rather viewed "invention" as its foremost aim' (1979, p. 47). The artists and architects who revealed these traits in their sketches came to epitomize the title of *divino artista*. Myths regarding their innate talents abounded, stressing their natural skills (Kris and Kurz, 1979). Such heroic architects were worshipped for their genius, and the value of work coming directly from their hands increased. This enhanced status of these artists and architects, and assisted in the retention of sketches, subsequently affecting the number that have been retained and held in archives through the years.

All of these factors attributed to the growing use of sketches and the general respect for evidence of inspiration and invention. The notion of architectural sketching was less practiced and respected in the periods prior to the Renaissance for various reasons. Sketches were not required since much architecture was envisioned by the Church who retained the templates of construction allowing only minor variations. These master builders were viewed as agents of God governed by the traditions of their guilds. In the years preceding the fifteenth century, these generations of craftsmen found little need to sketch and any sketches and drawings were inclined to consist of documents copying existing solutions. The few sketches that do exist appear minimal, diagrammatic, consisting of plan and elevation, and most likely were used for details or to communicate accepted construction methods. They show restraint and provide only the most pertinent information. In contrast, the creative building expansion spurred by Humanism and the relative economic stability encouraged the Renaissance architects to recognize the value of individual inspiration, and trust in their own imaginations and the images formed by their hands. Although retaining strong beliefs in God, these architects took responsibility for their actions and challenged themselves to new heights of aesthetic exploration. Certainly the availability of sketching media and the desire to explore and understand the constructions of antiquity rendered sketches more acceptable and plentiful.

Sketches by architects of the Renaissance and later reveal more fluid lines, extensive exploration of alternatives, plans, sections, and elevations rendered with detail along with use of three-dimensional views. These sketches often fill the page and overlap in the exuberance of design thinking. They are less self-conscious as they often leave mistakes, utilize expressive lines, and employ these images to attain knowledge about and understand the world around them.

Although similar developments in science, technology, and art were occurring in various parts of the world, other events kept architects from using or retaining sketches. Much of the Americas, Africa and Australia had not yet moved beyond nomadic tribes or the evolution of traditional vernacular architecture by the time of the Italian Renaissance. The Aztec civilization of Mexico built monuments and extensive urban structures. Laid out with geometry and precision, they must have developed extensive measuring systems. To document their work, the Aztecs utilized a form of *amate* fiber paper. Designing in the brief time period of approximately 1200–1400 AD, these builders devised combination drawings of plans and elevations, and represented scenes in a believable semblance of perspective (Serrato-Combe, 2001). Expansive ground drawings scar the mountains of Peru, but their use (and the tools for conceiving and executing such enormous drawings) is a matter of speculation (Kostof, 1985). The arrival of the Spanish erased much of this civilization and replaced it with European style; so very few of these artifacts remain.

The Chinese and Japanese built sophisticated architecture that depended upon strict rules pertaining to tradition and religious practices. This tight control of architectural expression limited the need for drawings and particularly sketches, although the arts of drawing and painting were tremendously refined. A descendant of vernacular type, the tearoom was developed as a style in Japan during the *Tensho* era, 1573–1592 AD. Much of the tearoom design has been attributed to the tea master Sen no Rikyu, celebrating a sense of space in Japanese architecture (Stewart, 1987). Drawings from Asia show representation of architecture that may be primarily pictorial. Sketches as conceptually exploring architectural intention are less common.

As a result of travel during the fourteenth, fifteenth and sixteenth centuries, imperialism affected the styles of architecture around the world. Originating primarily from Europe, the influence of the baroque and neoclassical styles appeared throughout the world. Without a developed architectural identity, the newly formed United States looked to Europe for models. The profession of architecture in the United States was not organized until the late 1800s. Builders and laymen copied buildings, prior to this time, from pattern books; therefore, sketches were not needed.

Many forces united to create an attitude toward sketching that suggested the individuality of the architect and the ability to provoke imagination as a creative endeavor. While most pre-Renaissance buildings contained some level of visual communication as part of the design process, little of this evidence remains. This fact may question whether the sketches were used to envision the project in its entirety before construction as may be expected of the profession. In cases where sketches convey less tangible information than solely recording or communicating, they inherently act as remnants of design process.

Drawings, although they are part of the construction process, do not always reveal the imaginative inspiration. Again, Wolfgang Meisenheimer expresses the emotion and allusions involved when a sketch tries to speak in terms of the undefinable. He writes about poetic drawings that embody the 'traces of the memory and the dreams of the drawer, outbreaks of temperament and wit, provocations of the observer, riddles, vague evocations or gestures of philosophical thesis . . . The transferals and interpretations which result from them move on all possible levels' (1987, p. 111). Thus the sketch, as a thinking instrument, carries the individual dialogue requiring the associative reflections that encourage interpretation and manipulation. The initiation and implementation of sketches into design process required an altered philosophical attitude making the Cinquecento a Renaissance for sketches as well as cultural thought.

POST-RENAISSANCE

This book begins with Renaissance sketches as a philosophical point of departure. Once identified as a means to visualize concepts, the use of sketches never waned. Although their uses developed at different times and in various forms around the world, they were used less or not at all in the construction of vernacular architecture. The story of the sketch extends from the perspective of Western Europe where their use was more prominent in the sixteenth and seventeenth centuries with baroque, French classicism, rococo and eighteenth century neoclassicism. The sketches from these periods reflect both the 'style' of the buildings and prevalent media for image manipulation. In general, they extensively used graphite, ink, and wash, with fluid strokes exhibiting the architect's great dexterity. The nineteenth century and early twentieth century movements in architecture expand to various parts of the world including parts of Asia and North America. Many of these sketches demonstrate the political, economic, and social climate of the world. The media had not changed remarkably but their manifestation was dramatically varied by individual architect, especially considering the ideological and polemical movements of the era. Modern architecture expanded into the International Style and, as the name implies, spread around the world with numerous cultural variations. The representative sketches reflect the stark geometric forms with ruled sketches in orthographic and axonometric projection.

The chapters have been organized chronologically, beginning with the architects of the Renaissance. Examples depend upon the availability of sketches, the prominence of the architect, representative examples of the architect's work, and finally sketches that display an interpretive premise for theoretical exploration. The illustrative examples have been arranged chronologically by the date of the architect's death. When trying to categorize the sketches and their architects into periods, it was realized that some architects span several movements in architectural theory, and clearly defy categories. For these reasons, the groupings follow a loose timeline.

THE SKETCHES AS ARTIFACTS

Each chapter begins with an introduction to the period, general social and political climate, ideals of the movements and/or architectural thought of the period, the tools and technologies available, and a brief survey of the education (or state of the profession) of the included architects. Also discussed is any similarity in technique or function of the sketches.

As a preamble to a discussion of architectural sketches it is important first to examine the compilation process for this collection of sketches. From the inception of this project the thesis was to present a historical survey of prominent architects using sketches as indicative of their design thinking. The selection of architects and sketches to include has been a difficult task requiring the consideration of numerous factors. The choice of architects relied on the availability of appropriate sketches and their interesting or unusual approaches to sketching as a process of design. This study included how the context, subject matter and physical look of the sketches may have affected an architect's repertoire of built work. These factors were revealed through exploring the media used, and how techniques facilitated and expressed the architects' intention.

The process of selecting the images to be discussed, either from direct observation in an archive or inspection of published sketches, involved evaluating the specific sketches considering a diversity of style and theme to be presented. Of primary concern was the attempt to locate sketches with a variety of techniques and content to present a wide range of approaches. Subsequently a sketch example from each architect was chosen because it epitomized the style or 'hand' of that architect. These conclusions were reached after inspecting as many examples as possible. Most sketches were chosen because they displayed a theory or reasoning inherently expressed in their form or technique. This meant attempting to locate a revelation or understanding of what that architect was thinking as manifest in the sketches. Also important was the uniqueness of the use, a direct link to a specific building or a connection to a feature in the architect's repertoire evident in the handling, such as smudges, pinpricks, erasures, circling of the sketches, eliminating by crossing out unwanted images or the drawing over specific areas for emphasis. With many of the sketches, this process began with observing the original sketches in an archival setting. Viewing the artifact firsthand revealed unique elements of process such as marks showing through from the reverse side of the paper, distinctive texture of the paper or fine guidelines difficult to view in photographs. Some sketches have been previously published and invariably represent the best examples of that architect's work available.

One of the major factors in choosing which sketches to include involved the availability of the collections. Some sketches obviously were chosen because all others had been destroyed for various reasons, such as the limited collection of sketches by Antonio Gaudi and the few ornament sketches saved by Louis Sullivan. Other architects such as Le Corbusier and Erich Mendelsohn meticulously reserved evidence of their beginning conceptual thoughts, and in these instances the selection was daunting because of the great number of existing sketches. These examples may reflect an attitude toward sketches. Some architects viewed the remnants of the process as valueless or, conversely, as a valuable artifact embodying their creative inspiration.

Another concern when selecting the sketches was the consideration for those that would reproduce well in publication. Numerous sketches that were considered exhibited brief beginnings, with only a few lines on a page, where the architect presumably rejected them for a fresh start. Comprising personal dialogue, the architects did not consider the images' beauty or communication qualities to anyone but themselves. Thus many of these sketches defy interpretation because of their briefness. An attempt was made to balance the number of sketches within the periods but also increase the number of examples in periods where sketches were more accessible. The techniques of the sketches by architects from within architectural movements are not necessarily visually consistent, because they each represent individual styles, commissions, themes and functions.

All of the sketches published in this collection are 'attributed to' the specific architect named by the various archives, unless otherwise mentioned. Authorship of the work has been reasonably determined from a combination of art dealers, collection donors and researchers. Although many of the sketches chosen for this collection have never been referenced in publication, it was possible to view numerous examples of an architect's technique and style of drawing to feel confident in the attributions of authorship. Sketches were avoided where authorship appeared doubtful specifically those that may have been rendered by a partner or apprentice. In archives around the world, there are many sketches 'in the school of' which may never divulge the hand that made them. In the case of Renaissance artist's sketches there is always the possibility that the images were drawn by an assistant in the workshop, as apprentices were regularly encouraged to copy the work of the master. However, with architectural sketches there may be less mistaken identification than with completed drawings. This may be partially because a less prominent architect could copy or render a famous professional's architectural 'style' or imitate a construction rendering, but sketches are unique conceptual thinking and thus difficult to reproduce. In this way, sketches can be perceived as more distinctively individual as compared to completed drawings that utilize conventional methods of representation. As an essence of thinking they are quick, expressive and unique to the individual architects and it is these traits that render them difficult to falsify. The act of miscrediting architectural sketches may stem from the melding of collections by several architects such as the case of John Webb having inherited sketches by both Palladio and Inigo Jones. The instances where architects were in partnership or a sketch is substantially brief may also make identifying authorship more complex. The most important aspect of this argument asserts that most architects felt that their sketches were part of a process and valueless compared to the built structure, consequently there has been little motive to claim false authorship. The problem was usually not intentional falsification but concerns the many images that have been separated from, or sold individually out of, collections.

An effort was made to obtain sketches by prominent architects through history and from around the world. As a history of architectural sketches, this collection focuses less on the architect's whole body of work, important accomplishments or theories, but rather targets the sketch as an artifact remaining as evidence of a place in history and as evidence of an architect's individual expression. The sketches were selected to represent a variety of styles, an array of media uses and a range of functions, for example sketches acting as travel companions, sketches entreated to contemplate construction details or sketches conjured to assist first conceptual inspiration. Primary importance involved the speculation about meaning for these architects in a process of design intention and to provide insight into the evolution of architectural sketches through history.

NOTES

1. Marco Frascari, Critical Conversations in Media, Drawing as Theory, ACSA Annual Meeting 2001.

BIBLIOGRAPHY

– (1892). *The Dictionary of Architecture: The Architecture Publication Society, volume II*. Thomas Richards.
Allsopp, B. (1959). *A History of Renaissance Architecture*. Pitman and Sons.
Aristotle translated by Holt, W.S. (1935). *De Anima and De Memoria*. Harvard University Press.
Barasch, M. (1985). *Theories of Art: From Plato to Winckelmann*. New York University Press.
Barzman, K-e. (2000). *The Florentine Academy and the Early Modern State: The Discipline of Disegno*. Cambridge University Press.
Benevolo, L. (1978). *The Architecture of the Renaissance*. Westview Press.
Blau, E. and Kaufman, E. (1989). *Architecture and Its Image. Four Centuries of Architectural Representation*. Canadian Centre for Architecture.
Bucher, F. (1979). *Architector: The Lodgebooks and Sketchbooks of Medieval Architects, vol. 1*. Abaris Books.
Calvino, I. (1988). *Six Memos for the Next Millennium*. Harvard University Press.
Casey, E.S. (1976). *Imagining: A Phenomenological Study*. Indiana University Press.
Casey, E.S. (1987). *Remembering: A Phenomenological Study*. Indiana University Press.

Coulin, C. (1962). *Drawings by Architects*. Reinhold.

Coulton, J.J. (1977). *Ancient Greek Architects at Work*. Cornell University Press.

Currie, S. (1998). *Drawing 1400–1600. Invention and Innovation*. Ashgate.

Dal Co, F. and Mazzariol, G. (1984). *Carlo Scarpa: The Complete Works*. Electa/Rizzoli.

Dalley, T. (1980). *The Complete Guide to Illustration and Design: Techniques and Materials*. Chartwell.

Evans, R. (1986). Translations from Drawing to Building. *AA Files*, 12.

Filarete translated by J. R. Spencer (1965). *Treatise on Architecture*. Yale University Press.

Gebhard, D. and Nevins, D. (1977). *200 Years of American Architectural Drawings*. Whitney Library of Design.

Gibson, J.J. (1979). *The Ecological Approach to Visual Perception*. Houghton Mifflin Company.

Gibson, J.J. edited by Reed, E. and Jones, R. (1982). *Reasons for Realism: Selected Essays of James J. Gibson*. Lawrence Erlbaum Associates.

Gombrich, E.H. (1985). *The Story of Art*. Prentice-Hall.

Gordon, D.J. (1975). *The Renaissance Imagination*. University of California Press.

Halse, A.O. (1952). *A History of the Development in Architectural Drafting Technique*. Doctor of Education Dissertation. New York University.

Hambly, M. (1988). *Drawing Instruments, 1580–1980*. Sotheby's Publications/Philip Wilson Publishers.

Hammond, J.H. (1981). *The Camra Obscura*. Adam Hilger.

Hewitt, M. (1985). Representational Forms and Modes of Conception: An Approach to the History of Architectural Drawing. *Journal of Architectural Education*, 39/2.

Hutter, H. (1968). *Drawing: History and Technique*. McGraw-Hill.

Kearney, R. (1988). *The Wake of the Imagination: Toward a Postmodern Culture*. University of Minnesota Press.

Kostof, S. ed. (1977). *The Architect*. Oxford University Press.

Kostof, S. (1985). *A History of Architecture: Settings and Rituals*. Oxford University Press.

Kris, E. and Kurz, O. (1979). *Legend, Myth, and Magic in the Image of the Artist*. Yale University Press.

Lauer, D. (1979). *Design Basics*. Holt, Rinehart and Winston.

McQuaid, M. (2002). *Envisioning Architecture: Drawings from the Museum of Modern Art*. The Museum of Modern Art.

Meisenheimer, W. (1987). The Functional and the Poetic Drawing. *Daidalos*, 25.

Merleau-Ponty, M. (1964). *Primacy of Perception*. Northwestern University Press.

Oechslin, W. (1982). The Well-Tempered Sketch. *Daidalos*, 5.

Pérez-Gómez, A. and Pelletier, L. (1997). *Architectural Representation and the Perspective Hinge*. MIT Press.

Pierce, J.S. (1967). Architectural Drawings and the Intent of the Architect. *Art Journal*, 27.

Porter, T. (1979). *How Architects Visualize*. Van Nostrand Reinhold.

Price, L. (1982). *The Plan of St. Gall in Brief*. University of California Press.

Randall, L. (1966). *Images in the Margins of Gothic Manuscripts*. University of California Press.

Robbins, E. (1994). *Why Architects Draw*. MIT Press.

Scheller, R.W. (1995). *Exemplum: Model-Book Drawings and the Practice of Artistic Transmission in the Middle Ages*. Amsterdam University Press.

Serrato-Combe, A. (2001). *The Aztec Templo Mayor: A Visualization*. University of Utah Press.

Smith, A. (2004). *Architectural Model as Machine*. Architectural Press.

Stewart, D.B. (1987). *The Making of a Modern Japanese Architecture, 1868 to the Present*. Kodansha International.

de Tolnay, C. (1972). *History and Technique of Old Masters Drawings*. Hacker Art Books.

Trachtenberg, M. and Hyman, I. (1986). *Architecture: From Prehistory to Post-Modernism*. Harry N. Abrams.

Vasari, G. abridged and edited by Burroughs, B. (1946). *The Lives of the Artists*. Simon and Schuster.

Vitruvius translated by Granger, F. (1934). *On Architecture*. William Heinemann.

Warnock, M. (1976). *Imagination*. The University of California Press.

White, J. (1972). *The Birth and Rebirth of Pictorial Space*. Harper and Row.

Wittkower, R. (1949). *Architectural Principles in the Age of Humanism*. University of London.

Wittkower, R. (1980). *Art and Architecture in Italy 1600–1750*. Penguin Books.

Wollheim, R. (1971). *Art and Its Objects*. Harper and Row.

CHAPTER 1

RENAISSANCE (1500–1650)

The Renaissance resulted in many innovations in architecture and parallel developments in techniques pertaining to drawings and sketches. Exploration of antiquity, and the dissemination of knowledge about its ideals, necessitated methods of communication and analysis. The emergence of paper as a medium to convey information was part of this exchange of ideas. As mentioned in the general introduction, attitudes toward sketching as a mode for exploration distinguished the Renaissance from traditional medieval practices. Renaissance workshops acted as educational facilities, encouraging competition and creativity. All of these factors affected architects' media manipulation and, consequently, the manner in which they thought about architecture.

It is important to briefly reiterate some of the sparks of early Renaissance thought that led to this movement. The Renaissance, from *Renascenta*, meant a revival or rebirth of classical culture and civilization (Allsopp, 1959). The Renaissance represented a paradigm shift from the Middle Ages which were considered with disdain. The Italians were reviving a period when Rome had been a powerful empire. Its fall left the region in disarray, its culture and language degraded. Revisiting this former age, the Italians believed, would provide standards of judgment that were indisputable. With the reuse of a little-known civilization, the excavation of antiquities supplied models for new ideals (Allsopp, 1959; Benevolo, 1978; Murray, 1963, 1978; Trachtenberg and Hyman, 1986; Wittkower, 1980).

At this time, Italy was comprised of city-states which were loosely associated under the Emperor and the Pope (Allsopp, 1959). These political units did not have the military strength to become independent so they owed their allegiance to Rome. This relationship depended upon diplomatic representation, requiring a certain amount of literacy; with this came scholarship. The ideal Renaissance statesman aspired to be competent, learned and cultured. This was a part of the concept of humanism, applied as a term many centuries later, which manifest itself in a reappearance of classical thought. Humanism suggested the civilizing qualities of being cultivated in Latin and Greek literary works (Murray, 1978). With this interest in antiquity, Vitruvius' *Ten Books of Architecture* was republished in approximately 1486, and a subsequent Italian edition was published in 1521.

The rereading of Vitruvius reinforced the concept of architects as persons of learning and practical experience, stressing diverse knowledge in multiple fields. Again, architects were not just craftsmen or masons, but could envision the building's form as well as direct its construction. The Renaissance architects studied elements of antiquity to understand their form. Brunelleschi constitutes an example; as a student of Roman structural techniques, he was said to have sketched many buildings in Rome. These sketches were a way to analyze and interpret antiquity, and humanists such as Alberti considered the art of architecture as dominated by proportions and mathematics (Murray, 1963, 1978). Such architects were scrutinizing ancient artifacts by drawing and measuring; they were taking notes so that they could reuse the imagery of antiquity; thus they were learning to speak in the language of classicism. This learning was seen as the key to a greater level of knowledge. Alberti, in the forward to his treatise, wrote that it was this learning that elevated the architect above the role of craftsman and identified them with the liberal arts (Blunt, 1958; Alberti, 1988). In this way, the educated architect could integrate all intellectual endeavors and could engage in diverse occupations such as observation of the heavens or building sundials (Benevolo, 1978). Ernst Cassirer stresses the combination of theory and practice that Renaissance thinking held for these artists: 'Just as the visual arts seek plastic formulas of balance, so philosophy seeks intellectual formulas of balance between the "medieval faith in God and the self-confidence of Renaissance man"' (1963, p. 76).

SKETCHES

Renaissance ideals, supportive of creativity and speculation, allowed sketches to become a common media for recording, communicating architecturally, visualizing, evaluating, and designing. As a brief preamble, this discussion presents some commonalities between the techniques and intentions of architects' representational media that can be observed through their sketches.

Drawing became the basis for the artistic endeavors of Renaissance architects. It was through the act of drawing that advancements in visual perception were developed. Brunelleschi's lessons, which described perspective construction, changed the way architects presented their proposals. It also changed their conception of the architectural artifact and, subsequently, architectural space. It proved easier for them to visualize the spaces they intended, since these were three-dimensional views rendered with relative spatial accuracy. The new (or renewed) codification of perspective construction greatly influenced painting as well as architects' methods of design.

The 'elevation' as a drawing convention dates to the early 1400s. It revealed the dominating features of the façade and made proportioning easier to explore with drawings (Murray, 1978). Remnants from medieval forms of representation, these drawings did not have contemporary concepts of construction as part of their language. In the mid-1500s, Leonardo was producing a prolific number of sketchbooks, evidence that the Renaissance artists/architects accepted drawing and sketching, and many practiced their skills with intense regularity. These skills were attained through maturity, allowing eye–hand coordination to be developed with practice. These architects recognized the value of such skills in allowing them to visualize unseen aspects of their architecture, but it was not until the end of the century did architects begin to draw monuments from antiquity for evaluation or recording (Murray, 1978). 'The development of such a technique of descriptive drawing is of fundamental importance to the way in which an architect visualizes buildings – to the very process of his thought – and the technique of architectural (as distinct from pictorial) drawing was in a critical stage of development at the end of the fifteenth century' (Murray, 1978, p. 12).

Humanism encouraged architects to believe in their identity as God-given rather than God-inspired; thus, they were less inhibited in the use of sketching as a creative act. As an artistic community they continually shared information and skills through the publishing of treatises, which were basically books of rules and advice for practice and theory. Through this collaboration, they perpetuated a collective interpretation of classicism. The rules supplied them with the basic elements, but drawing encouraged their interpretation and manipulation of these elements. The treatises prescribed architectural rules such as the orders – but they were indirectly advocating a theory of drawing.

The Renaissance architects obtained large commissions that they could complete in the span of their lifetime; thus, they needed the forethought provided by sketches and drawings to command many craftsmen and masons. The necessity to conceptually understand a building before its erection defined a new role for the master builder. Unlike the craftsmen of the gothic cathedrals, the Renaissance architect supervised construction partially because the project could not be finished by relying entirely upon traditional methods – innovative elements and details required intellectual foresight.

The Renaissance architects held allegiance to their individual patrons who were responsible for funding such large projects. The educated clients expected to be convinced of the validity of a project before it was undertaken. This required the architect's skills to both convey conceptual ideas and delineate convincing presentations. Comparatively, the patrons also felt the pressure of competition; their personal prestige was often tied to self-aggrandizing monuments of their accomplishments.

20

Simultaneously, these architects relied on their reputation and/or publication to enhance the success of their careers. They were compensated for their ingenuity and design abilities, unlike the medieval craftsman whose manual skills were valued above their intellect.

Thus in the late Renaissance, a standard was set for sketches and drawings, as vehicles of exploration and discovery. The sketchbook was a medium for thinking and visualizing. Although drawings reflected the study and tracing of elements suggested by Vitruvius (constituting a medium to study accepted principles) the sketch emerged as an impetus for creativity. Most architects were trained in painting workshops where they became highly skilled in quick conceptual sketching. They were able to achieve aesthetically beautiful and proportionally accurate imitations of nature. A master's drawings were both revered and copied by apprentices, as they became valuable in their own right (Kris and Kurz, 1979). Vasari was the first to collect (and thereby raise the status of) these works as artifacts to be held for prosperity, giving many Renaissance architects mythical reputations. The legends of these architects, such as Michelangelo and Leonardo, increased the value of their sketches.

Sketching/drawing styles and methods of representation varied, but they did have some similarities. Leonardo had an explorative and analytical style. His sketches contained the quality of observation; as he was attempting to understand through viewing. He was able to document empirical study, recording his curiosity by combining observed facts with aspects of his imagination (Cassirer, 1963). Peruzzi, da Sangallo and Vignola employed their sketches to work out details and visualize a future building. Each had tremendous skill in manipulating drawing media, especially in controlling pen and ink with very fine parallel lines for shading. Da Sangallo's drawings, from the sketches held in the Uffizi collection, exhibit many alternatives for fortification plans. Likewise, Michelangelo diagrammed the projectile angles of munitions in his plans for military fortifications, as evidenced by his many sketches in the collections of the Casa Buonarroti. He understood the volatility of his mannerist style, and many of his sketches were fluid expressions often rendered simultaneously with studies of human figures.

The Renaissance architects explored three-dimensional space through sketches, making quick perspectives to visualize form. Palladio often crowded drawings on the page, unconcerned if they overlapped or merged. Many of the sketches by Inigo Jones demonstrate a crude abstraction, with scratchy lines overworked and distorted. Each architect presented in this chapter utilized sketched images because, for them, they held an answer to a question. They believed in the power of the sketch to convey the technical details, dimensionality, spatial qualities, or conceptual beginnings necessary to their architecture. Using a trusted medium, they accomplished the skills allowing them to celebrate a personal dialogue. The tools at their disposal were important to this development.

MEDIA

Bambach, Ames-Lewis and Wright, all writing about the culture of the Renaissance workshop, elucidate the media employed for drawing and sketching. Until the middle of the 1400s, vellum was the most prevalent drawing medium. Vellum consisted of animal hide, soaked in lime, and subsequently scraped clean. To further prepare the drawing surface it was wetted, scoured with a gritty substance such as pumice, and stretched to dry in flat sheets. It was extremely sturdy, although expensive and not always available. As discussed in the general Introduction, paper later became the medium of choice. Although vellum was still available throughout the century, paper was less expensive and became continually more available to the Renaissance artist/architect. It was made in various thicknesses and in numerous tones of white, some even having pastel tints. As paper's quality and availability improved, artists and architects found that it performed well for conceptual exploration.

Following the use of the reed pen in ancient Egypt and Rome, the quill pen became predominant, since it was deemed more controllable. The quill could be cut in multiple ways for specific effects, and it allowed the renderer to alter line width by applying various amounts of pressure. Metal nibs for pens had been in use since the Roman period although these points had less flexibility and tended to rust (Turner, 1996). Inks were often used with wash for tonal qualities and shading, in both black and browns. Natural chalk was also available; it was an immediate medium that facilitated quick sketches, and could be purchased in tones of red, white, and black. In Italy, red chalk was known as *Sanguine* suggesting a reference to blood. It was useful to create soft tones for portraits. Charcoal, made from willow sticks, could be used for more detailed drawings. Its powdery quality permitted erasing, although it smudged easily. Graphite, from Bavaria, was available since the early thirteenth century. It was not, however, a popular drawing medium with artists and architects until the sixteenth century, when it was found in Cumbria, England. Learning the techniques and acquiring the skills to proficiently use these media were attained in the Renaissance workshops (Ames-Lewis and Wright, 1983; Vasari, 1945; Turner, 1996; Bambach, 1999).

EDUCATION; WORKSHOP CULTURE

Although Renaissance architects made pilgrimages to sites of excavated ruins to draw and measure the antiquities, most acquired their drawing skills in a prominent artist's workshop (Ames-Lewis and Wright, 1983; Vasari, 1945; Turner, 1996; Bambach, 1999). These workshops were organized for efficiency, to accomplish the many tasks necessary for painting, frescos, sculpture, or tapestry. The education of apprentice artists supported these endeavors. Bambach, Ames-Lewis and Wright describe the organization of these workshops.

A large workshop may have had many artists, craftsmen, and assistants, all working together to accomplish the tasks required for various projects. A successful master artist may have had many projects in the process of design, or at various stages of completion, at any one time. For example, assistants or apprentices might have been specialized in one or more of the numerous tasks involved in fresco painting. They were skilled in enlarging a sketch to the size of the finished fresco, which may have employed a grid for transfer. They (or a professional plasterer) applied the plaster in an amount equal to the work to be completed that day. They moved and assembled scaffolding, or ground and carried pigment to the site. The assistants and apprentices cut and joined the sheets of paper to be used for cartoons (full-scale templates for transfer), pounced the powdered charcoal through the cartoon onto the wet plastered surface, and assisted in the placing of these large templates. Painting and sculpture required comparable levels of effort. General workshop duties included grinding pigments, preparing charcoal sticks, texturing drawing surfaces, chipping outer layers of granite, or acting as models. As discussed earlier, these were the interdisciplinary tasks that encouraged a sense of *disegno*.

The education of an apprentice often took many years, and involved learning many skills. Promising young apprentices' education revolved around drawing. They first learned to draw using a silverpoint technique. A stylus, fashioned out of silver, was used to draw on a prepared surface. The stylus scraped a fine line of silver deposit that then oxidized to leave a faint line of consistent diameter. To achieve a bolder line the blunt end of the stylus was used. This technique required practice, since the silverpoint line was not erasable. To allow for such practice, the apprentices prepared the surface of a wood tablet that could be scraped off for reuse. Thus, silverpoint was used mostly for finished drawings, especially those to be retained in the workshop's archive. Other metals were used, but the line (being consistent) did not allow for a shading method other than cross-hatching. After learning sketching and drawing, apprentices were given other tasks to develop necessary skills. They were encouraged to study by drawing from a sculptured example, or by drawing each other. These exercises honed their skills in observation, trained their visual perception, improved eye–hand coordination, and allowed them to reproduce a natural looking figure exhibiting proper proportion. They imitated the master artist's style to learn from a great renderer, but also to provide consistency of style to the workshop's products. This was particularly important when finishing the background of a painting or transferring sketches for cartoons.

Using sketches as a trusted tool for imitation and an instrument for thinking, Renaissance architects developed skills that helped them understand antiquity as well as explore new directions within their individual repertoire. There is great variety in the way these sketches visually appear. This reflects their various intentions, stages in the design process, the skill level of each architect or the specific media selected.

FIGURE 1.1

Bramante, Donato (1444–1514)

Untitled, Uffizi, UFF 1714 A, Approx. 15.5 × 16.6 cm, Ink on paper

Bramante was one of the first of the great High Renaissance architects, influencing numerous prominent architects of Rome such as Peruzzi and Sangallo. He is best known for reviving the architecture of classical antiquity, which had begun with the works of Alberti (Allsopp, 1959). Vasari reported that Bramante spent much of his time studying and sketching the buildings in Rome (Vasari, 1907).

Born Donato di Angelo di Anthonio da Urbino/Pascuccio, it is speculated that he studied with Piero della Francesca and/or Andrea Mantegna. His first notable building was S. Maria Presso S. Satiro in Milan. In Rome, some of Bramante's most celebrated and influential projects were for Pope Julius at the Vatican, where he designed the Cortile di S. Damaso and the Cortile del Belvedere. With an interest in centrally planned churches similar to Leonardo, he also designed a Greek cross plan for St. Peter's with a vast central dome. His expressive building of the classical tradition was the Tempietto of S. Pietro in Montorio, 1502.

Bramante's design for the Tempietto was sited in the courtyard of the Church and Monastery of San Pietro in Montorio. It constitutes a diminutive temple acting as a Martyria, standing on the place presumed to be St. Peter's Martyrdom. Small and circular, it revisits antique forms appealing to contemporary Christians' preferences, crowned with a hemispherical dome resembling the Pantheon. This small monument displays simple proportions where the width of the dome is equal to the height of the interior cylinder (Allsopp, 1959).

This sketch on the facing page (Figure 1.1) exhibits a small shrine-like structure, representing an example of a centrally planned building. The sketch reads as an elevation of an octagon-shaped dome on a raised foundation. In plan, the building presented appears to be shaped in the form of a cross with small projections containing porches; it is vaguely reminiscent of Palladio's Villa Rotunda. Bramante's concern with the reference to a shrine led him to draw this sketch demonstrating its volume from the exterior, rather than interior space. Here, he used the porch to accent the central domed space, stressing the qualities of a monument, a temple from antiquity.

The building's organization describes an octagon within a Greek cross imposed within a square, but the sketch presents an image somewhere between a perspective and an elevation, as the face of the porch has been drawn slightly taller than the side porches. To stress the central altar and promote a three-dimensional effect, Bramante employs shading on the side of the octagon, further confusing the flat façade of the elevation. The sculptural figures on the roof have been drawn with the same lack of complexity as the scale figures standing on the stairs. Although the sketch does not appear to be hurried, Bramante describes the stairs with minimal detail. The set on the left display some definition, while the other set of stairs have been represented simply by double diagonal lines. This technique concentrates the focus to the center, and emphasizes the fact that the building was designed to be viewed equally well from all angles.

The sketch suggests a self-reflexivity, as it refers to the many centrally planned structures designed by Bramante. It also recalls the three-dimensional/volumetric qualities of Bramante's concern for a building's mass. The architectural historian James Ackerman wrote about the volume of Bramante's walls: '[W]e sense that where the earlier architect drew buildings, Bramante modelled them' (1961, p. 27). Although this design for a small building may not be directly related to the Tempietto, it is representative of a theme, one that Bramante explored throughout his career.

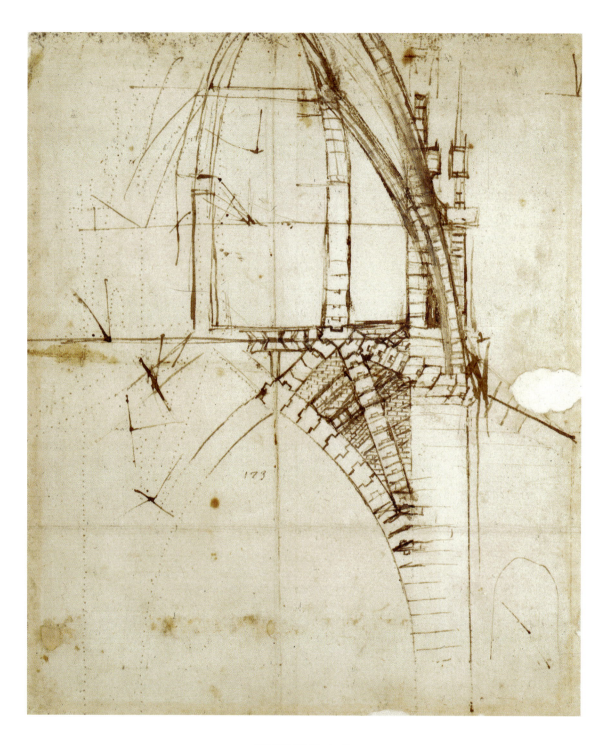

FIGURE 1.2

da Vinci, Leonardo (1452–1519)

Codex Atlanticus, studies for the tiburio of Milan Cathedral, c. 1487, Biblioteca Ambrosiana, f. 851 *recto*, 28.2 × 23.7 cm, Ink

It is impossible to discuss a history of architectural sketches without an example from Leonardo da Vinci, whose numerous sketchbooks reveal the genius of an architect, painter, sculptor, and inventor. Although he built or finished very little architectural work, he proposed designs for domed, centrally planned churches, fortifications, numerous mechanical inventions, and buildings in various scales from chapels to palaces to cities. At an early age he started in the workshop of painter Andrea del Verrochio. Throughout his career, Leonardo worked as a military engineer in Milan, in his own studio in Florence, and later in his life, on projects for King Louis XII in France. It was in Amboise, France, where he died in 1519. His works that remain include extensive sketchbooks, some sculpture, and paintings such as the *Mona Lisa, Virgin of the Rocks* and the fresco *The Last Supper* in San Maria delle Grazie, Milan.

A consummate observer, Leonardo took an empirical approach to satisfy his curiosity about the nature of the world, giving him the ability of 'sight and insight' (Janson, 1970). He felt that experience is acquired by the senses and, subsequently, that seeing involved an active process. Feeling a need to represent nature as he viewed it, his approach was opposed to that of universal beauty as discussed by Alberti. He viewed vision as the source of scientific truth (Barasch, 1999).

In 1487 Leonardo produced a model for the design of the dome of the Milan Cathedral. This page from his sketchbook, *Codex Atlanticus* (Figure 1.2), presents some of the design process for the *tiburio* of this cathedral. It shows the stacking of bricks or blocks to structure the light arches and buttresses. Typical of Leonardo's sketches, it is possible to view details of construction and connection, as the blocks are rendered with interlocking notches. As a design study, the sketch also displays rough beginnings and alterations, showing a centerline and horizontals to guide proportions. Only half of the construction has been detailed; Leonardo understood enough to move on to another drawing or a model. Perhaps he rejected how the proposal was progressing, or the sketch had simply served its purpose and could be set aside.

This page (f. 851 *recto*) has numerous identical stippling marks as the page f. 850 *recto*. These marks were presumably used as guidelines and also acted as identical templates to explore multiple variations for assembly and construction. The marks are in fact pinpricks that resemble the pounced guidelines of a cartoon used to transfer a design onto a fresco. Leonardo was well aware of the transfer techniques of cartoons using bilateral symmetry. It is evident that on other sheets from the *Codex Atlanticus*, he folded the paper to prick guidelines through both sides of the paper to perceive a symmetrical whole (Bambach, 1999). Evidence of a similar technique can be viewed on this page; a prominent crease down the center. The irregular spacing of the marks coincides exactly, strongly suggesting that at least part of each sketch was pricked simultaneously, or possibly, the pages were first folded and then pricked through all layers.[1] This points to an economy, in that Leonardo would not need to recalculate the *tiburio*, but make minor alterations to the structural form or the stacking of the blocks on identical sheets. In this way, one can view the architect/builder concerned with the solidity of the structure as well as the artist, utilizing known transfer techniques.

FIGURE 1.3

Peruzzi, Baldassare (1481–1536)
Study of a sepulchre, Uffizi, UFF 159 A, 12 × 13 cm, Brown ink and wash

A prominent architect of the high Renaissance in Rome, Baldassare Peruzzi's approach was influenced by the work of Bramante and Raphael. His peers respected him for his revival of the art of stage design, and for his expertise in the art of perspective drawing. Peruzzi arrived in Rome in 1503 from Siena. He began as a painter under Pinturicchio, and was commissioned in 1509 by the Sienese banker Agostino Chigi to design the Palace Farnesina. The palazzo reflects his strong sense of proportion and his interest in the principles of mathematics as set down by Alberti. Different in plan than other Roman palaces of the time, Villa Farnesina has two wings flanking a central loggia, containing frescos by Raphael.

Much of Peruzzi's experience was obtained in the Vatican Workshop assisting Donato Bramante, and, later, collaborating with Raphael until 1527 when he fled to Siena precipitated by the Sack of Rome. Bramante had envisioned a rebuilding of St. Peter's based on a Greek cross plan, and Peruzzi's plan suggested a variation (Allsopp, 1959). Other projects designed by Peruzzi individually or in collaboration, in addition to St. Peter's, include: fortifications near Porta Laterina and Porta S. Viene, Palazzo Pollini, San Nicolò in Carpi, and the Palazzo Massimo alle Colonne in Rome. He died in Rome in 1536, and Serlio, who included Peruzzi's drawings prominently in his treatise, heralded his influence on architecture.

This ink and wash sketch (Figure 1.3) demonstrates a three-dimensional study of what seems to be a sepulcher, or tomb chest, with an apsidiole form. This small projecting chapel structure consists of a self-contained entity, possibly planned for an interior wall of a cathedral side aisle. Drawn freehand in perspective, or a version of an elevation oblique, the sketch appears somewhat distorted, obviously not calculated or measured. Because this view employs washes for shadows and a completed composition, Peruzzi was able to interpret and evaluate the proposed solution. The sketch, then, suggests the importance for Peruzzi to quickly comprehend three-dimensional relationships. The sketch acted as a method of evaluation to represent either an image from his mind's eye or an emerging design solution. Although the ink techniques are minimal and scratchy, the sketch contains enough information to visualize the form as a whole.

Peruzzi must have understood the sketch as part of a process. Although showing the aedicule as a whole, the technique of the lines are quick and loosely constructed, suggesting not a solution, but a momentary snapshot of a thought in the process. The columns are straightened by additional lines in a method of 'making and matching,' numbers are sprinkled over the top and other façades, and pen-testing lines appear in the background (Gombrich, 1969, p. 29). These elements, which appear on and around the sketch, suggest the little value given the image by Peruzzi after the information was conveyed in a dialogue of the design process. Even though the columns are not straight and the distances between the columns are irregular, the sketch conveys a compositional whole, displaying proportions, relationships and symmetry. The ink wash provides depth that enhances the three-dimensional illusion, helping to judge the final effects of the whole. Being both a definitive view and a design in process, the sarcophagus/tomb-chest stand has been drawn and redrawn in a search for its relationship to the columns and figures. This reveals how the design was still fluid and could be reevaluated when seen in conjunction with other elements.

This sketch gave a quick proportional and compositional view to Peruzzi, allowing him to see the whole at a decision point in his thinking.

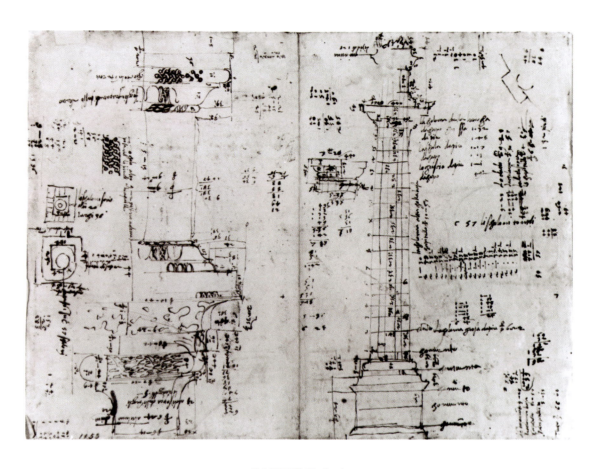

FIGURE 1.4

da Sangallo, Antonio the Younger (1483–1546) or (1485–1546)

Design for a freestanding tomb seen in elevation and plan, Uffizi, UFF 1153 A.v.,
11.1 × 15.5 cm, Pen and brown ink, brush and brown wash on tan laid paper

Antonio da Sangallo, born in Florence in 1485, was the nephew of two da Sangallo architects, Giuliano and Antonio the Elder. He trained under their tutelage before arriving in Rome in approximately 1503. Although obviously influenced by his uncles, his architecture proved to adhere to the classicism of the High Renaissance.

da Sangallo designed numerous architectural projects throughout his life, such as the interior of Capella Paolina in the Vatican, Palazzo Palma-Baldassini, Rome, in 1520, Palazzo Sacchetti, Rome, begun in 1542, and Palazzo Baldassini, which evokes the architecture of ancient Rome with its massive masonry. After a period as Raphael's assistant, in 1539 he became the chief architect for St. Peter's and supplied designs for the alteration of Bramante's plan (Musgrove, 1987). Although not executed, his plan advocated altering the Greek plan into a more traditional cathedral plan, considering liturgical requirements. For many years he was employed as a military engineer working on fortifications around Rome. Antonio da Sangallo died in 1546 in Rome, having spent much of his life working on St. Peter's.

With this page of sketches (Figure 1.4) da Sangallo appears to have been employing diagrams to calculate visually. The diagrams may have worked to serve his memory for difficult items such as numerous dimensions and proportions, or as simple outlines to frame his concentration of a specific subject. They may not have acted as an imitation, but instead were used to convey basic spatial relationships. Diagrams may be defined in mathematical terms as assisting to present a definition or 'to aid in the proof of a proposition.' Additionally, they can be outlines or abstractions that provide the basic scheme of something to reveal 'the shape and relations of its various parts' (OED, 1985). Similar to a definition of sketches, diagrams may help to isolate the essence of a concept or proposition.

On the right side of the page stands a column, giving just enough information to recognize it as such. A simple outline, the column has been overlaid with a grid and is accompanied by a series of numbers, possibly describing dimensions or calculations pertaining to the construction of the column. The left side of this page reveals an inverted column where the capital and base have been dimensioned but the shaft, having been foreshortened, reveals its relative unimportance. Around the periphery, as partial musings, are pen testing marks, capital carvings, small column elevations, and unfinished details of moldings and stairs. It is possible to view two tones of the brown ink used for this sketch, conveying a sense of the passage of time. This is especially visible where he crosses out particular numbers. It might be assumed that either the sketch was drawn at one time and altered later with a different mix of ink, or that da Sangallo freshly dipped his pen before crossing out the inappropriate numbers after reconsideration.

The 'look' of the column was obviously unimportant, as he avoided shadows or details. Slightly skewed to the right, vertical fluting extends beyond the capital top, suggesting that he began calculating the sections from the base. The section numbers can be equated with the long list of numbers viewed horizontally while they vary in individual dimensions. The horizontal section markings may represent the pieces intended for assembly in construction of the column or a key for the changes in the diameter or entasis. Most importantly, it was unnecessary for da Sangallo to carefully render the column because the brief outline acted to visually reference the spatial relationships. The left column also has been dimensioned, and here the details are small parts of the planned carving. These limited suggestions of ornament were enough for him to remember what had been planned for each portion.

FIGURE 1.5

Buonarroti, Michelangelo (1475–1564)

Base/molding profile studies for San Lorenzo (Basi di pilastro per la Sagreetia Nuova, scritte autografe), *c.* 1520–1525, Fondazione Casa Buonarroti, 10 A *recto*, 28.3 × 21.4cm, Red chalk, pen and ink (Sanguigna, penna)

Probably the most influential high Renaissance/mannerist architect, the design thinking used by Michelangelo was continually affected by his roles as a sculptor, painter, and architect. During the Renaissance, it was common for architects to use the human body as analogy (especially concerning proportion and geometry), but Michelangelo's theory of architecture looked instead to metaphors involving bodies moving in space and sculptural forms revealing shadow and light. Trained in anatomy, Michelangelo viewed architecture as more than external appearances; rather the movement in his architecture can be compared to nerve and muscle systems (Ackerman, 1961).

Michelangelo Buonarroti was born in Caprese, 1475. He began early in his life as a painter being apprenticed to the Florentine Ghirlandaio. Throughout his life, he was patronized by both the Medici family and the Church. He also received commissions from Pope Julius II in the Sistine Chapel and, later, from Leo X, Clement VII, and Paul III. In addition to his numerous sculptural and painting projects, his architectural projects include the Façade of San Lorenzo, the Medici Family Mausoleum, the Biblioteca Laurenziana, and Fortifications in Florence, the Palazzo dei Conservatori and the Palazzo dei Senatore on Capitoline Hill (Wittkower, 1980; Wallace, 1998; Summers, 1981; Murray, 1963, 1978).

In this freehand sketch (Figure 1.5) can be seen the design of bases for columns at San Lorenzo, resembling templates used to construct molding profiles. At the same time, Michelangelo was caricaturing a human profile. It may be possible to speculate that after drawing these bases several times, Michelangelo saw that they began to resemble a human face, so he hooked the nose slightly and added an eye. A few quick lines were enough to complete the figure in a surprisingly recognizable way. The eye and the hook on the nose are in the same tone of *sanquine*, and with the same hand pressure, so one can conclude that they were completed simultaneously with the profiles, rather than being a later addition.

It is unlikely Michelangelo originally intended to reference the human body with this design, but once he recognized the resemblance he could not resist completing the imagery. In the collection of sketches at the Casa Buonarroti, many sheets of his architectural details were drawn on the same pages as figure studies. Considering the culture of the Renaissance studio, drawings may have floated from hand to hand so that he might pick up the closest piece of paper with a blank spot and continue to draw, revealing an interesting crossover between the figure and architecture. It is interesting to contemplate that he saw little difference in the conceptual design of architecture as compared to studies of the human form.

This sketch contains numerous qualities distinctive of caricature. The imagination of the caricaturist demonstrates techniques of transformation and condensation to expose the true personality of their subjects (Kris and Gombrich, 1938). The transformation of features relies on the ability to recognize that 'resemblance is a prerequisite of caricature' (Kris, 1934, p. 298). It depends upon metaphors; it is the likeness, altered, to reveal related traits through visual allusion.

The action of adding human anatomy to a sketch is particularly interesting considering Michelangelo's theories, as most other architects would not have made similar mental connections. Here, though, the caricature involves a likeness, rather than the organic quality evident in his architecture. Since Michelangelo thoroughly understood the principles of *disegno*, it is possible to presume that his memories and imagination carried across disciplines.

33

FIGURE 1.6

34

de L'Orme, Philibert (between 1505 and 1510–1570)

Heliocoidal staircase in perspective, Attributed to Philibert de L'Orme, archive, *c.* 1505–1568, Musée du Louvre, INV 11114, *recto*, 38.2 × 24.3 cm, Brown ink, black lead, feather pen

Philibert de L'Orme may have been the first Frenchman to achieve the stature of architect in the modern sense, but he was profoundly located in the sixteenth century. de L'Orme visited Italy to draw and measure antiquity carrying much of what he learned back to France. Subsequently, he was the first French architect to consciously employ Renaissance ideals in his architecture. He was born in Lyon, somewhere between the years 1505 and 1510, into a family of master masons. In addition to learning skills in masonry, crucial to his education were his visits to the south of France and Italy to study antiquity, the most significant being his trip to Rome from 1533 to 1536.

His first significant commission came from Cardinal Jean du Bellay to design the Château St. Maur-lès-Fossés, where he was able to exhibit his knowledge of classical principles. In this case, his challenge was to bring classical architecture to France while accommodating local materials and traditions. The result was a plan somewhat French, incorporating classical Corinthian pilasters and ornament. By 1550 de L'Orme, then living in Paris, was placed in charge of all the royal buildings (except the Louvre) by Henry II. Examples of his numerous other architectural projects include Château Neuf, the chapel in Château Anet, and the bridge gallery across the Cher at Chenonceaux.

This spiral staircase (Figure 1.6) delineated in a confident hand is attributed to de L'Orme.[2] It is likely that he is the author, considering the many staircases known to be designed by him, that show similar technique. In the case that it is not, the image remains a compelling example, contemplating the difficulties for architects in visualizing a complex architectural element. The importance of this image for the Italian school in France comes from a reference in his treatises, *Nouvelles Inventions pour bien bastir et à petits Fraiz* and *Le premier tôme de l'Architecture*, that refers to Bramante's spiral staircase in the Belvedere. In chapter nineteen, de L'Orme states that bases and capitals of the columns should follow the sloping entablature, rather than be placed horizontally as in Bramante's design, and that architects should use coffering instead of brick on the underside of the vault (Blunt, 1958).

The technique of this sketch shows it was drawn primarily in single line. Each line seems rendered with slow precision. Although he was speculating on a three-dimensional view, there is very little use of shadow or texture. There are no perspective guidelines or evidence of orthographic construction.

Although de L'Orme was undoubtedly familiar with current development in perspective construction, this image has been drawn entirely freehand. To delineate it accurately would have been an extremely time-consuming endeavor. It is a very clear three-dimensional rendition presenting enough detail to visualize the complex stair. A spiral stair is very difficult to imagine, even more difficult to draw, and is very hard to explain to someone else. With this in mind, he may have felt the perspective complete (believable) enough that he started to detail the coffers and railings, even though they still appear rough and not consistent with the intended view. He was not worried that it was imperfectly constructed, but rather believed in the information he was receiving, and thus trusted in the power of the sketch. With the addition of letters inscribed on certain material surfaces, this image may have also been trusted enough to build from.

FIGURE 1.7

da Vignola, Giacomo Barozzi (1507–1573)

Elevation, sections sketch page, Uffizi, UFF 96 A.v., 30 × 44.5 cm, Ink and wash

Giacomo Barozzi, known as Vignola, was influential in both his role as an author and as a practicing architect. His work, having a strong foundation in classicism, was innovative, and made important contributions to the design of churches and palaces. He was born at Vignola, near Modena, in 1507 and died in Rome in 1573. His early education included studying painting and architecture in Bologna. In 1530 he relocated to Rome and spent much time drawing examples of antiquity (Murray, 1963). Although a contemporary of Michelangelo, much of his classicism descends from Bramante (Murray, 1963). Early in his career, Vignola worked at Fontainebleau in France where he first met Sebastiano Serlio. His first major design was Villa Giulia for Pope Julius III, a starkly blank façade with deep-cut rusticated stone accenting the door and corners. One of his early churches, the Church of Sant' Andrea, 1554, anticipates Baroque church design with its oval dome. The quintessential plan of the Gesú, begun in 1568, reveals a wide nave and barrel vault that consider the liturgical needs of the Counter Reformation. Vignola's legacy includes a treatise entitled *Regola delli Cinque Ordini d'Architettura*, 1562, which deals mostly with the classical orders and was widely distributed for many years after his death.

This sketch (Figure 1.7) by Vignola exhibits a mostly freehand page, crowded with various notes and sections. The sketch was used as a method to think through design, as it is strewn with dimensioning, details, and carefully drawn capitals and stairs, all in various stages of completion. It may represent work studied in one sitting but most likely represented a drawing returned to over time.

This working page has an uneven thickness of paper and scars from compass arcs that show through from the other side. One can see shadows of ink wash and a compass puncture from the *recto* that gives the page background and texture. As an example of a page used for thinking and discovering, one can see the various media of ink and wash, along with graphite used for guidelines. The smearing of the graphite suggests a drawing that acts as a 'medium' for design, considering both the meaning of medium as the physical media used to manipulate, and additionally suggesting the medium as substance or atmosphere in a magical sense. 'Medium' is both a means of conveying ideas or information and a substance through which something is carried or transmitted, allowing someone to convey messages between the spirits of the dead and the living (OED, 1985). With this in mind, the sketch becomes the medium of mediation, the place where ideas flow and intersect.

The largest image is a section, not completely rendered with poché. Molding profiles can also be viewed in section, rendered with wash to contemplate the three-dimensional illusion. A few of these images are drawn quite slowly in contemplation or carefully ruled. Although they are drawn slowly, they may display a thinking process as Vignola used the media to answer questions. As a medium or substance that encourages dialogue, it is possible to question which sketches were drawn first or last or even if they relate to the same building. This may be true especially since items as disparate as details of brick and spiral stairs question these relationships.

This sketch provides physical evidence of design thinking where Vignola was using various conventional and non-conventional modes of drawing. Here he was easily moving between different media and various techniques, almost as if he needed to conjure up the methods that best assisted him to visualize. This not-self-conscious free flow of ideas may provide insight into the 'medium' of Vignola's design process.

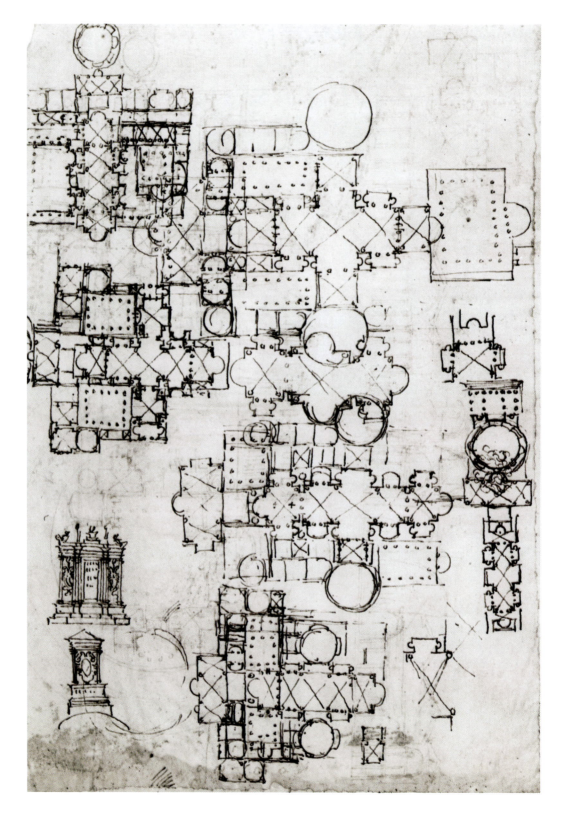

FIGURE 1.8

Palladio, Andrea (1508–1580)

Sketch page for the Baths of Agippa, and Hadrian's Villa, Tivoli, RIBA, VII/6R *verso*,
Approx. 7 × 10 in., Ink on paper

Palladio was born in Padua, near Venice, in 1508, as Andrea di Pietro dalla Gondola. His early exposure to architecture came both as a stonemason and a craftsman of ornamentation, working in the studio of Giovanni di Giacomo in Pedemuro. Later influenced by ideas of humanism, he studied the work of Vitruvius, Alberti, and other Renaissance treatises, writing his *Quattro libri dell'architettura* in 1570. His meeting with Sanmicheli strengthened this knowledge of classical structures, and his later association with Barbaro and Vasari helped him establish his ideas based on rules of proportion. Palladio's prestige in the architectural community was evident by his becoming a member of the Academy of Design in Florence in 1566. In 1570, after the death of Jacopo Sansovino, he became the architectural advisor to the Venetian Republic (Puppi, 1973; Wittkower, 1980; Murray, 1978).

Andrea Palladio's villas of the Veneto were based on harmonic proportions, symmetry, and the images of classical temple fronts. This antique monumentalism was influenced by his visits to Rome and by the work of Giulio Romano around the environs of Vincenza. In developing his architecture, he adapted the use of proportional ground plans and utilized a strong axis of penetration (front to rear) through his buildings. In his urban projects, the loggias reflected classical proportions, such as the Basilica in Vicenza (*Palazzo della Ragione*), where his new loggia was based on lessons of antiquity.

This page of sketches (Figure 1.8) shows images crowded across the page, as if one idea led quickly to the next, the sketches bleeding into one another and overlapping. These sketches seem to be variations on a theme, as they all contain similar floor area and organization. Some sketches seem more complete, while others were rejected and abandoned early in the process of exploration. In many places on the page, the lines are adjusted (drawn over) to suggest a form of *pentimento* – regret, or the recalibration of an idea. This technique references the comparison and adjustment of what is seen on the paper with what is seen in the mind's eye.

Specifically, on this page are found mostly symmetrical building plans, very distinctive of Palladio's architecture. As in many of his villas, there is a strong axis running through the center of the building. The columns are drawn very quickly and read as ovals and incomplete circles, showing the hurry of his thinking to sketch and visually evaluate the design. Included on the page are several elevations that seem to resemble a heavy column base, or altar, and a pediment/entablature detail. If indeed this sketch is meant to be a column base, it may be reminiscent of those heavy bases he used in the *Palazzo Porto-Breganze*, which are distinctive of his later, more sculptural, work.

Palladio seems to be manipulating combinations of circles and squares into various alternatives, without concern for the beauty of the sketch. In contrast are the wavy lines of x's that convey a slow, thoughtful movement of the pen. The technique and the possible purpose of these marks suggest that these x's were added later, at a time when Palladio was more intently evaluating the design, or when he began to think three-dimensionally.

Although decisively symmetrical, these building plans are each slightly warped and off-center. This reinforces the idea that the page of sketches was drawn in a state of concentration and, consequently, reveals a thinking process. It was not necessary for Palladio to view the plans square or lined up, it was more important to see the proportional relationships as he was designing. He was concerned with the relationships between these spaces and how they related to the whole.

FIGURE 1.9

Scamozzi, Vincenzo (1552–1616)
Study sketch of column capitals, Uffizi, UFF 1806 A.v., Ink, wash and graphite

The most prominent architect in Venice at the turn of the century, and a final holdout for classicism, Vincenzo Scamozzi represented the end of the Mannerist approach in northern Italy (Wittkower, 1980). At a time when aspects of the Baroque were starting to surface, his buildings constituted a reworking of Palladio's ideals, with strong theoretical basis in Pythagorean theory (Hersey, 1976). Born in Vicenza, he was the son of the contractor/carpenter/surveyor Gian Domenico Scamozzi. His first documented commissions were for a villa in Barbano for Girolamo Ferramosco (*c.* 1520) and Palazzo Thiene-Bonin (1572–1593). He moved to Venice in 1581, and finished Palladio's Villa Rotunda with minor alterations and completed renovations for Teatro Olimpico from 1584 to 1585. Scamozzi was widely traveled, visiting Paris, Prague, Salzburg, Rome, parts of Germany, and Venice, where he died in 1616. With a prolific architectural career, his later projects included large buildings such as Procuratie Nuove on the Piazza of San Marco and a commission for the Palazzo Contarini at San Trovaso on the Grand Canal in Venice.

One of Scamozzi's legacies includes his theoretical treatise, *L'idea dell'Architettura Universale*, 1615, which many historians agree represents the final codification of the orders. Despite its publishing date, the book clearly speaks to the previous century, as he finds both literary and historical evidence from antiquity to support his assertions. In the tradition of Vitruvius, Alberti, Filarete, Serlio, de Giorgio, and Lomazzo, the square was the essential element, and he illustrated his treatise with 'Man the Beautiful procreates both square and circle' (Hersey, 1976, p. 99).

This sketch (Figure 1.9) from the Uffizi Archives in Florence presents variations on column capitals in both ink and graphite. Although a freehand sketch, the column capitals appear more complete. The controlled crosshatch ink technique exhibits his great skill with pen and ink; rendered with shadows, the page of sketches was a way to visualize and understand, possibly even to locate a particular resolution. The attention to the 'look' of the images reveals his interest in presenting the capital's materiality and shape. This suggests that Scamozzi was rendering the proposals either to discover a form yet unknown to him, or to match an image in his 'mind's eye' (Gombrich, 1969; Gibson, 1979). The very detailed and conventionally classical appearance of the capitals reveals his intention to carefully work out the necessary details. The columns are not placed to investigate a structural composition; instead they overlap, and others are inverted. This implies he needed to see them in proximity for comparison. The method he used to draw alternatives questions how he employed the images to formulate decisions. Viewing these variations in some semblance of three-dimensional realism may have allowed him to compare visually the impression from his imagination.

To support this suggestion, Scamozzi began to sketch a capital, and at the point it became solidified, he abandoned the sketch for another attempt. It may have been a method to test the three-dimensional volume, as he would do with a model. Perhaps he was employing the sketch to replace a model, or as a precursor to the capital's sculpted form. Reinforcing this proposition, a small elevation presents the columns in context, referencing this comparison between detail and the larger picture.

A sketch may imply the quick capturing of escaping ideas, but in this case Scamozzi may not have been able to receive sufficient information from a brief sketch to answer his specific question. The finished qualities provided the necessary information to visualize the form for decision-making.

FIGURE 1.10

Jones, Inigo (1573–1652)

Studies of voussoired windows, after Serlio, 1618, RIBA, Jones and Webb, 76, 77, and 78, #76: 16.7 × 16.5 cm; #77: 8.2 × 19.8 cm; #78: 28 × 19.1 cm, Graphite, pen and brown ink with brown wash over scorelines

Credited with bringing Renaissance art and architecture to Britain, Inigo Jones' career involved painting, theatrical design, and architecture. Being the first English classical architect, he followed in the tradition of Palladio, Serlio and Scamozzi (Summerson, 1966). Inigo Jones was born the son of a clothmaker in 1573. After being apprenticed to a joiner, he began his career in the profession of 'picture-maker.' In the year 1605, he created his first theatrical designs for scenery and costumes with the playwright Ben Jonson. The production was *The Masque of Blackness*, the first of some 25 masques for the Stuart Court, and it began a long association of patronage with the British monarchy (Harris, Orgel and Strong, 1973; Summerson, 1966). The year 1508 exhibited his first architectural drawings and his second trip to Italy, which solidified his classical education. His first important work, presented in his translation of Venetian classicism for England, was the Queen's House in Greenwich. In his position as King's surveyor starting in 1615, he also designed projects such as Whitehall Palace Banqueting Hall, Somerset House, and St. Paul's Cathedral, Covenant Garden.

Inspecting Jones' architectural drawings throughout his practice, there are noticeable changes in his drawing style. The drawings completed soon after his return from the second trip to Italy most closely resemble drawings by Palladio, such as the use of underscoring enhanced with graphite. His annotated copy of *I Quattro Libri Dell Architettura* reveals extensive notes and some diagrams substantiating Jones' careful study of the text (Allsopp, 1970; Harris and Higgott, 1989).

This series of sketches of voussoired windows reveals how strongly Italian classical architecture and the treatises of Renaissance masters influenced Inigo Jones. On this page (Figure 1.10) are five windows studied in graphite, scored lines, ink and wash. The windows, although titled *voussoired*, do not consist of arches or vaults. To the left, a running script of cryptic commentary accompanies the window alternatives. The inscriptions contain references to Serlio in the design and analysis of the windows with such thoughts as '... the midel most is / bigger then thos / of the sydes by 1/4 / Serlio of gaates fo. 5. / and fo. 14; and: noat that in Serlio / ye Spaces ar more large ...' (Harris and Higgott, 1989, p. 96). Here Jones is directly comparing the dimensions of his design to that of windows used as examples by Serlio in his treatise. He is not copying the elements verbatim, but instead transforms the proportions to fit his own use. Experts on Jones, Harris and Higgot seem to concur that this sketch is not necessarily theoretical by suggesting that certain details point to a specific building project (1989).

Jones was employing a technique, used similarly by Palladio, where he scored guidelines that revealed concentrations of the wash. These score lines show especially in the openings of the windows, where he used them to find symmetry and to construct the geometry of the angled stone pieces. Jones used a straight edge for the guidelines but chose to work freehand for the analysis, possibly because it was a more efficient media to quickly study the proportions he was exploring.

Inigo Jones clearly referenced Palladio, Serlio, and Renaissance classicism as a model for his architecture, but he was able to creatively transform their principles and apply them to a particular building project. He was conscious of this fact as evidenced by his notes; he analyzed his divergence from an ideal, evoking advice from his forerunners for a solution that was contemporary to his practice. This page was not merely a travel observation, but a sketch that allows manipulative analysis of precedent.

NOTES

1. While Carmen Bambach (p. 170) argues that 'Both extant designs by Leonardo coincide closely in their outlines, but not precisely, proving that they are not direct prickings of each other.' I believe that irregularities of the points line up in some areas so precisely that they must have been pricked at the same time. Although I would concede that the drawing may have been initially and partially pricked and later altered as Leonardo's thinking process allowed him to transform ideas using the sketch.
2. As to attribution, I am apt to agree with Anthony Blunt's suggestion and am willing to ascribe the sketch to de L'Orme with the caveat that more research would decide the controversy (Blunt, 1958).

BIBLIOGRAPHY

Ackerman, J.S. (1961). *The Architecture of Michelangelo.* The University of Chicago Press.

Alberti, L.B. (1956). *On Painting* (Della Pittura). Yale University Press.

Alberti, L.B. translated by Rykwert, J., Leach, N. and Tavernor, R. (1988). *On the Art of Building in Ten Books.* MIT Press.

Allsopp, B. (1959). *A History of Renaissance Architecture.* Pitman and Sons.

Allsopp, B. ed. (1970). *Inigo Jones on Palladio: Being the Notes by Inigo Jones in the Copy of I QUATTRO LIBRI DELL ARCHITETTURA DI ANDREA PALLADIO, 1601.* Oriel Press.

Ames-Lewis, F. and Wright, J. (1983). *Drawing in the Italian Renaissance Workshop.* Victoria and Albert Museum.

Bambach, C. (1999). *Drawing and Painting in the Italian Renaissance Workshop: Theory and Practice, 1300–1600.* Cambridge University Press.

Barasch, M. (1985). *Theories of Art: From Plate to Winckelmann.* New York University Press.

Benevolo, L. (1978). *The Architecture of the Renaissance.* Westview Press.

Blunt, A. (1958). *Philibert De L'Orme.* A. Zwemmer.

Cassirer, E. translated by Domandi, M. (1963). *The Individual and the Cosmos in Renaissance Philosophy.* Barnes and Noble.

Fleming, J., Honour, H. and Pevsner, N. (1966). *The Penguin Dictionary of Architecture.* Penguin.

Gibson, J.J. (1979). *The Ecological Approach to Visual Perception.* Houghton Mifflin Company.

Gombrich, E. and Kris, E. (1940). *Caricature.* King Penguin Books.

Gombrich, E. (1969). *Art and Illusion.* Princeton University Press.

Gotch, J.A. (1928). *Inigo Jones.* Methuen & Co.

Harris, C.M. ed. (1977). *Illustrated Dictionary of Historic Architecture.* Dover Publications.

Harris, J. and Higgott, G. (1989). *Inigo Jones Complete Architectural Drawings.* A. Zwemmer.

Harris, J. and Tait, A.A. (1979). *Catalogue of the Drawings by Inigo Jones, John Webb and Isaac de Caus at Worchester College, Oxford.* Clarendon Press.

Hersey, G.L. (1976). *Pythagorean Palaces: Magic and Architecture in the Italian Renaissance.* Cornell University Press.

Holt, E.G. (1958). *A Documentary History of Art: Michelangelo and the Mannerists. The Baroque and the Eighteenth Century, Vol. II.* Doubleday and Co.

Hubert, S. and La Montagne, R. (1924). *The Art of Fresco Painting.* F.F. Sherman/Hugh Lanter Levin Associates.

Janson, H.W. (1970). *History of Art.* Prentice-Hall and Harry N. Abrams.

Kent, W. (1925). *The Life and Works of Baldassare Peruzzi of Siena.* Architectural Book Publishing.

Kris, E. and Gombrich, E. (1938). The Principles of Caricature. *British Journal of Medical Psychology, 17,* 285–303.

Kris, E. and Kurz, O. (1979). *Legend, Myth, and Magic in the Image of the Artist.* Yale University.

Lowry, B. (1962). *Renaissance Architecture*. Braziller.

Meiss, M. (1968). *The Great Age of Fresco: Giotto to Pontormo*. The Metropolitan Museum of Art.

Merrifield, [Mrs.] (1846, 1952). *The Art of Fresco Painting*. Alec Tiranti.

Murray, P. (1963). *The Architecture of the Italian Renaissance*. Schocken Books.

Murray, P. (1978). *Renaissance Architecture*. Electa Editrice/Rizzoli.

Musgrove, J. ed. (1987). *Sir Banister Fletcher's, A History of Architecture*. Butterworths.

OED (1985). *The Compact Edition of the Oxford English Dictionary*. Oxford University Press.

Pedretti, C. (1981). *Leonardo: Architect*. Rizzoli.

Puppi, L. (1973). *Andrea Palladio: The Complete Works*. Electa/Rizzoli.

Summers, D. (1981). *Michelangelo and the Language of Art*. Princeton University Press.

Summerson, J. (1966). *Inigo Jones*. Yale University Press.

Trachtenberg, M. and Hyman, I. (1986). *Architecture: From Prehistory to Post-Modernism*. Abrams.

Turner, J. ed. (1996). *The Dictionary of Art*. Grove.

Tuttle, R.J., Adorni, B. and Frommel, C.L. et al. (2002). *Jacopo Barozzi da Vignola*. Electa.

Vasari, G. edited and abridged by Burroughs, B. (1945). *Vasari's Lives of the Artists: Biographies of the Most Eminent Architects, Painters and Sculptors of Italy*. Simon and Schuster.

Vasari, G. translated by Maclehose, L.S. (1907). *Vasari on Technique*. J.M. Dent.

Wallace, W.E. (1998). *Michelangelo: The Complete Sculpture, Painting, Architecture*. Beaux Arts Editions.

Ward, J. (1909). *Fresco Painting: Its Art and Technique*. D. Appleton.

Ward, W.H. (1926). *The Architecture of the Renaissance in France, Vols 1&2*. B.T. Batsford.

Wittkower, R. (1949). *Architectural Principles in the Age of Humanism*. University of London.

Wittkower, R. (1980). *Art and Architecture in Italy 1600–1750*. Penguin Books.

CHAPTER 2

BAROQUE, FRENCH CLASSICISM AND ROCOCO
(1650–1750)

The baroque period experienced a greater prevalence of drawing than the Renaissance. Sketches continually proliferated, as architects were less dependent upon rules of proportion and enjoyed the freedom characteristic of baroque architecture. Growing access to paper products and continually more complex building programs perpetuated the need for sketching. A desire to express the more emotional states of architecture, and describe secondary endeavors such as theater set design, encouraged architects' visual communication. As reflective of construction practices, patronage, and baroque style, it is possible to assess traits common to the sketching techniques of late seventeenth century and early eighteenth century architects.

The name of the baroque style may have originated with the word *barocca*, describing an ill-shaped pearl (Trachtenberg and Hyman, 1986; Briggs, 1967). Although this connection is not completely substantiated, it may yet be an appropriate comparison, especially when seen from the eyes of the artists and architects of the seventeenth and eighteenth centuries. The 'pure' rendition of antiquity in Renaissance classicism and the mannerists' formalized expression led to a freedom in translation, and a more liberal transformation of classical elements.

The high baroque may have seemed an emotional distortion of Renaissance ideals (Millon, 1999). A definition of its form was manifest quite disparately in various regions of Europe. With Francesco Borromini and Filippo Juvarra, the baroque was an extension of the Italian Mannerist movement; the French created a more restrained version often referred to as baroque classical; and the German baroque, located primarily in Bavaria and displayed in religious architecture, acquired a more fluid interpretation called the rococo.

As a movement, the baroque began with a rejection of strict rules, and ceased when the participants felt restraint was again necessary, being weary of relatively uninhibited freedom. Renaissance space was stationary, with clearly ordered elements forming volume. Baroque, on the other hand, allowed form to extend from the surface of the walls to make exuberant and dramatic three-dimensional mass (Briggs, 1967; Millon, 1961).

The papacy in Rome adopted the baroque style, both in the funding and commissioning of projects of great scale, and in their eagerness to exalt the Church by creating a new style distinct from pagan Roman antiquities. The wealthy papal families were enthusiastic patrons, ready to exert their status through the building of churches and palaces. Because of the growing population and expanding boundaries of Rome, such wealth also built numerous villas in the hills around the city. This period of building held many advantages for art and architecture professionals, as wealth allowed cultural activities to expand. This architecture was of the same lineage as the Renaissance but was more expansive, using a complex vocabulary of ovals and ellipses, axial site layout, and interiors of marble, relief stucco, and lighting effects (Briggs, 1967; Millon, 1999; Hersey, 2000).

The seventeenth century was an age of reason (Ward, 1926; Kaufmann, 1955; Benevolo, 1970). France had become united under the monarchy after years of religious wars. The monarchy funded public works and commissioned royal building projects that employed architects, decorators, and craftsmen up to the time of the revolution. Academies in the various arts were founded, preparing guidelines for genuine French classicism (Trachtenberg and Hyman, 1986). French architecture assumed a relatively conservative approach. The baroque had moved north from Italy, but French architects were less invested in its ideals, transforming it to fit a 'national style' (Kaufmann, 1955; Norberg-Schulz, 1971). Partaking in very little exaggeration, these architects advocated a unified, symmetrical, and restrained exterior articulation. In contrast, interior decoration reflected the appearance of French rococo with mirrors and arabesque high relief.

The Germanic countries participated less in the Renaissance interest of antiquity because of their gothic tradition. However, with the building of churches throughout Bavaria, rococo style flourished across the Alps. Basically an architecture stemming from local expression, rather than royalty or the Catholic Church, resulted in interiors flooded with light displaying visionary ceiling paintings (Trachtenberg and Hyman, 1986; Briggs, 1967; Powell, 1959). The palaces of Austria also featured these sculptural effects with the designs of such architects as Johann Lukas von Hildebrandt and Johann Bernhardt Fischer von Erlach.

SKETCHES; INFLUENCES ON STYLE AND TECHNIQUE

Humanism extended literary scholarship into an age of reason. Music and theater thrived with wealthy patrons in attendance. Architects easily crossed between theater and architecture, as they had in the past with painting and sculpture. Juvarra was a baroque architect whose many drawings for theater sets show the fluid motion and illusionary fantasy of temporary stage production. Of great influence on these architects, the Bibiena family was producing imaginative scenery for musical theater and festivals. Similarly, Juvarra and Giuseppe Galli da Bibiena were creating fantasies that departed from contemporary experience, *vedute ideate* (Millon, 1999).

This interest in the theatre and its immediacy affected the sketching and drawing styles of baroque architects. The illusion of stage sets and the movement inherent in the media of theater encouraged a different attitude toward representation. Theater inherently had less structural significance and required less construction time. Based on illusion, it was attractive because of the immediate gratification in the display. It also secured the attention of the monarch, who had much leisure time for spectacle. Theatrical pageantry required both quick conceptual sketches and limited construction drawings. Unlike a static monumental structure, a theater set design was compelled to convey the emotion of the music or narrative being performed. This required more emotional sketches.

These architects' collaborations with playwrights necessitated a visual communication of intention. The spectacular illusions of the stage affected drawing style and encouraged a more expressive sentiment, very different than descriptive exterior elevations.

During this period, baroque painting was experiencing techniques in archaeological illusion, displayed later in the work of Gian Battista Piranesi. Ruined landscapes and architectural fantasy found a pinnacle in sixteenth century Rome and in seventeenth century Venice with artists such as Canaletto. *Veduta*, the intentionally deformed views of real places, and *capriccio*, the mingling of real and imaginary places, provided themes for a movement in painting (Millon, 1999). Rudolf Wittkower writes that, in the Renaissance, drawing was a method of analysis and observation, and that (especially in painting) it was a pretext to a finished work of art. But in the seventeenth and eighteenth centuries some artists left their paintings in unfinished states resembling sketches (Wittkower, 1980).

Baroque architects continued to view sketching as a means to an end, for communication, evaluation, or design. Giorgio Vasari writes that, at least in the case of painters, their first sketches exuded a 'fire of inspiration' that lost their freshness when fully rendered (Wittkower, 1980, p. 367). For baroque architects, there is no doubt that sketches were a generally accepted technique of the design process. The baroque period throughout Europe saw the extensive use of models, in much the same way that they were used in the Renaissance, for both design and presentation. Many of these extremely large models have been preserved, and numerous examples were painted and included elaborate, detailed interiors. Models may have been more understandable for laypersons, while sketches remained a language of the artistic and architectural professions – a sort of private dialogue (Millon, 1999). Although the Renaissance architect Filarete recommended in his treatise, that architects should sketch in the presence of their clients, the practice may have been limited (Filarete, 1965).

Gianlorenzo Bernini, as an interesting example, was a professional who successfully integrated sculpture and architecture, since not all baroque architects received training in secondary skills such as sculpture or painting. During this period, apprenticeships were a common method for architects to gain experience with some of these shops, specializing in architecture rather than various visual arts. Paper was continually more plentiful, evidenced by Johann Gutenberg's printed bible in 1456. The baroque historian Henry Millon explains that visual imagery was required to express certain emotions or conceptual intentions: 'Bernini's father before him had held that in drawing up a plan a good architect must always try to provide it with real meaning (*significato vero*), or an allusion to something exceptional, whether that something was drawn from reality or from the imagination' (Millon, 1961, p. 410).

The political climate, attitudes, and construction practices of the time influenced and affected the design processes and representational techniques of baroque architects. Many of the architects' drawings that survive were those of large buildings projects. They represent prestigious architects, members of a royal court or maintaining the trust of wealthy patrons. Several of them succeeded in reaching a position of status and prominence. These architects fraternized with politicians and ruling monarchy and in the case of France and the papal families in Italy, as members of royal courts. With this accessibility they were able to promote their skills and talents.

Presentation drawings became necessary instruments, persuading with seductive illusion, describing the intention of an architectural proposal. Drawings were a way to obtain a client's approval and funding. They furthered the architect's image as a magician, able to conjure up the majesty and splendor so important to their clients' purposes. They provoked dialogue, allowing the architect and client to speak a visual language. For example, the sketch by Carlo Fontana suggests two alternatives to engage the client in decision-making. The educated aristocracy could have formulated opinions on the future building, or at the very least desired knowledge of the proposed building's concepts and intentions.

Construction drawings, although probably not similar to those used today, were plentiful enough to accommodate large-scale projects, with their extensive interior ornamentation, individual articulation of traditional elements, and numerous details. Baroque building allowed for inventiveness – it required elaborate spatial organizations in plan, calculations of complex geometries, and the integration of sculpture with building components. Sketches were necessary to conceive of and work out these designs. Substantially more complex architectural solutions, such as Christopher Wren's extended three-part dome for St. Paul's Cathedral, dictated exploration through both drawings and sketches (Hersey, 2000). As demonstrated by Ange-Jacques Gabriel, coordination of a large staff of draughtsmen required extensive visual communication. Baroque architects continued to utilize models to both comprehend an intended solution and communicate form to others. These three-dimensional constructions were often highly detailed, even describing interior surface ornamentation as in the case of Wren.

A majority of the architects from this period acquired their skills and training as apprentices under the direction of established architects. With this experience, they were educated in established methods of representing buildings; plan, section, elevation, and perspective. A number of these architects obtained additional experience in the spectacle of theater design, where a sketch would suffice for construction of a set or translated into a costume's pattern. They viewed the sketch as less precious or definitive, allowing alterations and corrections to become a part of their process. Not all having emerged from a workshop tradition, they were yet able to develop the skills necessary for a design dialogue.

MEDIA

The materials trusted for sketching were quite similar to those employed in the Renaissance. The growing availability of paper decreased the physical value of the sketch, thus, the sketches could be rejected and restarted more readily. Graphite was substantially more prevalent, especially after 1662 when it reached mass production in Nuremberg as a form of pencil. Encased in a wooden holder, the medium substantially gained in popularity because of its convenience. Able to be applied directly to paper the pencil did not necessitate a prepared surface as silverpoint required. Eventually the graphite was mixed with clay and mechanically produced (Petroski, 1990). Comparable in softness to chalk, graphite moved smoothly across the surface of the paper. Graphite was also somewhat erasable, in that the distinct lines could be rubbed off or even intentionally smudged for shading.

Many baroque architects invariably chose to sketch with quill pen and ink. A substantially darker line (causing greater contrast), readability, and its smooth flow were most likely the reasons for this medium's popularity. Ink was permanent, which may have assisted architects to conclude design solutions. In most cases, though, these architects relied upon a variety of media. One medium could be corrected with another to differentiate an idea from a subsequent thought. A first draft could be laid out in graphite and alternatives displayed over the top in another medium. Inigo Jones, in the middle seventeenth century, had scored the paper with guidelines so as not to be distracted by their prominence, or perhaps because he realized the difficulties with erasure. François Mansart and Bernini, for example, sketched moving quickly between images, not bothering to stop and erase; they recognized the page of sketches was an entirely personal dialogue. It could be speculated they needed to reference earlier images and they did not care if the sketches intersected or overlapped. Juvarra, for example, employed ink wash in such a way that the brush became another sketching tool, rather than primarily a device to render tone and value. With the brush they could vary line thickness or weight from beginning to end of a single stroke, achieving more expressive images. Piranesi also found etching to be an accommodating medium for expression, determining it could be continually reworked and widely distributed throughout the printing process. This allowed him more easily to disseminate his theoretical propositions.

The seventeenth century witnessed the development of instruments of exact measurement, particularly those necessary for exploration in astronomy and navigation, as well as military engineering and land surveying. The documentation required for these endeavors spawned the emergence of technical drawing. Tools in common use by the 1600s were scale measures, protractors, compasses, set squares, and parallel rules. These tools were necessary for the accuracy required of orthogonal drawings (plan, section, and elevation). Fairly crude ruling pens had been available previous to the seventeenth century, when composite metals were used to make drawing tools. The non-corrosive metal instruments were also substantially more precise. Important for draughting a finished solution these implements often assisted the architect while sketching.

The architects of the baroque period found sketches served their design processes in various capacities, from the search for form to presentation and evaluation with a client. These sketches show increasing confidence in the media, evidenced by a substantial number of examples that have been preserved. Sketches also gained a wider acceptance, being used for such purposes as diagramming, calculating geometries and communicating to draughtsmen.

FIGURE 2.1

Mansart, François (1598–1666)

Alterations to the Hôtel de la Bazinière on the Quai Malaquais, 1653–1658, Bibliothèque
Nationale de France, Bib. Nat. Est., Hd 207a, p.6, 37 × 27.3 cm, Brown ink, black and red chalk

Although François Mansart preserved classical intentions using Italian Renaissance architects as models, his architecture work was tempered by the contemporary French culture of the seventeenth century. It is known that he owned a copy of Vitruvius' book and some examples of design by Vignola. His architecture was speaking a language of classicism, although there are no definitive records that he ever visited Italy.

Mansart was born in Paris in 1598 into a family of artisans; his father was a master carpenter. Most likely because of the death of his father when he was young, Mansart studied architecture with his brother-in-law Germain Gaultier. In 1623, at a young age, Mansart was working on his first architectural project for the façade of the Church of the Feuillants in Paris.

In 1626, he was commissioned to design the Château of Balleroy near Bayeu, and in 1635 he was given the large project to rebuild Château at Blois, the Orléans Wing. But it is the Château de Maisons-Laffitte in 1642 which may be viewed as the best example of his architectural style. This building features a high attic, distinctive of the French architecture of the time, and although it is named the *Mansart roof* he was not the first to use it. This building has a U shape plan, with a façade of pilasters and proportionally tall windows. The incorporation of small round windows, and an interior with ceiling carvings and moldings, expresses a less restrained interpretation of classicism.

This dense page of sketches (Figure 2.1) displays the design and study techniques used by Mansart to renovate a room in the Hôtel de la Bazinière. Mansart was commissioned to improve the town house by the son of Macé Bertrand de la Bazinière in 1653. The historians Allan Braham and Peter Smith, in their book on Mansart, mention contracts from the period, demonstrating that Mansart added two staircases and a *cabinet* attached to the garden side of the building (1973). This page demonstrates an interior elevation with a corresponding plan placed in the center. The large section is not a ruled drawing, but carefully delineated freehand. Around and on top of these drawings are many small study sketches and notes.

It would be logical to assume, from looking at this image, that Mansart first outlined the narrow wing of the house he was to alter and then proceeded to draw his modifications over the original image. The proposed *cabinet* has been attached to the left side of the room. The alternative details and capitals are presented at a smaller scale, and tiny sections can be viewed to the bottom right. The most compelling and revealing aspect of this sketch indicates that Mansart was sketching all of the alternatives on one page so as to continually reference the main image. It acted as a baseline or constant, the outside limits from which to respond.

This page becomes interesting as a device for decision-making. Mansart seems to have been evaluating and eliminating certain variations. Even though this sketch was partially rendered in chalk he did not bother to erase. Instead, he used strong diagonal lines to eliminate certain images that he no longer felt were valid. Many of the column capitals were only partially represented as he abandoned them to contemplate a new thought. A brief plan shows many changes and notes for the dimensioning of the space. As a renovation, certain constraints were placed on the solutions for his design. Again, the large outline/drawing may have acted as a boundary to his thinking, one that was easy to manipulate, alter, and continually reference throughout the process.

FIGURE 2.2

Borromini, Francesco (1599–1667)

Rome, Collegio di Propaganda Fide, studies for front windows, 1662, Albertina, Az Rom 913, 18.3 × 26.1 cm, Graphite on paper (*grafite tenera su carta da scrivere di discreta resistenza; filigrana: variante di quella al n. 6088 in Briquet II*)

Numerous of Francesco Borromini's design sketches carry the expression and passion for architecture that can be found in his built work. Displaying fluid lines and definitive vertical emphasis, his admirers continually stress his knowledge of Vitruvius and his foundation in classical architecture. He implemented classical elements, but in new combinations, employing dramatic lighting effects and integrating painting, sculpture, and architecture as a unified whole (Blunt, 1979).

The son of architect Giovanni Domenico Castelli, he was born at Bissone near Lake Lugano in 1599, acquiring the name Borromini later in life. Being related to Carlo Maderno, he found work carving coats of arms, festoons, decorative *putti*, and balustrades at St. Peter's (Wittkower, 1980). Subsequently, Maderno employed him as a draughtsman and, achieving some freedom of design during Bernini's directorship at St. Peter's, he started his architectural career. He brought with him skills as a builder and craftsman to design the monastery of S. Carlo alle Quattro Fontane. The façade consists of three concave bays separated from the rest of the corner site. The church displays an oval plan with four indented corners creating an interior undulating pattern of columns (Millon, 1961). The historian George Hersey suggests that it evokes a mannerist/baroque use of geometry, elongating and distorting circles to become ovals and ellipses (Hersey, 2000). Several of his other projects include Palazzo della Sapienza (1642–1662), Propaganda Fide (1647–1662), St. Agnese in Piazza Navona (1652–1657), St. John Lateran, and Church of S. Ivo alla Sapienza.

The many sketches from the collection of Borromini in the Albertina are primarily rendered in graphite. Most show the heavy usage that could be expected from drawings that are pondered. Demonstrating their use for contemplation over long periods of time, the graphite has been smeared and often partially erased. The compass seems to have been his constant companion, as the sketches are riddled with holes.

This early conceptual sketch (Figure 2.2) for the Collegio della Progaganda Fide exemplifies many of these traits. The page suggests that he was lost in thought, moving easily across the sheet between plans, elevations, and calculations. He tried several variations of a columned entrance, in a process of constant refinement. The smeared graphite designates the trial quality of this sketch page; it expresses how he participated with the sketches, just as he did with his architecture. He was not afraid to keep working on the same page even if it became dirty and smeared.

Borromini likely chose graphite because it was fast, expressive, and changeable. In contrast, pen and ink may have been too permanent, belabored, and slow (dipping the pen); it was a medium less erasable. These sketches are not careless, but rather deliberate in concentration. The *palimpset*, of his thinking shows how he was constantly reacting to an existing line with a new one. Reconsidered solutions can be seen in the darker alternatives for an entrance. Each time he decided on a better solution, Borromini tried definitively to emphasize it with a heavier lineweight. The reworking of the sketch and the rough texture of the paper stemming from erasure also shows in the darker marks around the altered areas.

From the liveliness of his sketches, one can imagine the passion he gave to his art. For him, the sketches were personal conversations and he did not care how they looked. He was absorbed in the dialogue of the image.

FIGURE 2.3

Webb, John (1611–1672)
Pavilion addition sketch, RIBA, JOI, WEJ [166], 20 × 32.5 cm, Pen and brown ink

John Webb's early architectural experience began when he left Merchant Taylor's School in 1628 and went to study/work with Inigo Jones at the time of the rebuilding of old St. Paul's (Bold, 1989). During the period of restoration Webb turned his attention to domestic architecture, finding commissions from both royalists and members of parliament. He designed Belvoir Castle in Leicestershire in 1655, Gunnersbury House in the late 1650s and Amesbury Abbey (Bold, 1989). Despite his years of experience, Webb was not awarded the position of Surveyor-General of the Office of the Works, but instead was presented with commissions for two very important buildings for the monarchy: Somerset House, 1661, for the Queen Mother and a new Royal Place at Greenwich, 1664 (Worsley, 1995). One of his final projects was a royal palace for Charles II at Greenwich. In this building Webb was able to refine his relationship to classical baroque with elements such as rusticated windows and walls.

Although Webb likely never traveled to the continent like his predecessors, he was educated in European architecture through treatises, engravings, and pattern books. Interestingly, his influence is also at least partially a legacy of drawings. When Inigo Jones died he left his books and drawings to Webb as well as a collection of Palladio's drawings.

The drawings and treatises in Webb's possession became part of his personal repertoire, as he was able to analyze their contents as they pertained to antiquity. This meant he was an architect who approached classicism not from firsthand archeological experience but from the ideal work of Vitruvius, Palladio, Jones, and to some extent Scamozzi. Giles Worsley writes that Webb studied Vitruvius and drew reconstructions of Roman antiquity, which 'could have been practical exercises to assist Webb to establish appropriate classical solutions to modern building types' (1995, p. 47).

This sketch by Webb (Figure 2.3) now in the collection of the RIBA, shows a plan and elevation delineated primarily with single lines. The simple organization consists of a central block and four hesitantly connected square 'wings,' supposedly an early proposal for the Queen's House at Greenwich (Harris, 1982; Bold, 1989). Webb seems able to comprehend the proportions, spatial relationships, and overall perception of this project using very few lines. However brief, the sketch appears not to be a search for form but a contemplative exploration, an assembly of building parts. Completed with pen and ink, this sketch was drawn in a minimal amount of time and with little concern for its appearance. The single weight lines were not meant to communicate construction but rather provide an outline of spatial relationships. The elevation's direct relationship to the plan shows that he was thinking about both simultaneously. With remarkably good proportions, it reveals elements distinctive of Webb's former constructions, forms from his palette or repertoire.

Relying on his memory of successful spaces he was able to view the organization in diagram form. The plan organization resembles Gunnersbury House, consisting of a square with wide bisecting hallways. The center portico elevation mimics the four-columned porch on Amesbury Abbey, with its rusticated base and heavy band between the first floor and the second. The sketch also displays similar vertical proportions to the façade at Amesbury Abbey, complete with cupola. A large forecourt organizationally connects this project to the finished Greenwich Palace. Similarly, in the design of Belvoir Castle, Webb configures the center block as an elongated rectangle, where the corners are suites of rooms consisting of four slightly attached pods.

FIGURE 2.4

Bernini, Gianlorenzo (1598–1680)

Sketch for the Fountain of Four Rivers, 1646–1647, Museum der bildenden Künste, Leipzig 7907r, 32.9 × 35 cm, Pen and ink, black chalk

Gianlorenzo Bernini was born in Naples in 1598. His father was a Florentine sculptor, and from an early age he showed creative talent. It was in Rome that Bernini lived, and completed most of his architectural and sculptural projects, until his death in 1680. His buildings represent the fluid and expressive qualities of the Baroque while revealing his interest in sculpture and theatrical design. Throughout his career, he received numerous projects for the Church, beginning with a commission for Cardinal Scipione Borghese. Although Bernini's beginnings were distinctly classical, the Baldachin for St. Peter's and his later churches such as St. Andrea al Quirinale describe the movement effects of the baroque. The elliptical piazza in front of St. Peter's is one of his most celebrated projects.

The use of preparatory drawings and sketches were typical of Bernini's design process (Wittkower, 1997). He employed preliminary sketches for creative inspiration. He did not believe in overworking a sketch, but instead moved to an empty space on the page to try out new thoughts. They became increasingly precise as he arrived at a solution; as they remained in the realm of exploration, of conceptual beginnings (Lavin, 1981).

This page of sketches is distinctive of Bernini's style and process. The Fountain of Four Rivers in Piazza Navona in Rome (Figure 2.4) is well known and one that has been discussed by historians Rudolf Wittkower and Irving Lavin. This sketch displays an important relationship between the architect/experienced sculptor who was concerned with the assembly of the stone blocks for carving, and the artist who was compelled to capture form on the surface of stone.

Pope Innocent X Pamphili, although first working with Borromini, accepted a design for the fountain in 1647 from Bernini. The fountain was to be located in front of St. Agnes and utilize an obelisk transported from the Circus of Maxentius. This sketch, from 1646–1647, shows images distributed densely across the page. Many are iterations for a sculptural base, showing the figures in abstract form. One can imagine Bernini drawing on the page left to right, since the sketches to the right appear more fully developed. The figures envisioned for the sculptural base all have the same theme, as Bernini was not searching for form, but refining his ideas. These (approximately) ten sketches seem to be expressing similar perspective views, as the diagonal opening in the center moves from bottom left to top right in each alternative. Some seem relatively unfinished as he moved on to the next iteration. Most of the figures were studied in profile and drawn abstractly, with heads represented only as circles, so that Bernini could visualize the composition using fast strokes combined with shading.

The most unique and interesting aspect of the page concerns the alternatives for the sculptural figures interspersed with sketches exploring possibilities of assembly and construction. Bernini was studying the connection between the obelisk and its base and considering how the plinth would be perceived. The fact that Bernini was both an architect and a sculptor has been revealed in the way he explored the stacking of the blocks, either carved out or balanced. He was discovering how the sculptural form could best be achieved, while accounting for ways to span the grotto-like opening in the center of the fountain.

Bernini was seeking the impressions of light and dark composing the sculptural form. The sketches show volume and massing rather than specifics, evoking the fluid movement of the sculpture so distinctive of their author's baroque style. The technique suggests how the fountain might look with water flowing over, or from, it. The expressive techniques of this sketch display Bernini's thinking, as he explored both the internal structure and the external carving.

FIGURE 2.5

Hardouin-Mansart, Jules (1646–1708)

Chateau de Clagny, niche sketch, Bibliothèque Nationale de France, B.N. Estampes Va 360 8, 12.9 × 15.3 cm, *Dessin a la sanguine*

As conferred Royal Architect in 1675, Premier Architect in 1685, and Superintendent of Buildings from 1699 until his death in 1708, Jules Hardouin-Mansart defined the style of architecture in the reign of King Louis XIV. Being the king's primary architect, he (along with a large staff of architects), perpetuated the pageantry and grandiosity of the royal court at a time when the monarchy was building with unprecedented magnitude. His buildings included work on Versailles in 1671, along with other châteaux and projects in the city of Paris such as townhouses, churches, and city squares.

Born in 1646, Hardouin-Mansart was a great nephew of the famous architect François Mansart. He started in the king's employ with garden projects around Versailles and proceeded to remodel the château in 1678. The most celebrated of his projects at Versailles is the Hall of Mirrors. Honoring Louis XIV's accomplishments, the hall contains mirrors juxtaposed with arched windows opposite and a decorated vaulted ceiling, all of which essentially transformed the old royal apartments with themed architectural decoration. These illusionary effects, although their elements are classical, typify the grandeur of the French classical baroque. Several of his other renowned projects include: the Hôtel des Invalides with Libéral Bruant, Château du Val in St. Germain and other urban scale projects, Place des Victoires, and Place Vendôme with both of the last two located in Paris (Ward, 1926: Briggs, 1967; Van Vynckt, 1993).

On this page (Figure 2.5) is a drawing of a niche for the Château in Clagney for Madame de Montespan, the mistress of Louis XIV. This dwelling was crucial to Hardouin-Mansart's practice since it afforded him an introduction to the king. The drawing appears carefully ruled with limited detail. Although ruled with straight lines, it fulfills the definition of 'sketch' as an outline, and also preparatory to something else.

The niche has been presented in elevation with a small half plan seen below. To the right, tight to the margin, has been displayed a section identified as a 'B,' providing an enlargement of the pedestal which is possibly holding a sculptured figure. Much of the ornament is sketched freehand, such as the two Corinthian pilasters that flank the niche, and likewise the panel above. Perhaps the image was used to sketch changes and details onto an unfinished elevation, much as an architect today would 'redline' a construction document. In this way, it may have served Hardouin-Mansart as a medium to think through a detail implementing the ruled elevation as a basis for changes. The niche could have been built from the drawing, but the ornament of the capitals and the figures are incomplete thoughts and would need another drawing to explain them fully. Also apparent is the formality of the sketch by labeling the refined piece as 'B,' Hardouin-Mansart was perhaps suggesting that the image be transferred to someone else for construction implementation or redrawing.

Hardouin-Mansart may have indeed been questioning the ability of an elevation to relate the whole story he needed to convey. He was certainly expressing the limits of the drawing by adding freehand shading lines to describe the depth of the niche.

For the architects of the classical baroque, architecture depended on a three-dimensional interpretation of wall using ornament. This page does not describe a section view which might have been a more important drawing to explain his thoughts to himself or others. With the employment of orthographic techniques such as elevation (which successfully facilitated Renaissance architecture), Hardouin-Mansart may have been reevaluating them as a way to achieve his goals.

FIGURE 2.6

Fontana, Carlo (1638–1714)

Design for façade of Santi Faustino e Giovita, 1652–1714, Metropolitan Museum of Art, NYC, 61.658.39 Neg. 271466, 271467, 57.4 × 37.2 cm, Sepia, gray wash and graphite

This page exhibits a double image representing the design process of the late high baroque architect Carlo Fontana. Although appearing as finished drawings, they reveal Fontana's habit to explore many iterations of a given design. These images convey a temporary or preliminary attitude rendering them a form of sketch. Since he viewed them as a series of alternatives, they suggest that it was his intention to eventually compare them in a process of decision-making.

Fontana was born near Como, Italy. Early in his life he moved to Rome, approximately 1650, and began work in Pietro da Cortona's workshop. Following that initial exposure to architecture, he was employed by Gianlorenzo Bernini for nearly a decade, participating in the design of the piazza in front of St. Peter's, and of Scala Regia. Although strongly influenced by Bernini as a young architect, Fontana also worked directly with Carlo Rainaldi on several projects. One which best reveals these architectural influences was the façade of S. Marcello al Corso (1682–1683).

Commissioned by both the papacy and private patrons, examples of Fontana's projects include: his first project with full responsibility, the church of S. Biagio Campitelli; a commission by Queen Christina of Sweden for the Teatro Tor di Nona and remodeling projects; Santa Maria in Trastevere and San Spirito dei Napolitani. In contemplating Fontana's legacy, Rudolf Wittkower theorized that Fontana led a reinterpretation of classicism, proposing that his architecture may have been anticipating neoclassicism (1958).

Demonstrated here (Figure 2.6) are two iterations of a decorative façade. The overall impression of the technique feels finished and ruled, although some of the upper panels have been left blank or include freehand sculptures. These unfinished panels suggest the 'in-process' qualities that make it comparable to a sketch. Fontana has provided two equally well-detailed alternatives for the decorative doorway. The page has been rendered with one option, with a slice cut through the paper above the door to secure a tabbed flap of an alternative solution. The additional flap resembles the dimensions of the door and lifts to open, as an interesting analogy to a door. When closed, the solution beneath is completely obscured. These two options have opposing themes; one rectilinear, and the other mimicking the arched niche above the architrave.

To assist with the interpretation of this sketch, numerous drawings by Fontana exist which demonstrate his prolific practice. In their catalogue, Braham and Hager write: 'The facility of the courtier, his wish to please and his willingness to compromise are especially apparent in Fontana's drawings; they show how he was capable of producing, with little apparent effort, any number of different designs in the hope of satisfying his patrons' (Braham and Hager, 1977, p. 19). For example, fourteen studies in the archive at Windsor show alternatives for the decoration of the piers at St. Peter's, with each proposal having been studied in a separate vignette.

The question arises: what intention or thought process compelled Fontana to add the paper door to this façade? If the extra door was a later inspiration, he could have either cut out and patched the previous, or glued the new solution over the old. He could have also redrawn the façade with the new configuration, as he had done previously. Perhaps Fontana himself had difficulties making decisions, or, as a diplomatic move, was trying to elicit some participation from his client. By replacing only the door, he was limiting the options. Although architects often sketch many visual possibilities for their own study, it seems more likely that this façade was meant for presentation. Otherwise, he would not have needed to attach the door to keep it from being lost.

FIGURE 2.7

Fischer von Erlach, Johann Bernhard (1656–1723)

Le Grunst Palace Royal sketches, Albertina, Inv. 26392 fol. 26, Codex Montenuovo,
Approx. 8 × 12 in., Pencil and ink on paper

Classically educated Johann Bernhard Fischer von Erlach, architect for the affluent Austrian monarchy, transformed the baroque into the more ornate rococo. Fischer von Erlach was born in Graz, Austria. As a young man he studied in Italy for almost a decade. There he worked under Phillipp Schor and discovered the writings of Vitruvius and other Renaissance architects. While studying the art of metals with G. F. Travani, he met the Jesuit Athanasius Kircher, stimulating a fascination with the archaeology of Egyptian artifacts. Returning to Vienna in 1678 – a time of prosperity and power for Austria – he was prepared to begin his career with the combined skills of an architect, sculptor, medallist, archeologist, and theorist. He joined the royal court in 1694, beginning a long relationship with both Joseph I and Charles VI. In 1705 Fischer von Erlach was appointed Chief Imperial Inspector of royal building (ensuring him royal commissions), a position he held the remainder of his life. His extensive travels in the early 1700s most likely prompted his writing of *Entwurf einer Historischen Architektur*, published in 1712 (Briggs, 1967; Benevolo, 1978; Millon, 1961).

Combining ancient lessons with the contemporary work of Italian baroque architecture, Fischer von Erlach's most celebrated project was Karlskirche in Vienna, 1715–1733. The lower portion of the façade evokes a classical theme, where he placed columns and a pediment resembling the Pantheon. Fischer von Erlach's other built work includes: Schönbrunn Palace, Kollegienkirche, Dreifaltkeitskirche, and the Frain Palace in Moravia for Johann Michael II.

From viewing the extensive collection of existing drawings and sketches by Fischer von Erlach a few general conclusions can be ascertained. His freehand sketches exhibit a light touch where the abstraction of the forms prevents lines from intersecting. They give the impression that he was holding the drawing media extremely loosely, as if it was independent of his hand.

The single line sketches (Figure 2.7) include details, elevations, and three-dimensional images. They are crowded on the page and seem to fill every available space. Drawn with both graphite and ink, it is probable that he moved easily between the two media. The subject matter of the page makes it remarkable. The axonometric and perspective sketches explore variations for the design of a very large project, seen from a bird's-eye view. The words written across the top in script read *Le Grunst Palace Royal July*. One can see vast walled gardens connected to a building complex. Constructed in perspective, one variation demonstrates a rectangular study, while the unfinished example in the foreground consists of an elliptical arcade. The page has been strewn with beginnings of ponds, follies and sculptural monuments.

The large scale of the projects required that Fischer von Erlach sketch quite small; it would seem that his technique grew out of necessity. An architect of Palaces, at some point in his design process he needed to envision each project as a unified whole. Viewing the geometries and relationships of the entire project answered questions pertaining to the composite vision. It has been recorded that Fischer von Erlach traveled to the Prussian court of Frederick I with a proposal for an extravagant palace (Van Vynckt, 1993). Although unable to gain a commission, a project of that size mandated tremendous vision and design exploration. Whether or not this sketch represents the beginning thoughts for this palace, the disparate alternatives seem to be conceived without a definitive site or program. They suggest a search for form in the manner of a fantasy, an attempt to entice or persuade. They could express the first search for a theme before a site was selected or surveyed. Typical of the baroque, controlling nature through parterres and walled courts, the site may actually have had the least influence on the design.

FIGURE 2.8

Wren, Christopher (1632–1723)

Studies of a dome with four-lobed drum, Guildhall Library Deposit, Downes 92, 31.4 × 19.4 cm, Pen and ink

Christopher Wren's education and influences stemmed from mathematical and scientific beginnings, rather than an architectural or artistic apprenticeship. He received a classical education at Westminster School and studied at Wadham College, Oxford, where he obtained experience in anatomy, mathematics, and astronomy. In 1665–1666 he traveled to France, but beyond this experience, his knowledge of the rules of classical design was gleaned from architectural treatises such as Vitruvius, and by observing built work by architects such as Inigo Jones.

After the plague and the Great Fire, Charles II initiated a rebuilding program. Wren was able to participate in this incredible opportunity to reshape the city of London. He accepted the position of Surveyor General of the King's Works in 1669 and became the Commissioner for Building Fifty New Churches in the city, and thus built a remarkable number of buildings in his long life. His relationship to the monarchy afforded him commissions for building Whitehall Palace, Kensington Palace, Hampton Court Palace, Middlesex, and the Royal Naval Hospital, Greenwich. He also designed nearly every church built between 1670 and 1700 in London. Among the most notable were St. Stephen Walbrook, Christ Church Newgate Street, St. Andrew Holborn, and, of course, St. Paul's Cathedral.

Wren's scientific background gave him a way to approach beauty by considering both structure and form. His skills in constructing the representative media of models and mechanisms precipitated his interest in architecture (Summerson, 1953; Downes, 1982). In 1666 he undertook proposals for the renovation of St. Paul's and completed drawings featuring a cone-shaped dome. The Great Fire in that same year changed the assignment to a rebuilding project. The dome that Wren favored was classical in form, towering over the crossing of the Latin cross plan. Due to Wren's interest in mathematics and particularly geometry, the dome was built as a set of three domes, the inner two being catenoids (Hersey, 2000).

Figure 2.8, presumably an early study of St. Paul's, features a hemispherical dome placed on a split sketch, displaying both the interior and exterior of the cathedral. Wren was using this sketch to think through construction, since it appears that the detail at the left received the most attention and was also studied in plan below. He seems focused on the wall that conceals the buttresses which support the inner dome and the construction of semi-circular buttressing structures (Fürst, 1956). By studying this configuration in section, Wren was able to understand the ramifications to both the interior and exterior.

This sketch shows only one internal dome, and it has been speculated by Viktor Fürst that this image was an early study, before the heightening of the dome was considered (1956). Although a section through the dome, Wren employs dashed lines for the inner structure. The relationship between inside and outside was very important to Wren. Since he needed to reconcile the interior effect with the structure, the combination of the three domes preserved the perspective illusion of height he was trying to achieve (Hersey, 2000). Wren the mathematician/geometer/astronomer was creating an optical system, much like microscopes and telescopes of scientific discovery. If sketches can be indicators of architectural intention, then this image may represent how he used media to understand design relationships. The dome, being of an unusual shape for London at this period, required Wren to thoroughly investigate its form and structure in various types of drawings before construction.

FIGURE 2.9

Juvarra, Filippo (1687–1736)

Stage scenery design for Ottoboni for his theater in the Cancellaria Palace, 1708–1712, V&A Picture Library, Museum #8426 (20); Neg. #66409, 20 × 27cm, Pen and ink and wash on paper

Filippo Juvarra's architecture reflects the late baroque period in Europe. Highly prolific, he built many palaces and grand churches, mostly in and around Turin. Early in his career, he found fame as a set designer, working for Cardinal Ottoboni on the theater for the Cancelleria. As a result of this experience, Rudolf Wittkower suggests that Juvarra's architecture continually utilized the resourceful theatrics of a stage designer (1980). Possibly influenced by the German and Austrian rococo currents in Europe, his work combines the flamboyant rococo style with contrasting Italian classical elements.

Juvarra was born in Messina to a family of silversmiths. His architectural training began with a classical education in Rome under Carlo Fontana. After his service to Cardinal Ottoboni, around 1714, he moved to Turin to work for Victor Amadeus of Savoy. He spent the next twenty years in Turin, producing such projects as the grand baroque sanctuary Superga in 1715–1731, the chapel of the Venaria Reale from 1716 to 1721, and palaces such as the Palazzo Madama, Castello di Rivoli, and the nearly French château style palace Stupinigi.

A typical example of Juvarra's drawing style can be found in the volume of drawings made in Rome for the theater at Cancellaria Palace of a baroque set design. This sketch (Figure 2.9) conveys his attitudes about the temporality and illusion of performance, especially baroque theater. It represents architecture that was animated by light and movement, qualities that show vividly in his pen and ink techniques.

This sketch contains busy, vibrating, and modulated lines that fill the page. The pen techniques show that his lines were rendered with great speed. This is noticeable because many lines double back on themselves in Juvarra's effort to draw the lines quickly and in parallel sequence. Besides the multitude of lines, other techniques reinforce the temporal expression of a stage set. The ink wash technique was probably applied after the pen, because in several instances it causes the ink lines to bleed. The wash was intended to render the image more three-dimensional by providing shadows. It enlivens the sketch as it dances with baroque activity. This was partially because the contrast of dark and light evokes the bright directional illumination of stage lighting.

The sketch exhibits the overly decorative style of baroque interiors. In the center stands a pavilion very reminiscent of Bernini's Baldacchino at St. Peter's in Rome. The Baldacchino was a stage for religious ceremony; likewise, the pavilion on the stage acts with central importance for Juvarra. The twisted columns, typical of baroque interiors, also helped to give Juvarra's set the fluid motion of theater.

Juvarra's sketch contains a horizontal ground line that may represent the edge of the stage. Below this edge has been drawn a small plan of the proposed set. The horizontal layers reveal his concern for the blocking of the stage, similar to the way actors position themselves in the space. He was exploring openings for performers to appear and disappear, considering both the illusion and the practicality of how they enter the stage from the wings. On the plan, Juvarra also diagrammed a diagonal view corridor to express the exaggerated perspective of the shallow platform. Looking back to the three-dimensional illusion, the sketch presents the space from a very low perspective point, one that might represent the view of the audience. This adds to the dramatic presentation of the spectacle and also allowed Juvarra to understand the perspective effect from the view of the audience.

BIBLIOGRAPHY

– (1959). *70 Disegni di Francesco Borromini dalle collezioni dell'Albertina di Vienna*. Instituto Austriaco di Cultura in Roma, Gabinetto Nazionale delle Stampe Farnesina.

Beard, G. (1982). *The Work of Christopher Wren*. John Bartholomew & Son.

Benevolo, L. (1978). *The Architecture of the Renaissance*. Westview Press.

Blunt, A. (1979). *Borromini*. Harvard University Press.

Blunt, A. (1981). *Art and Architecture in France, 1500–1700*. Penguin Books.

Bold, J. (1989). *John Webb: Architectural Theory and Practice in the Seventeenth Century*. Clarendon Press.

Bourget, P. and Cattaui, G. (1956). *Jules Hardouin-Mansart*. Éditions Vincent, Fréal.

Braham, A. and Hager, H. (1977). *Carlo Fontana: The Drawings at Windsor Castle*. A Zwemmer.

Braham, A. and Smith, P. (1973). *Francois Mansart, 2 Volumes*. A. Zwemmer Ltd.

Brauer, H. and Wittkower, R. (1970). *Bernini's Drawings*. Collectors Editions.

Briggs, M.S. (1967). *Baroque Architecture*. Da Capo Press.

Dircks, R. (1923). *Sir Christopher Wren, A.D. 1632–1723: Bicentenary Memorial Volume Published Under the Auspices of the Royal Institute of British Architects*. Hodder and Stoughton.

Downes, K. (1982). *The Architecture of Wren*. Universe Books.

Downes, K. (1988). *Sir Christopher Wren: The Design of St. Paul's Cathedral*. Trefoil Publications.

Filarete translated by Spencer, J.R. (1965). *Treatise on Architecture*. Yale University Press.

Fleming, J., Honour, H. and Pevsner, N. (1998). *The Penguin Dictionary of Architecture and Landscape Architecture*. Penguin Books.

Fürst, V. (1956). *The Architecture of Sir Christopher Wren*. Lund Humphries.

Hambly, M. (1988). *Drawing Instruments, 1580–1980*. Sotheby's Publications/Philip Wilson Publishers.

Harris, J. and Tait, A.A. (1979). *Catalogue of the Drawings by Inigo Jones, John Webb and Isaac De Caus at Worchester College Oxford*. Clarendon Press.

Harris, J. (1982). *The Palladians*. Rizzoli.

Hersey, G.L. (2000). *Architecture and Geometry in the Age of the Baroque*. The University of Chicago Press.

Hutchison, H.F. (1976). *Sir Christopher Wren*. Victor Gollancz.

Hutter, H. (1968). *Drawing: History and Technique*. McGraw-Hill.

Jardine, L. (2002). *On a Grander Scale*. Harper Collins.

Kaufmann, E. (1955). *Architecture in the Age of Reason: Baroque and Post-Baroque in England, Italy, and France*. Harvard University Press.

Lavin, I. (1981). *Drawings by Gianlorenzo Bernini, from the Museum der Bildenen Künste Lipzig, German Democratic Republic*. Princeton University Press.

Magnuson, T. (1982). *Rome in the Age of Bernini*. Almqvist and Wiksell.

Martinelli, V. (1982). *Bernini: Drawing*. La Nuova Italia.

Millon, H.A. (1961). *Baroque and Rococo Architecture*. George Braziller.

Millon, H.A. and Lampugnani, V.M. (1994). *The Renaissance from Brunelleschi to Michelangelo, the Representation of Architecture*. Rizzoli.

Millon, H.A. ed. (1999). *The Triumph of the Baroque*. Rizzoli.

Norberg-Schulz, C. (1971). *Baroque Architecture*. Harry N. Abrams.

Petroski, H. (1990). *The Pencil: A History of Design and Circumstances*. Knopf.

Pommer, R. (1967). *Eighteenth Century Architecture in Piedmont: The Open Structures of Juvarra, Alfieri and Vittone*. New York University Press.

Portoghesi, P. (1967). *Francesco Borromini*. Electa Editrice.

Powell, N. (1959). *From Baroque to Rococo*. Faber and Faber.

Scribner III, C. (1991). *Gianlorenzo Bernini*. H.N. Abrams.

Sedlmayr, H. (1956). *Johann Bernhard Fischer Von Erlach*. Verlag Herold.

Smith, P. (1969). *L'Urbanisme de Paris et l'Europe 1600–1680*. Thesis.

Soo, L. (1998). *Wren's 'Tracts' on Architecture and Other Writings*. Cambridge University Press.

Summerson, J. (1953). *Sir Christopher Wren*. The Macmillan Company.

Tinniswood, A. (2001). *His Invention So Fertile: A life of Christopher Wren*. Oxford University Press.

Trachtenberg, M. and Hyman, I. (1986). *Architecture: From Prehistory to Post-Modernism*. Abrams.

Turner, J. ed. (1996). *The Dictionary of Art*. Grove.

Van Vynckt, R. ed. (1993). *International Dictionary of Architects and Architecture*. St. James Press.

Viale Ferrero, M. (1970). *Filippo Juvarra scenografo e architetto teatrale*. Benjamin Blom.

Ward, W.H. (1926). *The Architecture of the Renaissance in France, Vols 1&2*. B.T. Batsford.

Wittkower, R. (1949). *Architectural Principles in the Age of Humanism*. Warburg Institute.

Wittkower, R. (1958, 1980). *Art and Architecture in Italy 1600 to 1750*. Penguin Books.

Wittkower, R. (1997). *Bernini, the Sculptor of the Roman Baroque*. Phaidon Press.

Worsley, G. (1995). *Classical Architecture in Britain*. Yale University Press.

Wren, C. (1965). *Parentalia; or Memoirs of the Family of Wrens*. Gregg Press.

CHAPTER 3

NEOCLASSICAL, NEOGOTHIC, BEAUX-ARTS (1750–1870)

The neoclassical movement cannot be viewed as a universally consistent doctrine that dominated a specific location. Not easily definable, it was prevalent throughout Europe and extended abroad to places such as the United States and Asia. This new (and renewed) view of antiquity was subject to extensive and varied interpretation, from archaeological neoclassical, neogothic, visionary/revolutionary neoclassical, English neo-palladianism, and Greek and Roman revivals. Although an extension of methods developed in the Renaissance and baroque, sketching techniques were varied reflecting media and intent. From the academy traditions of the Ecole des Beaux-Arts the concept of *esquisse*, the sketch as an organizational diagram, emerged.

Most refined in France, neoclassicism emerged out of baroque classical and was substantially transformed from that of the fifteenth century. In reaction to the apparent unrestraint of baroque architecture, neoclassical architects desired a return to what was perceived as the principles of architecture (Broadbent, 1980). Numerous late baroque architects never embarked upon pilgrimages to the antiquities of the south, but in the middle of the eighteenth century, James Stuart and Nicholas Revett traveled to record the antiquities of Greece. Similar versions of their findings were eventually published by Julien-David LeRoy in 1758 (Broadbent, 1980). This renewed view of antiquity, tempered by the rational thought of philosophers such as Decartes and Rousseau, emerged as a 'static method of design.' It was exemplified by principles of order, symmetry, and harmony, embodied in a French national style sponsored by the monarchy (Kaufmann, 1955; Trachtenberg and Hyman, 1986; Egbert, 1980). This restrained French classicism was partially influenced by the enlightenment ideal of humanity as innocent and rational, harking back to a perceived naïveté of early cultures and the 'primitive hut' (Trachtenberg and Hyman, 1986; Laugier, 1977).

The architectural historian Joseph Rykwert writes that the 'classic' for these philosophers and architects meant both antique and 'excellent and choice.' They believed in a unified and natural approach, in the sense of real or genuine (Rykwert, 1980; Broadbent, 1980). As a result of these attitudes, architecture displayed Greek, Roman, or Renaissance detail and/or the use of pure geometric form. Architects were much more prone to be concerned with the building's form than its construction techniques. The beaux-arts taught the conventions of symmetry and experience of the space, but the invariably accepted medium was masonry. The advent of iron as a structural building material, as introduced by Henri Labrouste, meant that architects were required to consider new methods of assembly. An evolution in building materials and construction toward the end of the nineteenth century required those on the site to rethink assembly; but architects also had to consider joints and connections.

This resulted in the production of sketches and drawings to explain and develop these innovations. Exploratory sketches and explicit drawings were required for resolution and clarification. Although architects (up to the middle of the nineteenth century) were still primarily concerned with form and not construction, some semblance of construction drawings appear in France at this time. Although Marc-Antoine Laugier writes about structure in his essay on architecture, he presents his theory in aesthetic terms (Laugier, 1977). Similarly, Eugène-Emmanuel Viollet-le-Duc's *Dictionnaire raisonné* contains a section describing historic masonry construction (Viollet-le-Duc, 1990).

Architectural theory proliferated and was widely distributed, with treatises such as Laugier's *Essai sur l'architecture*, advocating naturalness, simplicity, elemental geometric forms and lauding Greek architecture; Claude-Nicholas Ledoux's *L'Architecture considéré sous le rapport de l'art, des moeur set de la legislation*, the first volume in 1804; Colin Campell's *Vitruvius Britannicus*; and *The Castle of Otranto: A Gothic Story* by Horace Walpole. These volumes were less about rules for the orders and the consequent methods of drawing, and more about character and the expression of architecture. Two developments of neoclassicism that directly influenced architects' drawings and sketches were the Ecole des Beaux-Arts, with strong rules for graphic representation, and the polemical fantasy images of the visionary/revolutionary architects such as Claude Nicholas Ledoux and Etienne-Louis Boullée.

SKETCHES; EDUCATION AND DESIGN PROCESS AT THE ECOLE DES BEAUX-ARTS

During the eighteenth century, academies of the arts were prevalent. State sponsored education of architects began in 1671 when Louis XIV's minister, Colbert, formed the Académie Royale d'Architecture with Jacques-Francois Blondel as its chief professor. The pedagogical foundation was built on the concept of ordered schemes and the aesthetic experience of buildings (Trachtenberg and Hyman, 1986; Drexler, 1977). As a method to control building for the monarchy, it advocated correct rules of proportion, harmony, order, and symmetry that would insure beauty (Egbert, 1980). After a period of turmoil in the late 1700s the school was transformed into the Ecole des Beaux-Arts. Closed in the late 1960s, the Ecole's method of education evolved; although rendered in various forms its general methods remained constant. A student matriculated the second class after successfully passing an entrance exam, usually a small design project. Students organized their own studios under a practitioner, who was usually an architect holding an association with the Ecole. These ateliers were the primary source of education, although lectures on theory and building assembly were available to the students. Students progressed through the school by acquiring points for placement in design competitions. These competitions consisted of several types – monthly sketch problems, decorative sketch problems, those limited to a space of nine hours, and several more formal competitions culminating in the most coveted competition: the Prix de Rome. One student per year was given this award of a stipend to study in Rome.

The organization of the competitions was particularly important. It was representative of an educational method and the development of drawing conventions. In the short monthly competitions, specific issues such as interior decorative problems were explored. These projects were sketch problems, completed within a limited time. The Prix de Rome, however, was divided into several stages of competition. Although the stages and requirements evolved over the years, a short sketch problem was given to a large number of students, usually thirty, to narrow the field to a group of eight. Each of these remaining contestants, after receiving the program, was sequestered *en loge* (in a small cell) to prepare a generalized *esquisse*. This consisted of an organizational *parti* usually presented in the form of plan, section, and elevation. Embodying the conceptual solution, the *parti* was compared with the final rendering for consistency. This method forced the students to make decisions quickly and to express themselves clearly to the jurors ranking their solutions. The *esquisse* was used to quickly visualize the solution, express the character of the building, and compose the page. Although mostly freehand, the *esquisse* was not the loose first thoughts of a sketch, but a rough rendered drawing that conveyed the essence of the solution. Prior to the *esquisse*, most students sketched variations of possible organizations called '*pre-esquisse*' or quick abstract explorations. The *esquisse* was required to be drawn on opaque paper, although tracing paper could be used for design exploration. The plan, section, and elevation were drawn to scale, and most competitors left time to render these drawings with pale washes. As a generalized concept, the design was not about ornament or detail, but rather the requirements of the program and the arrangement and proportions of spaces and elements (Harbeson, 1927).

The group of eight was ranked and allowed to continue to the next stage of the competition. After submitting their *esquisse*, the students traced (or in some way recorded) the essentials of their project. They then returned to their respective *atelier* to elaborate and render the scheme over a period of approximately three months. The formal renderings were submitted in conventional style, using only plan, section, and elevation (Egbert, 1980). The drawings were mechanically constructed abstractions of the building so that they could be easily comprehended by the jurors. The competition system was a way for the students to quickly formulate a solution to a specific program, one that was acceptable and proper according to the theories taught at the school. They were not buildable projects, in that they stressed character, proportion, and composition, with less emphasis on building materials and contemporary technology (Middleton, 1982). Character, originating with the classical tradition in art, was of three kinds: general character, not necessarily connected to the building program, meaning association with historic expression; type character, referring to the building's type; and specific character, ideas arising from each building's distinctive qualities (Egbert, 1980).

The length of attendance at the Ecole des Beaux-Arts was indeterminate. It often took several attempts before a student won the Grande Prix, and the competition was open only to French citizens. Invariably, the winners returned from Rome to careers in royal service. Those who never won the Prix de Rome, as well as the foreigners in attendance, left the school when they felt they had acquired sufficient architectural knowledge to begin practice or to continue their education with an apprenticeship. All of these young architects carried into practice the Ecole's method of both a '*pre-esquisse*' to find an appropriate *parti*, and the *esquisse*, which expressed the essence of the organization. Along with skills in design theory and rendering, these factors affected architects' process for many years to come.

VISIONARY/REVOLUTIONARY/RADICAL ARCHITECTURE

Emil Kaufmann called the architects Etienne-Louis Boullée, Claude-Nicholas Ledoux, and Jean-Jaques Lequeu revolutionary architects (1952). He was referring not to their political stance but rather to how they expressed the ideals of the great thinkers of their century. Their objectives 'were the expression of character, the creation of atmosphere, and the division of the composition into independent units' (Kaufmann, 1952, p. 434). They chose to express themselves through the monumentality of form. Like Laugier, they advocated the paring down of form to basic necessity, a purism that avoided all ornament. It was believed that this simplicity and naturalness resulted in beauty. The work of these architects was distinctly reminiscent of Gian Battista Piranesi's *carceri*: visions of prisons, ruins, cenotaphs, exaggerated monuments, and public works projects. Ledoux was able to build a few of his designs, such as the Saltworks at Arc-et Senans, but a large portion were disseminated primarily as illustrations for theory books. As paper architecture, these drawings were easily reproduced and distributed; as theoretical endeavors, they carried less functional responsibility.

The visionary/revolutionary architect's theoretical proposals captured dramatic perspective views, intensifying the grandeur of the architecture. Drawing techniques such as eliminating background conveyed a specific message, free of unnecessary details. Ledoux's fantasy architecture consisted of simple geometry and primarily displayed function. He utilized perfect cubes and spheres to describe large and smooth architectural form. Boullée employed atmospheric techniques to provide a context of emotion, but his images lacked environmental context. The massive masonry façades were often represented from a corner with high perspective points. Strong beams of light flooding the interior spaces enhanced the dramatic effect. In contrast, Lequeu imagined decorative follies with an eclectic mix of orders and in various states of ruin. These visionary/revolutionary sketches and drawings as theoretical arguments raise particularly important issues for the study of architects' media.

MEDIA

Many media and techniques preferred by the neoclassical architects were more refined versions of traditional tools and methods. New media were also continually developing. Paper became steadily more available, especially after the mid-nineteenth century when wood pulping was prevalent. Previously, paper was composed of linen or other rag fibers (Hutter, 1968). Beaux-arts architects regularly traced drawings with translucent paper, a technique they learned as students at the Ecole.

While attending the Ecole des Beaux-Arts it was required that the competition *esquisse* be completed in ink on opaque paper, and they were commonly articulated with pale gray, green, pink, or brown washes. The final rendered projects, *rendu*, were presented on extremely large sheets. These pages became ever larger through the years, commonly displaying sections and elevations approximately two meters long. Media such as pen and ink, graphite, watercolor, and wash were commonly used along with brushes, compasses, rulers, and straight-edged guides. Sepia ink was produced near the end of the eighteenth century and became so common that most brown inks were labeled sepia (Hutter, 1968). Charcoal and graphite images were fixed with a solution composed of diluted lacquers and it may be speculated that architects did likewise. Rubber was imported to Europe from India, which facilitated erasing, during the eighteenth century.

Sir John Soane and Karl Friedrich Schinkel commonly sketched in ink, having the patience and skills necessary to control this difficult medium. Although pen and ink required frequent dipping of the quill, the technique may have allowed momentary pauses for contemplation. Marks appear frequently in the margins of their sketches; places to rest a pen in thought. Washes are another definitive medium; since the contrast on the paper was easy to read, they created an instantaneous three-dimensional view that revealed volumetric qualities. Since elevations were easier to proportion and dimension, but lacked the three-dimensional illusion of perspective, washed shadows could imitate a perspective view to some degree. The ink and wash example by Soane indicates this technique.

The sketch by Henri Labrouste, who was trained at the Ecole, reveals early sketch diagram techniques to find compositional direction. Fantasy etchings by Piranesi were developed from archeological investigations, while those by Boullée emanated from an ideological approach. Unsurprisingly, these sketches are quite different from one another. Piranesi's evokes the nervous and dismal qualities of underground spaces while Boullée's sketch argues for an abstract and emotive future.

These architects of the neoclassical period envisioned the future of architecture – on paper – within their own ideological and educational framework.

FIGURE 3.1

Piranesi, Giovanni Battista (1720–1778)

Villa of Hadrian: Octagonal room in the Small Baths, Metropolitan Museum of Art, 1994.20, Neg. 258027, 39.4 × 55.3 cm, Red chalk with charcoal

It would be impossible to examine the architectural drawings of the neoclassical period without a discussion of Giovanni Battista Piranesi. Despite his architectural apprenticeship, he may not be viewed as an architect in a strict sense, considering the few commissions attributed to him (Tafuri, 1987). However, he was extremely influential due to his prolific distribution of archaeological, reconstructive, and fantastical architectural etchings, engravings, and sketches distributed throughout Europe. Embracing the inventiveness of baroque illusion, he also defended the return to Roman antiquity.

Piranesi was born near Mestre in 1720. The son of a stonemason, he first worked with his architect uncle Matteo Lucchesi in Venice. Apprenticed to Giovanni Scalfurotto, he also received training as a stage designer. In 1740, he went to Rome as a draughtsman to Marco Foscarini, the Venetian ambassador at the court of the new Pope Benedict XIV (Wilton-Ely, 1978). He traveled to archaeological excavations at Herculaneum and in 1743 he published the series of architectural fantasies *Prima Parte dei Architetture e Prospettive* (Wilton-Ely, 1993). Piranesi printed his various reconstructions and *capriccio* such as *Opere Varie* and *Trofei di Ottaviano Augusto* and in 1756, following thorough research, four volumes of *Antichità Romane* (Wilton-Ely, 1993). The popular distribution enjoyed by these texts may be compared to those by Alberti, Palladio, Serlio, and Vitruvius, all several centuries earlier. In his visual statements, Piranesi advocated the practical usage of antiquity combined with skilled archaeological speculation and exaggeration. He was a proponent of Roman antiquity, rather than Greek, and many who have analyzed his work suggest that his images, especially the *Carceri* (fantasy prisons), display a political and social polemic (Tafuri, 1987; Wilton-Ely, 1978, 1993).

An incredible number of his drawings and prints remain. They range in media from ink and wash sketches to etchings and detailed engravings, and are surprisingly loose and fluid. This sketch (Figure 3.1) was not a preliminary sketch associated with the *Carceri*, but contains a similar theme – excavated, subterranean, and dominated by a series of large arches. The sketch was drawn on heavy paper using graphite guidelines and studied with brown, waxy crayon.

Both the theme and techniques of this sketch resemble concepts of the grotesque. Although a comprehensive definition of the grotesque may be elusive, the author Geoffrey Harpham writes that contemporary grotesqueries hover between the known and the unknown, and contain elements of ambivalence, deformation, transition, or paradox (1982). These elements become visible in the grotesque as fragmented or jumbled. The underground, excavated, and prison themes of Piranesi's work suggest the early use of the word referring to *Grottesche*, the ornamental arabesques found in Roman excavations that connote the underground, burial, or secrecy (Harpham, 1982). A description of grotesqueries as being both bizarre and beautiful seems to fit Piranesi's imaginative scenes.

The unfinished qualities, especially where patterned brick above the doors transforms into the underside of arches, help to give this sketch a transitory feeling. Paradoxically, although the scene appears to be underground, it contains light and articulation not usually associated with subterranean space. The quickness of the lines, and the squiggles that resemble figures, reinforce the fragmentation. Similar to the *Carceri*, this technique lacks any place of stability, and the composition continuously keeps the observer's eyes in motion. Due to the ambiguity of the grotesque, the sketch is not false, but may in fact be real to the extreme; so full of emotion that it allows the observer's imagination to speculate (Harpham, 1982).

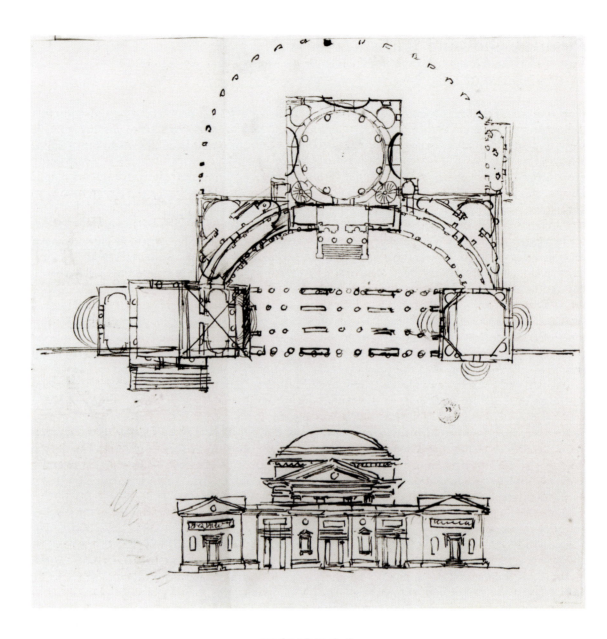

FIGURE 3.2

Adam, Robert (1728–1792)

House plan and elevation, 1755–1756, Sir John Soane's Museum, Adam Vol. 9/33 *verso*, 31.1 × 40.5 cm, Pencil and brown ink

Robert Adam was born in Scotland in 1728. His father was an architect, merchant, and primary builder in Edinburgh. Young Adam attended the University of Edinburgh, receiving a classical education, and in 1754 he embarked on the Grand Tour to Italy. There he explored antiquity, studying with and befriending the French architect Jacques Louis Clerisseau and the architect and archaeologist Giovanni Battista Piranesi. This education greatly influenced his approach to architecture and in 1758 he returned to London to practice, with his brother James, until his death in 1792. During their years of practice they completed many domestic projects, a few of the most well known being Luton Hoo in Bedfordshire (1766) and interiors for the houses Syon (1762) and Osterly (1763) (Rykwert, 1985).

The neoclassicism of Robert Adam was founded in archaeology, a method of looking at antiquity from discoveries in Italy. Roman antiquity as the creative impetus was an alternative to the Palladian style practiced in England. Traveling to Rome meant for Adam, and the other architects which embarked on the Grand Tour, that he knew his models well and could reuse the language in his inventive architecture (Kostof, 1985). Particularly known for his interior architecture, Adam made use of neoclassical antiquity in the way he clustered rooms of various geometric shapes, utilized 'interior columnar screens,' integrated Etruscan motifs, and employed aspects of sixteenth century Italian Renaissance design, especially in the 'movement' or visual rhythm, of classical façades (Trachtenberg and Hyman, 1986; King, 1991).

In this sketch (Figure 3.2) one can view a plan and an elevation of a country house. The sketch does not appear to be preparation for a specific building. It is particularly revealing, however, because it shows the intense way that Adam used his sketches as a method of design evaluation. The organization of the plan shows curved arms protruding from a central dome and an entrance screen (reminiscent of the Osterly House) with four rows of paired columns. Each pavilion at the end of the symmetrical arms reveals a different solution, possibly an indication that Adam was trying different forms to see which best fitted his overall concept.

Adam does not erase or cross out rejected forms, but draws over the previous thought; such constant reworking is displayed in the new niches by the dome, the changes in the shape of the porch, the alternatives for the ends of the arms, and the variations of the entrance screen. He was checking and reworking, watching for proportional and spatial qualities as he tried possible solutions. He needed to reinforce the new lines and drew them darker, even using poché on a new wall for emphasis. His interest in neoclassicism shows in his concern for symmetry, yet Adam seems comfortable working each side differently to experiment with variations. For example, he may have extended the arms on the left side of the sketch simply because the paper provided more room to draw. The elevation does not correspond to any version of the plan exactly, which may suggest that it was an aspect of the design process and not a conclusion. It may have acted as a 'test,' providing Adam a chance to pause and study the design.

This sketch may have been meant for discovery, as it was not tied to any of Adam's completed work. As many of his later houses were organized with some version of 'wings,' notably the Langside House of 1777 and the Jerviston House of 1782. His design for the Gosford House of 1791 also featured a large central dome similar to the one displayed in this sketch, along with paired columns and a dominant pediment over the center space.

FIGURE 3.3

Boullée, Etienne-Louis (1728–1799)

Cenotaph, in the shape of a pyramid, 1780–1790, Bibliothèque Nationale de France, Ha 57 FT 6, 4/237 IM.281 Plate 24, 39 × 61.3 cm, Ink and wash

With a similar penchant for drawing illusion as Piranesi, Etienne-Louis Boullée built little but as an educator, theoretician and illustrator, he was a dominant figure in neoclassical visionary/revolutionary architecture.

Boullée's father was the Parisian architect, Louis-Claude Boullée, who encouraged his son's education in architecture and drawing. Continuing his education in 1746, he studied with Boffrand, Lebon, and Le Geay, where he learned the architecture of the French classical tradition. Over the next several years (1768 to 1779) he designed numerous houses such as Pernon, Thun, Brunoy, and Alexandre, and he built or rebuilt Château Tassé at Chaville, Château Chauvri at Montmorency, and Château de Péreux at Nogent-sur-Marne, all in the proximity of Paris. Later in life, Boullée became a member of the Institut de France and was nominated a Professor of the Ecole Centrales (Kaufmann, 1955).

As discussed in the introduction, Boullée, along with Ledoux and Lequeu, have been united under the title of visionary/revolutionary architects. They were attracted to theoretical arguments, which they displayed in their fantastic and monumental illustrations utilizing geometric shape and symbolism. Boullée's fantasy images demonstrate massive, dynamic forms, substantially larger and more impressive than the monuments of Greece and Rome (Kaufmann, 1955).

This drawing (Figure 3.3) portrays a starkly simple pyramid with two unadorned columns, all bathed in stormy modeled light. Although all architectural illustration envisions the future, Boullée's fantasy consciously moves beyond the realm of possibility into a simplicity and scale unrelated to function or technology. Fantasy as a concept evokes the magical and suggests an extended associative capacity, whimsical invention, divination, and the expansive qualities of pure possibility (Casey, 2000). The art historian David Summers writes that during the Renaissance, *fantasia* was related in meaning to *invenzione*. Although similar to the term 'invention,' its original meaning derives from a technical term from rhetoric. *Invenzione* was primary in the five-part division of rhetoric, and consisted of '…the finding out or selection of topics to be treated, or arguments to be used' (Gordon, 1975, p. 82). Although viewed from a later period, Boullée represents an interesting connection between creative inspiration and the development of argument.

The fantasies were intended for his architectural treatise *Architecture, Essai sur l'art*, begun in 1780. In this essay, he wrote about what funerary monuments or cenotaphs meant to him: 'I cannot conceive of anything more melancholy than a monument consisting of a flat surface, bare and unadorned, made of a light-absorbent material, absolutely stripped of detail, its decorations consisting of a play of shadows, outlined by still deeper shadows' (Rosenau, 1976, p. 106).

Boullée employed the atmospheric qualities of the wash to create dramatic lighting effects, giving grandeur to the otherwise simple pyramid. He may have been attempting to persuade viewers of his beliefs, subconsciously convincing them of the sketch's possibilities, and of the argument as a theoretical position for architecture. Concerning the use of pyramids as a conscious choice for a theoretical discussion, he said 'I have given the Pyramid the proportions of an equilateral triangle because it is perfect regularity that gives form its beauty' (Rosenau, 1976, p. 106). The choice of the mystical shape of the pyramid for his cenotaph obviously connects it to the great society of the Egyptians, encouraging a comparison to the monumentality of his architectural ideals. The character of the atmospheric effect also 'proves' his theory by means of emotional seduction, and positions this sketch as a powerful instrument of persuasion.

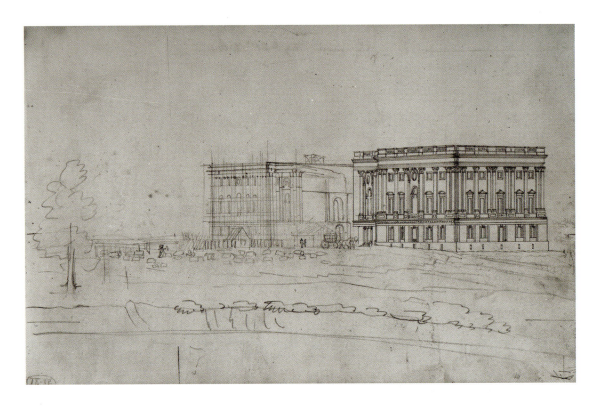

FIGURE 3.4

Latrobe, Benjamin Henry (1764–1820)

US Capitol under construction, seventh set, Maryland Historical Society, 1960.108.1.9.12, August 1806

Benjamin Henry Latrobe introduced the United States to a neoclassical language for monumental building. Born in 1764, in Yorkshire, England, he received a classical education. He attended the University of Leipzig and subsequently traveled throughout the continent, especially in Italy and France. Upon his return to England, he continued his education with the engineer John Smeaton and, later, in an architectural apprenticeship with Samuel Pepys Cockerell. With family connections in the United States, he initially moved to Virginia. Latrobe's first projects in the United States included the Bank of Philadelphia, a Greek revival structure; Sedgeley, a gothic revival house built in 1799; and engineering projects such as the Philadelphia Waterworks pumping station with its strong reference to Ledoux.

Latrobe relocated his practice to Philadelphia and other projects ensued such as the United States Customs House in 1807–1809 and Baltimore Cathedral from 1804 to 1808. As surveyor of public buildings, his most prominent and influential building came with the opportunity to design the Capitol building in Washington, DC. He designed a suitably imposing Pantheon-domed structure with alternating pilasters and windows, a rusticated lower level, and a Roman/Greek temple entrance (Norton, 1977). Sustaining a dialogue with Thomas Jefferson, he also contemplated appropriate architecture for America's emerging political system. He was prepared, with his knowledge of historical revival in Greek, Roman, and gothic styles, at a time when the United States needed public and political identity and was searching for symbols in the form of monuments.

Latrobe was deemed a skilled draughtsman, clearly able to explain his ideas visually (Van Vynckt, 1993). He constantly carried a sketchbook to record his travels, often rendering scenes in watercolor. This image from a sketchbook (Figure 3.4) may have been a travel companion, but it displays the Capitol building under construction. Delineated with a light hand, it appears brief and unfinished. Interestingly, the sketch remains less finished where the building appears less complete. Details of the completed section have been rendered darker and with more precision. Sketchy stacks of building materials, wagons, and temporary tents appear in front of the structure. The sketch contains mostly single lines and describes little context, barring a few brief trees and shrubs in the foreground.

With Latrobe's habit of carrying a sketchbook, the question arises of why architects draw when traveling. They may feel a need to capture a scene as a memory device, or perhaps they wish to analyze an element that is foreign to their experience. Curiously, Latrobe was sketching his own building during construction. One can speculate that he viewed the sketch as an architect's analysis, contemplating how the project was progressing. He may have used the sketch as part of a job survey or as a way to oversee the project's construction. Possibly divided between his roles as construction supervisor and detached observer, he may have absent-mindedly sketched during a free moment. This project, being unarguably his most identifying and most time consuming work, was likely a source of great pride. Consequently, the sketch may have been produced to record its emerging form. It also may represent his habitual technique of observation; a situation where Latrobe was unable to understand the building without drawing.

Since Latrobe was spending most of his time at his practice in Philadelphia, his intent may have been to carry the progress home for his own recollection or to inform someone else – the invention of the photograph was still several years in the future.

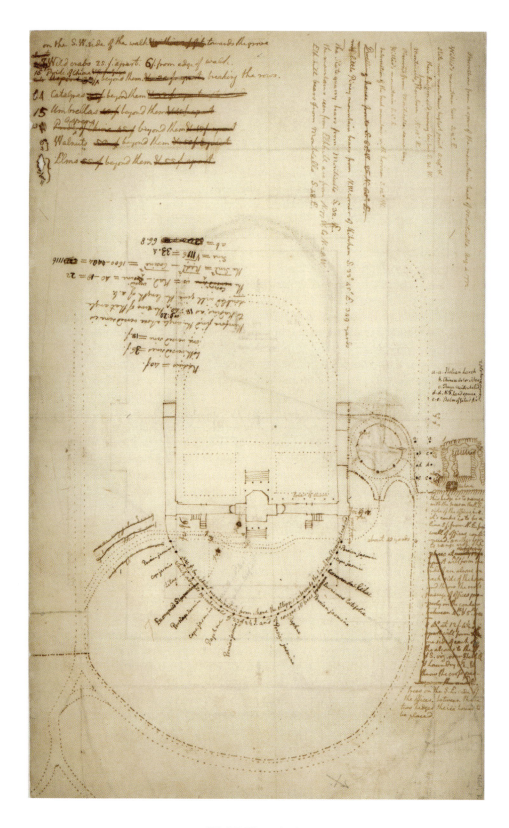

FIGURE 3.5

82

Jefferson, Thomas (1743–1826)

Monticello: mountaintop layout (plan), Before May 1768, Massachusetts Historical Society, N61; K34, 22.8 × 36.9cm, Ink, with a few additions, much later, in pencil

Although able to conceive of a building's design through drawings, Thomas Jefferson may be considered an amateur because of his lack of formal education or an apprenticeship in architecture (Norton, 1977). Considered the United States of America's first architect, Jefferson's education was classical and included the study of law. Known for his extensive library, Jefferson owned works by such authors as Vitruvius, Alberti, Palladio, Scamozzi, De L'Orme, Stuart, and Gibbs. He also acquired volumes concerning the practical aspects of building such as Halfpenny's *Practical Architecture* and a builder's dictionary.

America's architectural style had been a Georgian derivation called colonial, until Jefferson instigated the federal style (Trachtenberg and Hyman, 1986). With his political stature, holding the offices of both Secretary of State and President, he was able to influence the style of building for the new Capitol in Washington. Jefferson designed few projects in his lifetime; the campus of the University of Virginia, and the Capitol building for the state of Virginia, based on the Maison Carrée in Nîmes (Guinness and Sadler, 1973). The building of his home, called Monticello, became his most recognized architectural achievement. This hilltop estate references Palladio with a Greek temple façade and a central octagonal dome perched atop the symmetrical one-story brick structure.

Of the drawings by Jefferson housed in the Coolidge Collection, many are studies in the unforgiving medium of pen and ink. They appear diagrammatic in nature, due to their preparatory and simplistic quality. Wall thickness has been represented with single lines, unlike the heavy poché and nuance of detail and materiality found in drawings by Borromini, for example. As an architect with little construction experience, Jefferson studied classicism through model books to produce his designs.

This page (Figure 3.5) is a freehand planting plan for the grounds surrounding Monticello. Several areas have been erased and redrawn throughout the decision process. A single line describes the house while the proposed driveways are dotted without guidelines. Notes on the page prescribe the mathematical calculations for the site's geometry. The most interesting aspect of this page is Jefferson's notes to himself for both the location of the trees and the identification of their species. The simplicity and use of words give this sketch its diagrammatic quality since diagrams typically provide the most pertinent information while omitting the superfluous.

The semicircular row of trees noted as Lilac, Persian Jasmine, and Daphne has instructions whose wording follows the curve. From this one may speculate that Jefferson was intending to be absent at the time of the trees' planting; therefore, he needed to identify clearly their types. If this diagram was indeed meant to instruct workers, it would be unlikely that they could calculate the actual geometries per his notational instructions. As a diagram to document his thinking, it was limited by Jefferson's ability to render trees with enough detail so as to identify their species. Especially in plan, the trees would appear quite similar no matter how competent his rendering skills. It might also be suggested that he would be available for the planting and the purpose of the diagram was for his own reference. Studying the organization and symmetry of the different species could best be accomplished by recording their positions. The sketch could assist Jefferson to plan ahead, ordering or digging the trees before location. He may also have identified the trees knowing that when the work began, their location and identification could be confusing. The purpose of the sketch, then, was not to visualize the aesthetic qualities of the composition but rather to act as a memory device and a document to organize the planting.

FIGURE 3.6

Soane, Sir John (1753–1837)

Sketch of a design for the south side of the Lothbury Court, Bank of England, November 9, 1799, Sir John Soane's Museum, Soane 10/3/6, 56.5 × 68.4 cm, Pencil, pen and brown ink with pink, brown, and gray washes

The contemplation of a page by Sir John Soane initiates a discussion of the sketch as a form of 'rough draft.' Revealing Soane's neoclassical intentions, this sketch presents the formalization and subsequent correction of an image intended to be altered. He required the draft to act as a medium for an evaluative design dialogue.

An architect of both private country houses and the largest architectural commission in England of his time, the Bank of England, Soane emerged from humble beginnings. He was born in 1753, a country bricklayer's son, which gave him early exposure to the building trades. Schooled at the Royal Academy of Arts starting in 1771, he met George Dance the Younger and James Peacock, Surveyor, who encouraged him to visit Rome, 1778–1780. On this excursion he also stopped in Paris and visited antiquities in southern France, Naples, and Sicily (Darley, 1999; Richardson and Stevens, 1999).

Sir John Soane began his practice with the design of country houses, but in 1794 public commissions ensued starting with the House of Lords. Other projects followed, such as the Royal Entrance to the House of Lords, Law Courts, the Privy Council Chamber at Whitehall, and the Board of Trade. An advocate of French neoclassical architecture, he was influenced by the work of Borromini, Piranesi, and projects by his former employer George Dance (Richardson and Stevens, 1999; Darley, 1999).

The design and building of the Bank of England was a long and complex project, beginning with Soane's appointment as Surveyor to the bank in 1788. After completing many parts of the building, in 1797 he began the design of Lothbury Court. Soane produced numerous schemes in drawing form for the Roman-inspired courtyard and its façades, reworking the façade many times over a period of two years (Schumann-Bacia, 1989; Trachtenberg and Hyman, 1986). This sketch, dated November 9, 1799, and labeled as a design for the south side of the Lothbury Court (Figure 3.6) is a slow, deliberate, freehand ink drawing with pencil guidelines and numerous erasures and corrections.

Sketches cannot necessarily equate first conceptual thoughts with finished work, but they do capture the process of ideas followed by evaluation and alteration, a process not altogether linear (Jenny, 1989). Architectural sketches, as compared to unfinished manuscripts, are distinctly part of a design process that encourages possibilities and remains indeterminate. Soane's extensive design process may indicate that he worked through various façade iterations viewing the sketches as rough drafts. Since the sketch was completed in the definitive medium of ink, it is possible that image was meant to be a finished document and upon inspecting the form he made changes. As an erasure technique, one can see that ink had been scratched off the surface where Soane changed his mind. The two arched niches are delineated disparately on a symmetrical façade as he searched for alternatives. Dimensions were changed as Soane used this sketch for design exploration. The ink wash and scratchy shadows helped him to visualize the three-dimensional aspects of the façade. On the margins of the page, Soane studied and eliminated possible details, thoughts he certainly would not have included on a finished document. He dated the sketch to recall the latest option. This was especially important considering the many versions of this design and if he left the design for a few days while attending to other projects. This sketch represents a 'compositional' stage of the process; it constitutes the incomplete and changeable 'pre-text' as he was not searching for new constructs, but visually editing a proposed rough draft (De Biasi, 1989).

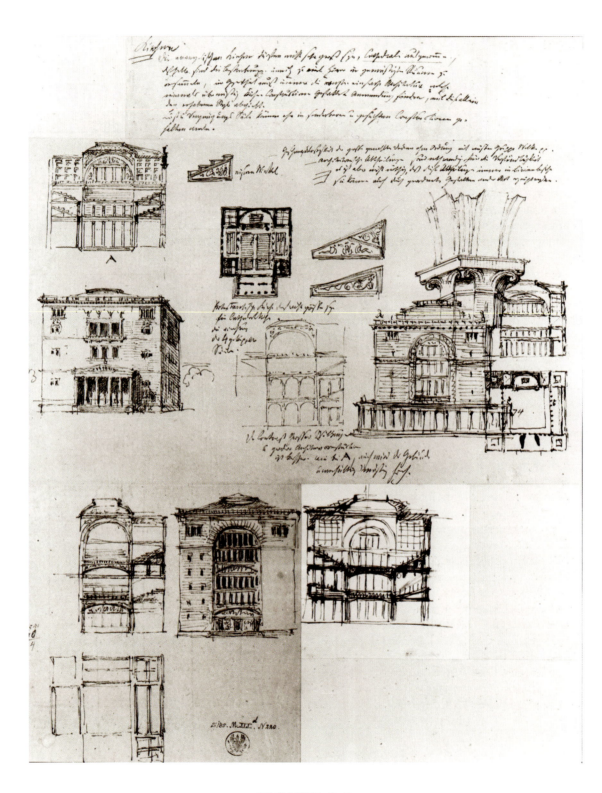

FIGURE 3.7

86

Schinkel, Karl Friedrich (1781–1841)

Sketches of a church at Grundriß Square, 1828, Staatliche Museen zu Berlin, SM 41d.220, 40.3 × 30.3 cm, Black ink

Karl Friedrich Schinkel, a prominent Prussian neoclassical architect, was born at Neuruppin/Mark Brandenburg in 1781. After the death of his father in 1794, the family moved to Berlin. Deciding that architecture was his interest, he joined the studio of David Gilly to study with he and his son, Friedrich Gilly. Schinkel subsequently enrolled in the first class of the Bauakademie and from 1803 to 1805 he embarked on a journey through Saxony, Austria, Italy, and France to view examples of architectural antiquity.

Schinkel's first major project was a commission by Friedrich Wilhelm III to design the Neue Wache at the Platz am Zeughaus. In 1821 he designed the Schauspielhaus in Berlin with its symmetrical wings, double entablature and raised pediment, all distinctive of his creative use of the neoclassical. His architecture evoked the Greek and Roman but reflected his own interpretation of classicism. One of the buildings he designed in Berlin was the Alte Museum in the Lustgarten, along with planning the development of the area. The distinctive element of this project, executed between 1824 and 1830, was a long colonnaded façade fronted by a large open plaza, giving the building a classical, monumental context.

This page of sketches for a square church (Figure 3.7) exhibits a search for form in plan, section, and elevation. It also conveys Schinkel's use of memory as a device in his design process, expressed through his freehand sketches. They are in some ways dependent upon memory since thoughts, images, and experiences, all part of the architect's whole being, determine what the sketch will be. Body memory, interpretation, and even specific items that are retained in memory over other experiences influence what each architect sketches.[1]

The quick, often uncontrolled process of sketching reveals how memory influences the form of the images. The haphazard placement and the heavy lines for correction are evidence of a thinking process. Schinkel uses his memory both to remember aspects of antiquity and to be reminded of the form of his earlier projects.

The square shape of this church is reminiscent of a Renaissance Palazzo with its heavy cornice and frieze. The center is open, so as to be an atrium or interior courtyard also evoking the Renaissance Palazzo theme. Other details speak of Schinkel's concern for history, such as the Pantheon-like portico, very similar to the Villa Medici at Poggio a Caiano by Giuliano da Sangallo. The tall, central space, possibly three to four stories, terminates in a domed oculus skylight.

The sketches also convey Schinkel's memory of his own earlier design projects, by the way he repeats certain elements in a new context. The image on the right shows the same square church, but on the lower level a long, colonnaded, raised portico surrounds it. One is distinctly reminded of the long colonnade on the Alte Museum, not yet completed at the time of this sketch, but possibly still very much in Schinkel's mind. The portico, rendered on the alternative to the left, is reminiscent of the façade of his earlier work, the Neue Wache, designed approximately twelve years earlier. These elemental shapes are reflective of the neoclassical style, but they are reused in creative ways, distinctive in his design.

FIGURE 3.8

Pugin, A.W.N. (1812–1852)

Details on the Avignon travel sketches, The Metropolitan Museum of Art, 35.33.3, II 16, p. 6
sketchbook, 15 × 10 in., Graphite and ink on sketchbook page

Extremely prolific for his short life, Auguste Welby Northmore Pugin designed a daunting amount of churches, along with furniture, metalwork, interior decoration and publications on gothic revival architecture. Having very little formal education and almost none in architecture, Pugin succeeded to learn about architecture through observation and sketching.

Born in London in 1812, his father was an illustrator, sometime draughtsman for John Nash, and producer of books on archaeological gothic revival. The elder Pugin also had a great influence on the future architect, teaching him drawing and taking him on excursions to both the continent and English medieval sites (Atterbury, 1994 and 1995). In 1835, he met Charles Barry and subsequently started work on the design of interiors for the Houses of Parliament, a project he would continue most of his life. Converting to Catholicism that same year had a great impact on his architectural career. Pugin's zealotry concerning church liturgy lead him to his most celebrated work, the design of religious buildings, and over thirty churches and cathedrals throughout England and Ireland that exhibit medieval and gothic sources. A few examples include the Cathedral of St. Chad, 1839–1840, the Roman Catholic Cathedral of St. Wilford, Hulme, 1839–1842 and the Roman Catholic Cathedral of St. George, Southwark, 1850.

Pugin's numerous travels to the continent were a source of inspiration to him; there he was able to sketch, observe and find sources/models for his architecture. He produced untold sketches using pocket sketchbooks. His publications expound practical rather than theoretical subjects, acting as copybooks, a few of these publications being *Gothic Furniture, The True Principles of Pointed or Christian Architecture*, and *A Treatise on Chancel Screens and Rood Lofts*.

This page (Figure 3.8) from a sketchbook contains details from a trip to Avignon. The page has been covered with pencil and ink studies of selected parts of ecclesiastical buildings. The architectural elements have been carefully sketched using pencil guidelines, and the fragments of details are randomly placed across the page. Although seemingly without an ordering system they have not been located haphazardly; each has been oriented upright and regular to the page. As fragments of tracery, columns, rose windows, and molding profiles they are all sketched with precision. Because they are freehand some of the carvings are irregular, and in several instances the sketches are unfinished. Where elements are repeated it was unnecessary for Pugin to draw every duplicated column.

These sketches were part of his education since he was drawing to understand. For example, the two columns located at the center of the page have column sections inscribed in their shafts. This suggests he wished to be reminded of their octagonal shape, a view difficult to render with an elevation drawing. The carefully imitated details were teaching him the fundamentals of medieval architecture, as if the page was a test of his comprehension.

The relatively small sketches were made with patience and with tremendous skill in observation. It could be speculated that Pugin was interested in accurately recording the essentials of gothic and Romanesque architecture to take home with him. Travel sketchbooks are often recording devices to remember the sights, but these sketches appear to be made with the intention similar to a visual dictionary. Pugin's architecture used many elements of the gothic and these sketches became references for details in his many church designs. This sketchbook resembles a medieval copybook, where Pugin was retaining the templates for reuse.

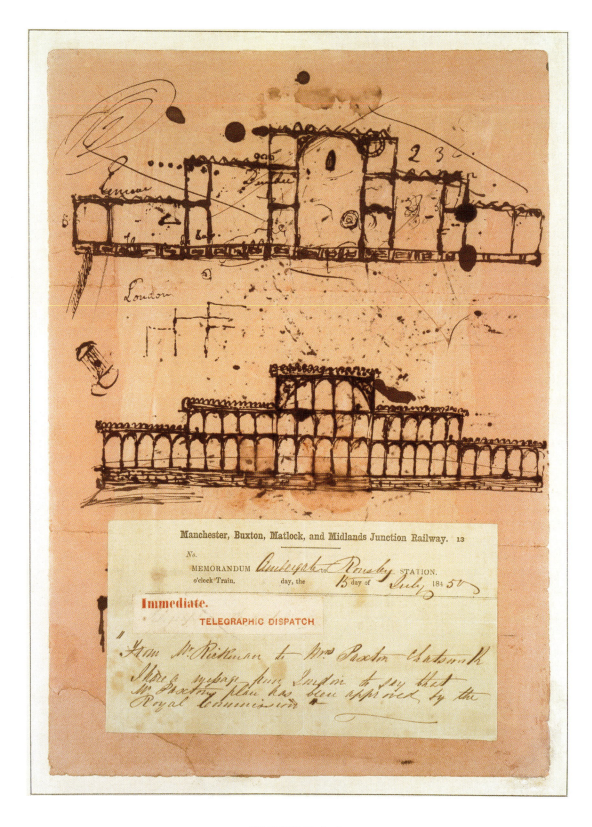

FIGURE 3.9

Paxton, Joseph (1801–1865)

Crystal Palace proposal end elevation and cross-section sketch, June 11, 1850,
V&A Picture Library, CT 14412, Pen and ink on blotting paper

A businessman and gardener, Joseph Paxton designed the most prominent example of exhibition architecture of his era. Born near Woburn, England, Paxton received little formal education. Starting work early in life as a gardener, he moved in 1820 to the gardens at Woodhall, Hertfordshire (Chadwick, 1961).

Paxton was ambitious; he became a successful businessman, railway investor, and bridge builder. It was in the design of glass structures that he was most innovative. His interest in horticultural building design began with the Great Conservatory at Chadsworth and the additional pavilions on the grounds. These conservatories were mostly constructed of glass and wood, where he developed ridge and furrow systems for the roofs (Chadwick, 1961). With a concern for tropical plants imported to England, Paxton refined the greenhouse with roof ventilation and heating elements beneath the floor.

The Industrial Revolution, which coincided with the rise of wealth and power of Great Britain, initiated London's international exhibition of 1851. Henry Cole proposed to Prince Albert an industry and commerce exposition. After rejecting all of the competition entries, the steering committee (made up of engineers and architects) proposed a design that proved unpopular (Beaver, 1986). As time was short, Paxton submitted a glass and iron structure composed of standardized parts that could be quickly assembled and taken down (Beaver, 1986; McKean, 1994).

Named the 'Crystal Palace' by the magazine *Punch*, Paxton's huge exhibition hall communicated 'the new relationship established between the technical means and the desire for prestige and the expressive aims of the building' (Benevolo, 1971, pp. 101–102). Crystal Palace, was nearly one third of a mile long (1851 feet), contained 900,000 square feet of glass, and 3300 iron columns. It was constructed of twenty-four foot repeating bays set upon a raised wood slat floor.

Having a short time to conceive of an appropriate solution, Paxton sketched this section and elevation (Figure 3.9) on blotter paper while attending a railway meeting (Chadwick, 1961). The sketch shows a three-tiered structure with ridge and valley roof panels and a floor heating system utilized in his earlier projects. This minimal sketch appears remarkably similar to the final construction. This may in part be due to the restricted time allowed for design, but it also reveals how Paxton relied on his former experience to find a solution. The flat roof with wavy lines can be more easily explained by understanding his previous conservatory projects; it was not necessary to detail the elements with which he was already familiar. Although the sub-floor heating system was ultimately not included in the Crystal Palace, the sketch gives the essence of the arched iron structure and tall, central, nave-like space. Surrounding Paxton's sketches, the page shows spare notes, scratchings, and inkblots that reveal the prior use of the paper as a railroad desk blotter. The ink bleeding into the paper from the bold lines suggest a high level of confidence. The absorption of the ink into the blotting paper means he sketched slowly with a certain amount of accuracy and experience. This project depended not on complex relationships of spaces but rather upon rapid assembly (approximately five months) and Paxton's knowledge of the fabrication of iron components. With these components as a 'kit of parts,' the brief sketch could easily replicate the entire building. This sketch may be the only one Paxton completed to describe the building as a whole, since it was necessary to translate the idea so swiftly into construction drawings. The simple lines were able to provide the necessary information and capture the essence of his conceptual thinking.

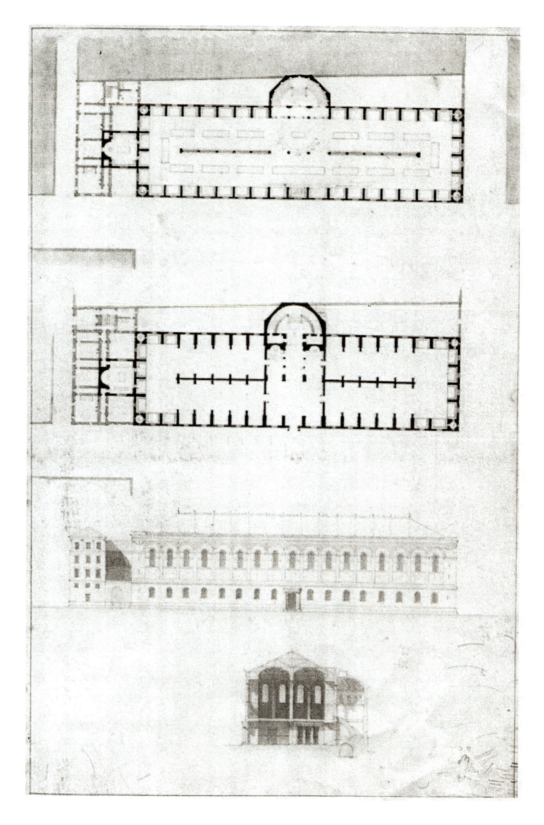

FIGURE 3.10

Labrouste, Henri (1801–1875)
Preliminary project for the Bibliothèque Ste-Geneviève, Paris,
Bibliothèque Nationale de France, 1839

Henri Labrouste emerged from the tradition of the beaux-arts and heralded an era of modernism with the use of functional building materials. Born in Paris, he followed his brother Théodore with architectural education at the École des Beaux-Arts. Henri joined the atelier of Vaudoyer and Lebas in 1819 and advanced to the first class within a year. He won the Grand Prix de Rome in 1824 and studied three Greek temples at Paestum. Returning to Paris, his controversial project disturbed the faculty at the Ecole, who were committed to a sculptural 'universal vocabulary' of the orders (Middleton, 1982). With its unorthodox conclusions, Labrouste's project examined the construction of these temples, revealing that, in addition to stone construction, stucco and wood articulation and polychromatic decoration were used (Middleton, 1982).

Over the subsequent years, Labrouste directed an atelier and in 1842 began the design of the Bibliothèque Ste-Geneviève. The library, with minimal decoration, can be read as the binding of a book with the names of authors prominently displayed on the exterior. The long, thin, barrel-vaulted building was constructed of masonry with exposed iron columns on the interior. Using a rational approach, Labrouste combined his traditional training with structurally efficient, contemporary building materials. In 1854 he was appointed architect of the Bibliothèque Nationale. The first part of the project required expanding the Palais Mazarin and Hôtel Chevry-Tubeuf. Again Labrouste employed an iron framework, using glass floors between the stacks and roofing the building with nine domes set on slender iron columns.

Although appearing rendered, this drawing (Figure 3.10) suggests an example of a beaux-arts *esquisse*. It consists of the typical preliminary orthographic drawings of plan, section, and elevation for the Bibliothèque Ste-Geneviève, Paris, 1939. As a stage beyond the initial search for organization, the content and format are consistent with a competition that would solidify a decision about direction (*parti*). There are several indications on the page that point to this assessment. At the bottom of the sheet are several short ink lines showing how Labrouste tested his pen. This checked if the ink was flowing (not dried at the nib) and to avoid the ink blob that often collected at the end during the time the pen was not in use.

On the elevation are a series of calculations indicating he was using the image to consider dimensions. An arched opening, sketched in graphite, has been added to the low connector between the two buildings. Freehand corrections show on the stair in plan and the lower level on the cross-section. These changes suggest the illustration represented the initial *esquisse* that was further developed after a process of evaluation. It would be possible to speculate that Labrouste was referring to this page while developing the design (the final *rendu*). Being the less valuable drawing (a sketch), it served its purpose as a *parti*, he could make corrections and used it as a blotter for his pen.

Understanding the abbreviated schedule for competitions at the Ecole des Beaux-Arts, the techniques of this sketch comparatively reveal the quickness inherent in a search for form (Harbeson, 1927). Quickness as expounded by Italo Calvino, involves a certain speed, economy, and wit (1988). The concept of the *parti* epitomized economy, displaying the whole organization as efficiently as possible. Time allotted to the search for form was extremely short – the *parti* was required to reveal a complete perception of the space, conveying its rationale. The academics at the Ecole may have referred to this intelligence as character, but the logic and perception may be of distinction in this case.

NOTES

1. The whole body is involved in the act of memory, since memory, and especially body memory, is *a priori*; constantly at work, never inoperative. See Casey, E. (1987). *Remembering: A Phenomenological Study*. Indiana University Press, and the suggestion of the body as 'habitual,' Merleau-Ponty, M. (1962). *Phenomenology of Perception*. The Humanities Press. Also see Yates, F. (1966). *The Art of Memory*. University of Chicago Press.

BIBLIOGRAPHY

Atterbury, P. and Wainwright, C. (1994). *Pugin: A Gothic Passion*. Yale University Press.

Atterbury, P. ed. (1995). *A.W.N. Pugin: Master of Gothic Revival*. Yale University Press.

Beaver, P. (1986). *The Crystal Palace: A Portrait of Victorian Enterprise*. Phillimore.

Benevolo, L. (1971). *History of Modern Architecture*. MIT Press.

Broadbent, G. (1980). Neo-classicism. *Architectural Design*, 25, 2–25.

Calvino, I. (1988). *Six Memos for the Next Millennium*. Harvard University Press.

Carter, E.C., Van Horne, J.C. and Brownell, C.E. eds (1985). *Latrobe's View of America, 1795–1820: Selections from the Watercolors and Sketches*. Maryland Historical Society by Yale University Press.

Casey, E. (2000). *Imagining: A Phenomenological Study*. Indiana University Press.

Casey, E. (1987). *Remembering: A Phenomenological Study*. Indiana University Press.

Chadwick, G.F. (1961). *The Work of Sir Joseph Paxton*. Architectural Press.

Cohen, J.A. and Brownell, C.E. (1994). *The Architectural Drawings of Benjamin Henry Latrobe, Vol. 2*. Yale University Press.

Dal Co, F. and Mazzariol, G. (1985). *Carlo Scarpa: The Complete Works*. Electa/Rizzoli.

Darley, G. (1999). *John Soane, An Accidental Romantic*. Yale University Press.

De Biasi, P. (1989). What is a Literary Draft? Toward a Functional Typology of Genetic Documentation. *Yale French Studies*, 89, 26–58.

De la Ruffinière du Prey, P. (1982). *John Soane: The Making of an Architect*. The University of Chicago Press.

Dean, P. (1999). *Sir John Soane and the Country Estate*. Ashgate.

Denison, C.D., Rosenfeld, M.N. and Wiles, S. (1993). *Exploring Rome: Piranesi and His Companions*. The Pierpont Morgan Library and the Canadian Centre for Architecture.

Drexler, A. ed. (1977). *The Architecture of the Ecole Des Beaux-Arts*. The Museum of Modern Art.

Egbert, D.D. (1980). *The Beaux-Arts in French Architecture*. Princeton University Press.

Fleming, John (1962). *Robert Adam and His Circle*. Harvard University Press.

Gordon, D.J. (1975). *The Renaissance Imagination: Essays and Lectures*. University of California Press.

Guinness, D. and Sadler, J.T. (1973). *Mr. Jefferson, Architect*. Viking Press.

Hamlin, T. (1955). *Benjamin Henry Latrobe*. Oxford University Press.

Harbeson, J.F. (1927). *The Study of Architectural Design*. Pencil Points Press.

Harpham, G.G. (1982). *On the Grotesque: Strategies of Contradiction in Art and Literature*. Princeton University Press.

Hind, A.M. (1922). *Giovanni Battista Piranesi: A Critical Study*. Holland Press.

Hofer, P. (1973). *Giovanni Battista Piranesi*. Dover.

Hutter, H. (1968). *Drawing: History and Technique*. McGraw-Hill.

Jenny, L. (1989). Genetic Criticism and its Myths. *Yale French Studies*, 89, 9–25.

Kaufmann, E. (1939). Etienne Louis Boullée. *Art Bulletin*, 21, 3, 212–227.

Kaufmann, E. (1952). Three Revolutionary Architects: Boullée, Ledoux and Lequeu. *Transactions of the American Philosophical Society*, 42, 431–564.

Kaufmann, E. (1955). *Architecture in the Age of Reason*. Harvard University Press.

Kimball, F. Essay and Notes (1968). *Thomas Jefferson, Architect: Original Designs in the Coolidge Collection of the Massachusetts Historical Society.* Da Capo Press.

King, D. (1991). *The Complete Works of Robert and James Adam.* Butterworth Architecture.

Kostof, S. (1985). *A History of Architecture, Settings and Rituals.* Oxford University Press.

Laugier, M-A. translated by W. and A. Herrmann (1977). *An Essay on Architecture.* Hennessey and Ingalls.

Lemagny, J.C. (1968). *Visionary Architects: Boullée Ledoux Lequeu.* University of St. Thomas.

MacDonald, W. (1979). *Piranesi's Carceri: Sources of Invention.* Smith College.

McKean, J. (1994). *Crystal Palace: Joseph Paxton and Charles Fox.* Phaidon.

Mead, C.C. (1991). *Charles Garnier's Paris Opéra: Architectural Empathy and the Renaissance of French Classicism.* MIT Press.

Merleau-Ponty, M. (1962). *Phenomenology of Perception.* Humanities Press.

Middleton, R. (1982). *The Beaux-Arts, and Nineteenth-century French Architecture.* MIT Press.

Millenson, S.F. (1987). *Sir John Soane's Museum.* UMI Research Press.

Millon, H.A. (1961). *Baroque and Rococo Architecture.* George Braziller.

Millon, H. (1999). *Triumph of the Baroque: Architecture in Europe, 1600–1750. Rizzoli.*

Norton, P.F. (1977). *Latrobe, Jefferson and the National Capitol.* Garland Publishing.

Papadakis, A. ed. (1983). *John Soane.* Academy Editions.

Pérouse De Montclos, J. (1974). *Etienne-Louis Boullée, 1728–1799: Theoretician of Revolutionary Architecture.* George Braziller.

Pundt, H.G. (1972). *Schinkel's Berlin: A Study in Environmental Planning.* Harvard University Press.

Richardson, M. and Stevens, M. eds (1999). *John Soane, Architect.* Royal Academy of Arts.

Riemann, G. and Heese, C. (1991). *Karl Friedrich Schinkel, Architekturzeichnungen.* Henschel Verlag.

Robison, A. (1986). *Piranesi, Early Architectural Fantasies: A Catalogue Raisonné of the Etchings.* National Gallery of Art / The University of Chicago Press.

Rosenau, H. (1976). *Boullée and Visionary Architecture, including Boullée's 'Architecture, Essays on Art'.* Academy Editions.

Rowan, A. (1988). *Robert Adam.* Victoria and Albert Museum.

Ruskin, J. (1907). *The Stones of Venice.* J.M. Dent.

Rykwert, J. (1980). *The First Moderns.* MIT Press.

Rykwert, J. and A. (1985). *Robert and James Adam: The Men and the Style.* Rizzoli.

Schinkel, K.F. (1989). *Collection of Architectural Designs by Karl Friedrich Schinkel.* Princeton Architectural Press.

Schumann-Bacia, E. (1989). *John Soane and The Bank of England.* Princeton Architectural Press.

Scully, V. (1969). *American Architecture and Urbanism.* Frederick A. Praeger.

Snodin, M. ed. (1991). *Karl Friedrich Schinkel: A Universal Man.* Yale University Press.

Stampfle, F. (1978). *Giovanni Battista Piranesi: Drawings in the Pierpont Morgan Library.* Pierpont Morgan Library / Dover.

Stroud, D. (1984). *Sir John Soane, Architect.* Faber and Faber.

Summers, D. (1981). *Michelangelo and the Language of Art.* Princeton University Press.

Tadgell, C. (1978). *Ange-Jacques Gabriel.* A. Zwemmer.

Tafuri, M. (1987). *The Sphere and the Labyrinth: Avant-Gardes and Architecture from Piranesi to the 1970s.* MIT Press.

Trachtenberg, M, and Hyman, I. (1986). *Architecture: From Prehistory to Post-Modernism.* Harry N. Abrams.

Turner, J. ed. (2000). *The Grove Dictionary of Art.* St. Martin's Press.

Van Horne, J.C. and Formwalt, L.W. (1984). *The Correspondence and Miscellaneous Papers of Benjamin Henry Latrobe.* Maryland Historical Society.

Van Vynckt, R.J. (1993). *International Dictionary of Architects and Architecture.* St. James Press.

Vasari, G. (1960). *Vasari on Techniques.* Dover.

Vasari, G. translated by De Vere, G.D. (1979). *Lives of the Most Eminent Painters, Sculptors, and Architects.* Abrams.

Viollet-le-Duc, E-E. translated by Whitehead, K.D. (1990). *The Foundations of Architecture: Selections from the Dictionnaire Raisonné*. G. Braziller.

Watkin, D. (1996). *Sir John Soane: Enlightenment Thought and the Royal Academy Lectures*. Cambridge University Press.

Wedgewood, A. (1985). *A.W.N. Pugin and the Pugin Family*. Victoria and Albert Museum.

Whiffen, M. and Koeper, F. (1981). *American Architecture 1607–1976*. MIT Press.

Wilton-Ely, J. (1978). *The Mind and Art of Giovanni Battista Piranesi*. Thames and Hudson.

Wilton-Ely, J. (1993). *Piranesi as Architect and Designer*. Yale University Press.

Yates, F. (1966). *The Art of Memory*. University of Chicago Press.

CHAPTER 4

AMERICAN NEOCLASSICISM AND THE EMERGENCE OF THE SKYSCRAPER (1870–1920)

One might question why this small group of Americans deserves their own chapter. As late-nineteenth century architects, they approached modern architecture with less fervor than their European counterparts. Henry Hobson Richardson, Louis Sullivan, Richard Morris Hunt, and Stanford White practiced with one foot in the past. Their high Victorian gothic and Renaissance revival allusions, use of materials and connection to the development of tall buildings led them tentatively toward the modern.

Although Sullivan believed that buildings needed to express their function, he never felt unified with the dedicated revolutions of Adolf Loos or Le Corbusier in Europe. Considered innovative in the design of tall buildings, Sullivan could not refrain from the decorative. He incorporated steel framing but lacked a conceptual expression of the new notion of the skyscraper. America's greatest contribution to the inception of modern architecture was the steel structural system. The historians Henry-Russell Hitchcock and Philip Johnson, in their book *The International Style*, disappointingly describe these architects as the 'half moderns' (1996). Unable to fully identify with the neoclassical architects of France, yet incapable of embracing a consistent belief in a modernist ideal, they reside in a moment of transition, at the cusp of a new era.

The sketches of these architects illustrate their unique position and affinity to past styles. Much of their visual expression reflects their education in the beaux-arts tradition. Remarkably poignant, these sketches typify their concerns and beliefs, reflecting the natural world in the case of Louis Sullivan and the stark minimalist essence of the gothic revival with Richardson. Hugh Ferriss' sketches boldly demonstrate the emotion of the evolving social and political period, heralding the monumentality of the 'new city' of tall buildings, while romanticizing the solidity of masonry construction. A brief summary of American architecture at the close of the nineteenth century and the emergence of the skyscraper will set the stage for a discussion of these architect's sketches.

For twenty years following the Civil War, architecture in the United States was mainly classical and gothic. During this period, the country was undergoing an enthusiastic building program including many governmental projects. Described as the second empire baroque, these monumental buildings had strong horizontal layering, mansard roofs and classical elements (Roth, 1979).

The great fire in Chicago in 1871 offered a tremendous opportunity. Burning 1,688 acres of wooden buildings, the need to rebuild was pressing (Douglas, 1996; Charernbhak, 1981). The 1880s were characterized by industrial and technological expansion. Industry was standardizing track gauge, huge corporations were providing electricity, the oil company of John D. Rockefeller was formed, and the emergence of the steel industry provided the materials to construct tall buildings. The small and bounded business district of Chicago produced the commercial building as a type, which quickly spread to New York City. These tall buildings satisfied the need for office space and efficiency in rapidly expanding cities. Contemporary construction of a steel frame clad with a curtain wall, the development of elevators and fireproofing, and advancements in environmental control systems, set the stage for the birth of the skyscraper (Goldberger, 1982; Huxtable, 1982).

Regardless of these potential advancements, American architects were still focused stylistically on Europe for direction; thus, the new tall buildings resembled neoclassical or gothic structures stretched in the middle. The first building to demonstrate these qualities and the first true skyscraper was the Home Insurance Building designed by William LeBaron Jenney in Chicago, 1883–1885. Other tall buildings followed including Richardson's Marshall Field Wholesale Store in Chicago, 1885–1887, and Sullivan's Wainwright Building in Missouri, 1890–1891. The architectural critic Paul Goldberger suggests that in Chicago, architects were more interested in structural honesty, while in New York City their concern was the historic appearance of the buildings (1982). Two buildings that predicted a modern approach were the Monadnock Building in Chicago and the Reliance Building, both by Daniel Burnham and John Wellborn Root. These structures substantially eliminated ornament, and the Reliance Building's façade was designed with a large amount of glazing.

The tall buildings of Chicago and New York City were not entirely commercial. Architects such as Hunt were designing tall apartment buildings and for many years the tallest building in New York City was Trinity Church. The wealthy industrialists, desiring vacation homes, initiated a contrasting scale of building in seaside communities such as Newport, Rhode Island. Influenced by Japanese architecture, these architects were building wood domestic architecture in the period between 1840 and 1876. Much of this was basically Queen Anne style. Vincent Scully describes this architecture as 'stick style,' identified by their rambling asymmetrical shape, large wrapping porches, gabled roofs and, most distinctive, a complex wooden frame and wall surface divided into panels (1955). Richardson expanded this repertoire, using a shingled exterior for his Newport houses from the early 1870s. The shingle style houses, often with recessed porches, were popularized by the architectural firm of McKim, Mead, and White during the 1880s. Many were published in magazines such as *Harpers*. Additionally published as picturesque sketches in *American Architect*, two 1880 sketches by Emerson capture the fluid, painterly technique, expressing his design intent. They presented an illusion of modeled light on the shingles. Scully suggests the style of sketching used to represent these buildings by White and Emerson resembles the blurred forms and reflective light of the French impressionist painters.

EDUCATION

American architects were looking to Europe for inspiration. A few of them had traveled to France for education, either at the Ecole des Beaux-Arts or a technical school such as Jenney. The number actually trained abroad were few, as the vast majority were apprenticed with architects influenced by French neoclassicism. William Rotch Ware, editor of *American Architect*, was an advocate for the necessity of architectural schools that would teach precedent. Having attended the Ecole himself, Ware's purpose was 'to raise the standing of the architectural profession, to draw a sharp line between builders and architects, and to make it clear to the world that the architect was an educated gentleman' (Scully, 1955, p. 51). He was concerned about the self-educated architect, reflective of the newly formed American Institute of Architects which was established with the role of the professional architect at its foundation. In response, several schools of architecture were formed at this time, the first being Massachusetts Institute of Technology in 1868, followed by the University of Illinois (1870), Cornell (1871), Syracuse (1873), University of Pennsylvania (1874) and Columbia (1881) (Roth, 1979). In most cases the system of education in these schools reflected beaux-arts tradition.

The gentleman architect, especially those educated in this system, viewed architecture primarily as an artform and depended heavily on builders' knowledge of construction and structure. Leland Roth writes concerning the relationship between architect and builder, especially considering the houses of the shingle style: 'It was then common practice to leave much to the discretion of the contractor, and the clause in building contracts, "to be finished in a workmanlike manner," expressed what was to builders like the Norcross brothers a sacred duty which they executed with exacting care' (Roth, p. 167). Architects' drawings did not include explicit details, so understanding between a builder and an architect were dependent upon reputation and skill. Drawings needed to convey intent, but left much to the contractors' judgment.

The architects designing tall buildings, however, met with issues of construction and engineering. Several of these innovative architects obtained their education in technical schools or engineering offices. Jenney had received training in engineering at the Ecole Centrale des Arts Manufactures in Paris and Root had studied engineering in New York (Douglas, 1996). Obviously, architects' offices varied from small to large, but the partners in large architectural firms began to specialize. As Dankmar Adler jovially acquired commissions, Sullivan was concerned with design, especially ornamentation. Similarly, Burnham, with strength in the organizational aspects of architecture, managed the firm while Root was reportedly the design partner (Douglas, 1996). Because the size and scale of his projects were expanding, Richardson terminated drawing and instead sketched his ideas, trusting his draughtsman to the technical drawing. In this way, the sketch, in addition to a personal dialogue, extended its role to intra-office communication. With the popularity of magazines publishing homes of the wealthy, sketches became a mode of advertisement and dissemination of style. As mentioned earlier, these sketches also propagated an emotional atmosphere to promote a style.

MEDIA

In the late nineteenth century, publication in the form of magazines connected the architects of the world. Heavily illustrated, these contemporary 'pattern books' transmitted style across the country and between continents. In 1896 Sullivan published his essay 'The Tall Office Building Artistically Considered' in *Lippincott's* magazine. It was this article that delineated the parts of a tall building and likened them to a column, specifying the base, mezzanine, repeated floors/shaft, and the attic column. The proliferation of architectural discourse also widely distributed drawing styles and techniques. Many proposed, and completed, buildings were portrayed as sketches to suggest textural or atmospheric impressions.

Although basically similar to previous generations, the tools and materials of this period available to the architect were considerably refined. Paper had been manufactured since the late eighteenth century and could be purchased in large sheets or rolls. The precision of ruling pens and other drawing instruments were constantly being improved. Presentation drawings were rendered with ink wash and watercolor. Draughting was precise and detailed using t-squares, triangles, and ruling pens (Hambly, 1988). Sketches relayed information concerning the design of details in the case of Sullivan's carefully explored floral ornament. The initial conceptual musings as illustrated by Richardson's brief sketch resemble a *parti* diagram describing the essence of the project. A fast and efficient method to visualize, pencil and pen and ink continued to assist in design. With an abundance of architectural and popular periodicals, architects such as Ferriss were able to successfully sway public opinion with their dramatic and emotional visions of the contemporary city. The use of pencil shading to achieve lighting effects made the sketch an atmospheric communication tool. The expansion of urban construction helped promote such skills, raising awareness in the minds of Americans that architecture was a factor in the image of the city. The American neoclassical architects depended upon sketches to conceive, envision, and detail their continually more complex building explorations.

FIGURE 4.1

Richardson, Henry Hobson (1838–1886)

Small sketch from west, preliminary sketch, All Saints Episcopal Cathedral (Albany, NY), 1882–1883, Houghton Library, Harvard College Library, HH Richardson Papers, ASA F3, 10 × 13 cm, Graphite on tracing paper

The 1850s produced many high Victorian gothic buildings, and Henry Hobson Richardson's early work reflects this influence. By the early 1870s, Richardson came into his own style, distinguished by heavy masonry and arched entrances, such as two projects in Massachusetts, the Hampden County Courthouse in Springfield and the Thomas Crane Public Library in Quincy. Richardson utilized a creative and individual approach to Romanesque that some describe as eclectic (O'Gorman, 1987). It was this approach that caused his work to be named the 'Richardsonian Romanesque.'

Richardson was born at Priestly Plantation in St. James Parish, Louisiana, in 1838. He began his higher education at Harvard in 1856 and gained admission to the Ecole des Beaux-Arts in 1860. Following the end of the Civil War, he returned to New York where he received his first independent commission, the Church of the Unity in Springfield, Massachusetts. Upon winning the competition for the design of the Trinity Church, he completed such projects as the Haydon Building, the Cheney Building in Hartford, and those representing his more mature works, the Ames Memorial Library Building at North Easton, Austin Hall at Harvard, and the Allegheny County Courthouse in Pittsburgh. After a long illness, Richardson died in 1886 at the age of forty-seven.

This sketch from Richardson's hand (Figure 4.1) expresses his first thoughts for the All Saints Church in Albany, 1882, and acts as a *parti* for the project. Because of his beaux-arts education, Richardson used a process of design learned from the Ecole in Paris, the *esquisse* (O'Gorman, 1987). Working on many projects at one time, Richardson would provide small sketches to be given to draftsmen for development. The senior draftsmen knew Richardson's intentions as they drew the designs (Ochsner, 1982). In this way, the sketch represented his concept for the project and communicated it to those in his office.

The project for which this sketch was the impetus was an invited competition designated to be in the gothic style (O'Gorman, 1987). Interestingly, Richardson's early sketch and the final drawing differ quite significantly. The sketch, in elevation, has similarities to his heavy railroad buildings with their massive stone and rounded arches. It displays a distinctive shape comprised of a main peaked roof flanked by two smaller versions. The shape resembles a pyramid, so much so that it may be possible to inscribe a simple equilateral triangle over this building. The technique of the sketch is minimal, using an economy of lines and lacking in detail. The arches in their simplicity consist of a series of 'm's' and the lines are mostly singular in weight. The three Roman arches are not perfectly round, but convey enough information so they did not need to be corrected. Very small and brief, the sketch acts an idea diagram and only considers the elevational *parti*. Although it shows a ground line, the image is lacking in context, another indicator that the sketch is a beginning impression.

In contrast, the competition drawing is an elevation much more reminiscent of the gothic style, although not entirely gothic. The peaked roofs were pared down to resemble spires and the façade has vertical windows and a rose window. The symmetry is obvious and striking with the three major arched entrances reminiscent of Notre Dame in Paris. This dichotomy between the sketch and the competition entry reveals how Richardson expressed his belief in the heavy materiality of the Romanesque as opposed to the lighter, vertical, gothic image expected for the competition. It is interesting how he allowed an early concept to become modified through design development to conform to the competition requirements.

FIGURE 4.2

Hunt, Richard Morris (1827–1895)

Sketch for the base of the Statue of Liberty, The Museum of the American Architectural Foundation, Box 1865, 11⅛ × 7⅜ in., Graphite, ink, and wash on paper

Richard Morris Hunt, the first American architect to have attended the Ecole des Beaux-Arts in Paris, brought back a French classical monumental architecture pervaded by idealism combined with practicality. Hunt's architecture was an eclectic blending of neogothic, neogrec and French neoclassical influence, contrasted by the picturesque wood frame cottages he designed in Newport (Stein, 1986). He was influential in the founding of the American Institute of Architects in 1857 and was its third president (Baker, 1980).

Hunt was born in Vermont in 1827. After his father's death, the family left for an unintentionally extended twelve-year trip to Europe. While living in France, Hunt applied to the Ecole des Beaux-Arts and was accepted in 1846. He chose the atelier of Hector Martin Lefuel and during his last years in Paris worked with him on the Pavillon de la Bibliothèque of the Louvre. He traveled widely while living in Europe, a practice he continued throughout his life. Returning to New York City in 1855, he started his practice designing small projects and instructing students in an atelier atmosphere. His first notable project was the Studio Building completed in 1858, a space designed particularly for the needs of artists. He was well established by the 1860s, designing skyscrapers and apartment buildings. Several of his numerous buildings include the Stuyvesant Apartments, the Tribune Building skyscraper in 1876 and monuments such as the Seventh Regimental Monument in Central Park (1873). Later in his life, he was commissioned to design large mansions for wealthy families as the Biltmore in Asheville and summer cottages in Newport, and then the Administration Building for the World's Columbian Exposition in 1893.

Most likely because of his strong relationships in France, Hunt took part in the planning for the Statue of Liberty in the early 1880s. With the sculpture by the artist Frédéric Auguste Bartholdi begun, a Franco-American Union was gathered to manage the project. Hunt was named architect and construction was begun on the pedestal in 1884 (Baker, 1980; Trachtenberg and Hyman, 1986). Hunt's challenge was to connect the star-shaped foundation of Fort Wood with the sculpture. He chose to design a rusticated stone base with a parapet cornice as a firm setting for the statue. Since he was attempting to unify the look of the fortress with the smooth texture of the sculpture, the rusticated base became more refined as it ascended acts as this transition.

This sketch (Figure 4.2) captures one iteration in his design exploration. Detailing the rusticated stone with graphite pencil, the remainder of the sketch consists of ink and wash over graphite. Proportionally the pedestal commands a larger portion of the composition than that of the final solution. It appears elongated and distorted possibly because the pedestal was his concern and he wanted to visualize its articulation. The previously resolved issue of the sculpture, less of his concern, could be vaguely placed with wash. The statue remained part of the composition but the emphasis of this sketch was to design the base. The details of the rustication and the proposed columns over a loggia space have been more carefully articulated, substantially more than the background. The right side of the page shows an enlarged detail of the stone coursing, again reinforcing his interest. In this case, interpreting Hunt's intention may be obvious. The purpose of sketches differs as to the questions being asked. Here Hunt was concentrating on one aspect of the design, not trying to visualize the whole, which may have left the entire composition disproportionate. Interestingly, once built the pedestal became a dominant feature of the composition. Invariably necessary to lift liberty into the air, it still prevailed.

FIGURE 4.3

White, Stanford (1853–1906)

Freehand sketches of large estates, Avery Architectural and Fine Arts Library, White DR 35, SW46:19, 4.74 × 7 in., Graphite on paper

An American architect with an eclectic style, Stanford White was a partner in the successful firm of McKim, Mead and White. White was originally intending to study painting, but was counseled to consider architecture. In 1872, after receiving a degree from New York University, he found work with the architectural practice of H. H. Richardson in Boston. Richardson had attended the Ecole des Beaux-Arts and his design process reflected that education. As an apprentice, White was exposed to Richardson's Romanesque since Trinity Church was being constructed during his tenure in the firm. It was in Richardson's office that he met his future partner, Charles Follon McKim. In 1878, White traveled to Europe for a period of almost a year. Upon returning from Europe he joined McKim and Mead as a third partner, replacing the retiring William Bigelow. In a scandal that almost overshadowed his prolific architectural career, he was fatally shot at the age of fifty-three.

The following are a few of the projects for which he was the partner responsible; the Methodist Episcopal Church in Baltimore, 1887, the New York Life Insurance Building, Omaha, Nebraska, 1890, Judson Memorial Church, Washington Square, 1888–1893, the Metropolitan Club built between 1892 and 1894, and Tiffany and Company in New York City, 1903–1906. Throughout his career, White designed numerous shingle style homes for the rich and famous. The precedent for his neoclassical architecture employed elements from the past, arbitrarily including Châteauesque, French provincial, Venetian, French and German Renaissance, in unique combinations and variations.

This example of a sketch by Stanford White is remarkably playful (Figure 4.3). Johann Huizinga and Hans-Georg Gadamer outline the philosophical aspects of play as having boundaries to sketch against, being representational, an all absorbing endeavor, conveying a method of learning and displaying a give and take of dialogue. Considering a definition of play, White found intelligibility in this image. He was quickly sketching the building's form conceived in his mind's eye while learning about the building in the process. As it emerged on the paper, he could visualize its potential. Play also involves representation as White was imagining this project, he was seeing the building rather than the paper as a substitute (Wollheim, 1971). He was consciously accepting boundaries, never sketching anything other than the building, providing a ground plane and a sense of perspective. The verticals as possible columns on the porch have been sketched so quickly they have transformed from columns to resemble n's and m's. These lines seem to skip off the page in some instances and in other cases they appear continuous. This implies he could not stop long enough to lift the pencil off the page. As another aspect of play, White was engrossed in the action of the play, the dialogue of the 'give and take.' He could draw one line and it responded with another as his mind interacted with the image. The sketch facilitating discourse shows a softer pencil lead over a first general outline. The latter demonstrative roof and balustrade are more forceful in an effort to obliterate the original roof expression. It is possible to surmise the areas of the design that most concerned him at the moment.

In a catalogue of projects by McKim, Mead and White, Leland Roth includes a project coordinated by White, the A. A. Pope Residence in Farmington, Connecticut. The building with its strong eave balustrade and taller central portion seems to strongly resemble this sketch by White. Roth indicates that the project was influenced by the Pope's daughter Theodate who had architectural education and participated with the design. With this in mind, White's sketch may also represent a mode of communication and discussion between two architects.

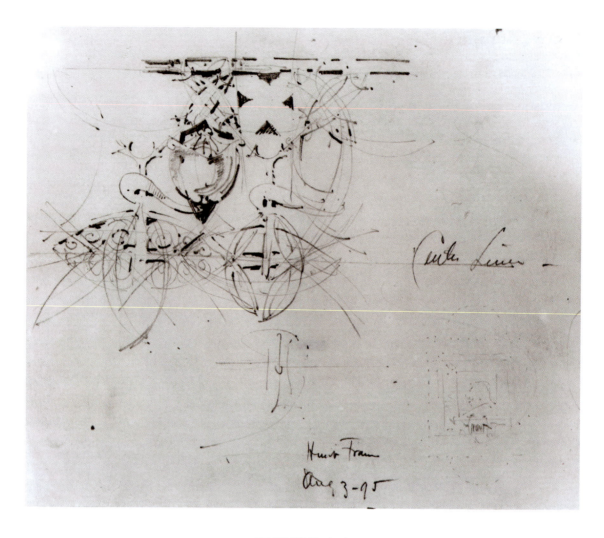

FIGURE 4.4

Sullivan, Louis (1856–1924)

Study of ornamental frame for Richard Morris Hunt memorial portrait for *Inland Architect*, August 7, 1895, Avery Architectural and Fine Arts Library, FLLW/LHS 123, 17 × 20.3 cm, Pencil on paper

Known for his 'evolutionistic' botanical style, Louis Sullivan was born in 1856 (Twombly and Menocal, 2000). He entered Massachusetts Institute of Technology in 1872. Sullivan was briefly employed by Frank Furness and later moved to Chicago to work with William Le Baron Jenny before enrolling at the Ecole des Beaux-Arts in 1874. Disappointed by his experience in Vaudremer's atelier, Sullivan instead spent his time studying Paris architecture and traveling to Rome and Florence. In 1879 he started with Dankmar Adler as a freelance draughtsman in Chicago. This firm eventually became Adler and Sullivan and was influential in the development of the skyscraper and the building of Chicago. Sullivan's role in the firm involved the 'composition of façades and the design of ornamentation' (Twombly and Menocal, 2000, p. 84).

Upon the closing of his firm shortly before his death in 1924, Sullivan moved all of the firm's architectural drawings to storage. Of these drawings, he retained approximately 100 sketches consisting largely of botanical and geometric ornament. These sketches make up the entirety of drawings by Sullivan found in collections today (Twombly and Menocal, 2000). Why Sullivan chose these particular images is a matter of speculation. They may have reflected a more direct expression of his inspiration, creativity, or personal architectural style.

Sullivan's architectural style involved massive volumes contrasted with intricate ornamentation. Narcisco Menocal writes about Sullivan's use of ornament: 'Louis Sullivan's concept of architectural and ornamental design was based on a belief that the universe was sustained by a cosmic rhythm. Change, flow, and one entity turning into another were effects of a universal becoming. ... In that scheme, beauty emerges from a never-ending transformation of all things into new entities' (Twombly and Menocal, 2000, p. 73). The ornament was, for Sullivan, an enhancing part of otherwise straightforward steel frame buildings.

This study, from 1895, is an ornamental frame for the Richard Morris Hunt memorial portrait (Figure 4.4). It is typical of Sullivan's studies for ornament, displaying intertwined organic shapes, composed of light guidelines with darker areas for detail. It appears to be a running band of foliage; the top edge and the indicated centerline suggest a linear pattern, one that would be repeated across the frame. This centerline reveals that the sketch is only half of the intended ornament. It was not necessary for Sullivan to complete the entire frieze, as he was able to make a judgment from a small section. This became his point of decision, whether to continue or reject the proposal. By using an underlying geometry, the ornate and complex foliage pattern could appear loose and haphazard, yet it could be precisely duplicated.

When drawing the negative space (the shadows) rather than the positive outline of the foliage, Sullivan was simulating and testing a future three-dimensional effect. The sketch, consistently undeveloped across the page, resembles a doodling that did not need to be completed.

Although this sketch represents only a small detail of ornament, it may be central to understanding Sullivan's architecture. It seems to act as appliqué to the functional spaces, in such a way that the ornament becomes the skin on the steel frame. Sullivan's buildings reflect the 'organic' on two different levels – in the way the architecture developed, and the allusions to nature found in the ornament. This, coupled with his desire to retain such sketches as evidence of his design, assists to understand the focus of Sullivan's architecture (Andrews, 1985).

FIGURE 4.5

Ferriss, Hugh (1889–1962)

Crest of Boulder, Hoover Dam, The Power in Buildings series, September 14 (between 1943 and 1953), Avery Architectural and Fine Arts Library, NYDA.1000.001.00010, 30.7 × 23.3 cm, Charcoal on tracing paper on board

Although Hugh Ferriss was from a different generation than Louis Sullivan, he represents the attitudes of the architects designing buildings scraping the skies of American cities. Primarily an illustrator, it is important to include him in this section because he did much to promote the future of cities with his drawings and sketches of emotive and dramatically lit urban structures.

Born in St. Louis, Missouri, he received a professional education in architecture from Washington University. A school immersed in beaux-arts teaching methods, he graduated in 1911. After completing school he journeyed to New York City to work for Cass Gilbert. A licensed architect, Ferriss found work rendering buildings for architects such as Harvey Wiley Corbett. Paul Goldberger writes that Ferriss became interested in New York City's new zoning ordinance, and in 1916 he drew a series of five drawings describing building mass and the pyramid shapes that the ordinances implied. 'Ferriss's drawing style became a crucial factor in shaping the priorities of the 1920's: his visions of the impact of the zoning law were to affect the age as much as the law itself, as masonry buildings endeavored to take on the feeling of sculpted mountains, their shape suddenly more important than their historical detail of even their style' (Goldberger, 1982, p. 58). Preparing his visions for a utopia, he exhibited 'Drawings of the Future City' in 1925 and in 1929 he published *Metropolis of Tomorrow*. Continuing to illustrate for a wide variety of architects he commented that his purpose was to convey a certain aspect of reality in an exciting way when the project was in still primarily in the architect's mind (Leich, 1980). Later in his life he received a grant to travel the United States recording important contemporary architecture, resulting in the book *Power in Buildings*.

The buildings in Hugh Ferriss' drawings were not of his design but in a sense he created the method by which they would be comprehended. They could be considered sketches by virtue of their conceptual qualities. Ferriss resembles the futurist architect Sant'Elia who seduced an ideal and appealed to an emotional position. In the *New York Times*, Peter Blake reviewed the show Power in Buildings and wrote: ' ... Ferriss speaks (and writes) softly, but carries an awfully big pencil'. Blake was implying their dynamic vision but also their powerful meaning (Leich, 1980, p. 31).

This sketch from the Power in Buildings series (Figure 4.5) presents a dramatic view of Hoover Dam. In a reversal, strong light is emitting from below exaggerating the height of the observation platform. The stark slope of the concrete mass fades away into emptiness further evoking this perception. The lone figure helps the viewer comprehend the immense scale. On close inspection the sketch is entirely freehand utilizing the ambiguous texture of a pliable media. Ferriss was known to have implored soft pencil, charcoal and crayon, subsequently removing the medium for highlights with a kneaded eraser or a knife. The use of smudged soft crayon produced an eerie foggy halo. In this case the soft medium presented both less defined edges and high contrast. Not a preparatory sketch like others in this book, the design by Gordon B. Kauffmann has been transformed by the hands of Ferriss. The sketch puts the viewer in awe of the dam's ability to extract power and the sheer magnitude of its size. It suggests the light emitting from below represents the glow of the generating electricity.

Hugh Ferriss lived until modernism had reached a peak, but his methods strongly speak of an architecture of masonry, of mass and solidity. His sketches were less about accuracy and more about seduction in an attempt to influence the perception of architecture.

BIBLIOGRAPHY

Andrews, D.S. (1985). *Louis Sullivan and the Polemics of Modern Architecture*. University of Illinois Press.

Baker, P.R. (1980). *Richard Morris Hunt*. MIT Press.

Baldwin, C.C. (1976). *Stanford White*. Da Capo Press.

Charernbhak, W. (1981). *Chicago School Architects and their Critics*. UMI Research Press.

Douglas, G.H. (1996). *Skyscrapers: A Social History of the Very Tall Building in America*. McFarland and Co.

Elia, Mario Manieri (1996). *Louis Henry Sullivan*. Princeton Architectural Press.

Fleming, J., Honour, H. and Pevsner, N. (1998). *The Penguin Dictionary of Architecture and Landscape Architecture*. Penguin Books.

Gadamer, H-G. (1989). *Truth and Method*. Crossroad.

Goldberger, P. (1982). *The Skyscraper*. Alfred A. Knopf.

Hambly, M. (1988). *Drawing Instruments, 1580–1980*. Sotheby's Publications.

Hitchcock, H-R. and Johnson, P. (1996). *The International Style*. W.W. Norton.

Huizinga, J. (1970). *Homo Ludens: A Study of the Play Element in Culture*. Harper and Row.

Huxtable, A.L. (1982). *The Tall Building Artistically Reconsidered: The Search for a Skyscraper Style*. Pantheon Books.

Landau, S.B. and Condit, C.W. (1996). *Rise of the New York Skyscraper, 1865–1913*. Yale University Press.

Leich, J.F. (1980). *Architectural Visions, the Drawings of Hugh Ferriss*. Watson-Guptill.

Menocal, N.G. (1981). *Architecture as Nature: The Transcendentalist Idea of Louis Sullivan*. University of Wisconsin Press.

Morrison, H. revised by Samuelson, T.J. (1935, 1998). *Louis Sullivan: Prophet of Modern Architecture*. W.W. Norton and Company.

O'Gorman, J.F. (1987). *H.H. Richardson, Architectural Forms for an American Society*. The University of Chicago Press.

Ochsner, J.K. (1982). *H.H. Richardson, Complete Architectural Works*. MIT Press.

Pokinski, D.F. (1984). *The Development of the American Modern Style*. UMI Research Press.

Roth, L. (1973). *A Monograph of the Works by McKim, Mead and White, 1879–1915*. Benjamin Blom.

Roth, L.M. (1979). *A Concise History of American Architecture*. Harper and Row.

Scully, V. (1955). *The Shingle Style, Architectural Theory and Design from Richardson to the Origins of Wright*. Yale University Press.

Stein, S.R. (1986). *The Architecture of Richard Morris Hunt*. The University of Chicago Press.

Sullivan, L.H. (1924). *The Autobiography of an Idea*. Press of the AIA, Inc.

Trachtenberg, M. and Hyman, I. (1986). *The Statue of Liberty*. Penguin Books.

Twombly, R. (1986). *Louis Sullivan: His Life and Work*. Viking.

Twombly, R. and Menocal, N.G. (2000). *Louis Sullivan: The Poetry of Architecture*. W.W. Norton and Company.

Van Vynckt, R. ed. (1993). *International Dictionary of Architects and Architecture*. St. James Press.

Wodehouse, L. (1988). *White of McKim, Mead and White*. Garland Publishing.

Wollheim, R, (1971). *On Art and its Objects: An Introduction to Aesthetics*. Harper and Row.

CHAPTER 5

THE TURN OF THE CENTURY EUROPE AND ITS INFLUENCES, PRELUDE TO MODERNISM (1870–1910)

The architects discussed in this chapter are generally considered premodern, although many of them have been credited with initiating elements of a modern style. After the decline of the widespread neoclassical influence, architecture was undergoing transition. At the turn of the twentieth century, the technology of world travel facilitated the transfer of knowledge and thus carried architectural ideas between countries. Industrialization, growing urban areas, and relative economic stability all contributed to divergent thinking. These changing environments saw European influence penetrate into India and Asia. Such transition also allowed for the emergence of new styles, such as the Arts and Crafts movement in Britain; Art Nouveau, beginning in France, Belgium, and Spain; and Secession in Austria. The United States suspended tradition by initiating construction of the tall building and encouraging development to the western regions of the country. Japan opened its ports to trade and consciously set a path toward westernization known as Meiji.

This period of transition also affected these architects' use of sketches and drawings. Some of these architects used techniques found in traditional sketches. Others such as Adolf Loos converted his sketches in tune with his straightforward approach to architecture. Many of these architects experimented with untested building materials that led them to find new ways to represent the material's use. Most of these architects depended upon sketches to resolve more complex relationships between materials' form and conceptual statements.

ARTS AND CRAFTS

As a result of extensive industrialization, architectural theorists as early as Pugin criticized the machine's part in the destruction of the human's 'spiritual and physical well being' (Naylor, 1971, p. 15). Begun in England, the Arts and Crafts movement was championed by several prominent theorists such as John Ruskin who advocated the worth of the working populace. He was not against technology and believed in 'organic principles that could be emulated by both art and industry' (Naylor, 1971, p. 23). In 1849 he published *The Seven Lamps of Architecture*, which laid out principles for the ethical use of materials. He followed this with *Stones of Venice* in 1851 and 1853. These books became a foundation for the Arts and Crafts doctrine (Naylor, 1971; Makinson, 1977). Although C. F. A. Voysey contributed concepts of simplicity, it was William Morris, in the 1860s and 1870s, who launched the movement. It promoted an egalitarian view of the arts, as the luxury of handcraftsmanship was affordable only to the wealthy. Morris was against industry and he also declined to imitate styles from the past. He admired the medieval process of craft, but not its style (Trachtenberg and Hyman, 1986). Like Ruskin, he supported respect for laborers; he felt the designer or architect should obtain an intimate knowledge of materials and understand their properties. This relationship with materials should be acquired from hands-on experience (Naylor, 1971).

The Arts and Crafts influenced the work of Charles Rennie Mackintosh in Scotland and Edwin Lutyens in England and spread throughout Europe and into the United States. Josef Hoffmann's work reveals the movement's influence, and the American architects Greene and Greene continued to practice its principles into the early 1900s.

ART NOUVEAU

Similar to the Arts and Crafts, Art Nouveau advocated craft and rejected standardization. But in using wrought iron and glass, this movement reflected the abilities of an industrialized society (Borsi and Portoghesi, 1991). Intending to evoke emotions, the Art Nouveau artists and architects formed fluid lines resembling whiplash curves and tendrils. They designed sinuous patterns and gracefully graphic posters. Architects employed a three-dimensional translation of the style, using iron primarily for biomorphic decoration. Although inspired by nature, they denied exact imitation of natural forms (Borsi and Portoghesi, 1991; Aubry and Vandenbreeden, 1996; Trachtenberg and Hyman, 1986). The Art Nouveau imagery flowed through the buildings in the form of stairs, balconies, and framing for doorways and windows. Mainly decorative, the style translated easily to furniture and utilitarian objects. In a tangential way, the writings of Viollet-le-Duc validated the movement's use of wrought iron (Trachtenberg and Hyman, 1986). The transforming of materials suggested the capacity of technology, and exemplified modern machine production. As a rejection of traditional architecture, Art Nouveau gave wealthy clients culture directly connected with industrialization (Borsi and Portoghesi, 1991). After beginning in the decorative arts, the style emerged in architecture in the early 1890s and was called *Stile Liberty* in Italy and *Jugendstil* in Eastern Europe, but faded soon after 1910. Hector Guimard, in France, and Victor Horta, in Belgium, designed some of the most cohesive Art Nouveau projects.

SECESSION

In Vienna, at the time of the Franz Joseph I celebration in 1897, exhibitions were planned by conservatives that excluded many of the more radical artists and architects. In response to this omission, several of them organized a group called the Secession. They soon published a magazine called *Ver Sacrum* that expressed the need for art and called for a new look at art and architecture. They presented their first exhibition within a year of their founding. This display of work proved to be so successful that they collected sufficient funds to build an exhibition hall. The result was the Vienna Secession building, located near the Naschmarkt and Karlsplatz, designed by member Josef Maria Olbrich (Latham, 1980; Fergusson, 1997). The simple geometric shape was crowned by a dome of gilded metal leaves.

This association of artists and architects was not a group united by style, but by a common philosophy. They advocated an all-encompassing artistic environment, declaring: 'To the time its art. To art its freedom' (Fergusson, 1997, p. 13). This rallying cry called for art to be modern, and allowed artists to choose a suitable expression. For the architects, this meant that the building should both adhere to its function and celebrate it, rather than hiding it (Latham, 1980). Besides Olbrich, other Viennese architects active in the Secession were Otto Wagner and Josef Hoffmann.

MEIJI

In 1854, American and European ships arrived in the ports of Japan. Fifteen years later, in 1868, the last shogun was replaced with an imperial government. The Emperor's aim was to modernize Japan by adopting culture and technology from abroad. His goals included organizing a military force, changing the boundaries of social classes, and centralizing the government. This period 1868 to 1912 launched Japan's transition. Called Meiji, the era embraced architectural styles from the West, especially European (Stewart, 1987). Following 1850, European-style architecture was constructed in Japan, modified by the local climate, availability of technology, and the influence of local custom (Stewart, 1987). In addition to buildings designed by foreigners, Japanese architects were constructing projects in a pseudo-western style called *giyofu*, such as the Kaichi school (1876) by Seiju Tateishi; the Tsukiji Hotel for foreigners (1868) and the First Mitsui Bank Headquarters (1872) by Kisuke Shimizu II. In the early 1870s, the Ministry of Technology opened a school staffed with professors imported from Europe. The *giyofu* buildings were often composed of Dutch, British, and Italian elements combined with such things as Japanese-style tile roofs. These unique compositions were described as 'carpentry [attempting] to mimic buildings constructed of masonry' (Stewart, 1987, p. 27).

Many artists and architects were influenced by the influx of Japanese culture into the West. In the late 1880s, the impressionist painters and Art Nouveau graphic artists found inspiration in the graceful *Ukioye* woodblock prints. As an example, Josef Hoffmann, along with the Secession artists, utilized aspects of Japanese art. The Arts and Crafts architects, especially Greene and Greene, were attracted to Japanese culture because of the well-crafted and exposed joinery, which reinforced their notion of the craftsman/laborer.

The legacy of these architects has been associated with the architecture of the turn of the century. In most cases, this period was a prolific and identifying period of these architects' careers, even though the pessimistic years following World War I did not sustain their individual styles to any extent. Despite the short span of time during which these projects were built, their effects were profound.

For these architects who share simultaneous time periods and overlapping influences, their sketches have both similarities and differences. The Art Nouveau and Secession architects benefited from their close association with graphic and fine artists. They acquired strong sketching skills, which developed from practice, education, and innate talent. Many of these designers, such as Mackintosh, studied in art schools. Others, such as Wagner, appeared to have a natural skill for representing designs in two dimensions. His fluid strokes in ink seldom required erasure and conveyed his conceptual explorations clearly. He obviously enjoyed sketching as he used these hand images extensively. This can be seen in the many variations of his designs, all explored thoroughly through images.

Some of these architectural styles were literally three-dimensional manifestations of art movements; many of the architects discussed in this chapter could easily shift between the two. For example, the graphic techniques practiced by Hoffmann can be viewed in his sketches. Throughout his career, he moved between designing architecture, domestic objects, posters, and furniture, and the bold outlined style conveyed his thinking in both dimensions.

In contrast to those of the neoclassical period, these architects were concerned with knowledge of and control over the construction process. This interest in details and technology was reflected in their sketches: Horta diagrammed acoustical reverberation angles, architects of the Arts and Crafts worked closely with the craftsmen, and the office of Greene and Greene studied material assembly. Needing to communicate directly with their contractors, the Greenes probably sketched to work out details as well as direct construction. Sketches were an efficient method to test ideas and explore material interactions. Undoubtedly, these in-depth investigations required additional construction drawings, which meant more sketches to work out the details. The architects of these movements were also commissioned to provide consistent design for interiors, objects, and furniture. The conception of these additional features required extensive study in two dimensions. Although there were remnants of beaux-arts education, many architects studied in art or technical schools. Their skills in practical arts prepared them for manipulation of materials and gave them a holistic attitude toward design.

Many architectural commissions were obtained through competitions. Sketches played a vital role in conceiving and illustrating potential projects. A skillful sketching style would help sell a project and make it more easily understandable. A seductive hand sketched perspective could quickly convey ideas of volume and spatial qualities to jurors. The use of color and texture added depth to the images, visual cues that clients could comprehend.

As in other periods, architects' intentions affected the manner of representation; the sketches reflected their beliefs and ideology. Mackintosh's light hand would sketch the delicate tracery of nature, such as flowers. Loos' sketches to alter hard-lined plans may suggest his critical attitudes. Gaudí found a way to utilize the inherent curve of hanging chains in his sketches, elements important to his structural forms. The Art Nouveau architects needed to use soft pencils to evoke the fluid lines of their forms, holding them loosely to achieve the continuous smooth arcs that defined the tendrils of their architecture. In contrast, Lutyens boldly sketched to cover the page, inserting images onto every empty space.

Unrestricted by the orthographic projection practices of the beaux-arts, these architects investigated concepts using a variety of techniques. They sketched in perspective, as well as the conventions of plan, section, and elevation. Their tools were substantially more sophisticated. Ink pens improved in quality and were easier to obtain; fountain pens proved to be more controllable than traditional dipped pens. Industrialization made such items continually more precise and available. Mass media encouraged the dissemination of architectural theory and practice, and influences from various parts of the world could now be widely considered. As eclectic as their architecture, these architects practiced differentiating techniques using various media. Although approaching sketches differently they each depended on them to explore the complexities required of the unprecedented architecture.

FIGURE 5.1

Olbrich, Josef Maria (1867–1908)

Sketch, Staatliche Museen zu Berlin, Hdz 10092, Ink on paper

As a founding member of the Secession movement in Vienna, Josef Maria Olbrich devoted his life to the arts, including architecture, interiors, furniture, and functional objects. He epitomized a designer in constant dialogue with his media, and his distinctive sketching style displayed fluid and confident visual expression.

Born in Troppau, he arrived in Vienna in 1882 to attend the Staadtsgewerbeschule, studying in the building department, and obtaining additional education at the Spezialschule für Architektur at the Akademie der Schönen Künste. Olbrich's skills were recognized by Otto Wagner during an Academy exhibition in 1893. He began work with Wagner, accepting the position of chief draughtsman for the Stadtbahn Project.

Olbrich's association with the Viennese artists and architects of the Secession proved crucial to his future. The prominence of his design for the Secession Exhibition Building and the group's ensuing exhibitions led to his invitation to Darmstadt's *Mathildenhöhe* by the Grand Duke, Ernst Ludwig, in 1899. Olbrich designed most of the structures on the site, being given the freedom to develop an experimental architectural laboratory. Over the next few years, he designed numerous houses and small projects in and around Germany, his largest being the Leonhard Tietz Department Store in Düsseldorf (Latham, 1980).

Olbrich's association with the Secessionist artists and his experience in the synergetic activity in Darmstadt demonstrated his commitment to the arts. Olbrich's architecture was based on abstract geometric forms with sparse appliqué for decoration, unlike the fluid expression of nature, through the entire building, as used by the Art Nouveau architects. He also felt an affinity for the Arts and Crafts movement, having contact with architects in Britain (Latham, 1980).

This quick but elegant sketch (Figure 5.1) confirms Olbrich's confident control of pen and ink. The expression of movement conjures up the dynamic experience of exhibition, creating a restless quality. The images are executed with near-perfect freehand perspective and the symmetrical façades are guided by just a few horizontals and verticals, sketched without erasing.

When observing a selection of his sketches, several examples show that he often diagrammed twenty or more small, obsessively neat elevation illustrations on a page. Other sketches in his repertoire are incredibly vigorous, lithe, and expressive. Olbrich was passionate about sketching as his sketches emit qualities of quickness, being both fast in a matter of time, intelligent, and thoughtful.

Described by the Italo Calvino as a concept which illuminates the meaning of quickness, *Festina Lente* literally means 'hurry slowly.' An apparent contradiction, the chiasmus inherently has the power to induce a greater understanding. Since Olbrich's images were sketched quickly, they have more information and may contain greater insight than images produced more slowly. In fact, they do convey something substantially perceptive by virtue of their speed (Calvino, 1988). The exuberance of the lines revealing an illusion may help to seduce and convince the observer of the sketch's potential. Although this sketch leaves many details vague, the whole impression has been communicated.

As a Roman adage, *Festina Lente* has had various meanings throughout history, often representing a need to resolve issues from contradictory positions (Lyons and Nichols, 1982). Olbrich may have been trusting the intuition of his subconscious, allowing the images to flow before his conscious mind could evaluate them for appropriateness. Quick lines often designate precise meaning, and in this example Olbrich was demonstrating the quick thinking of his imagination.

FIGURE 5.2

Wagner, Otto (1841–1918)

Perspective sketch, Vol. 021/30 *verso*, Museen der Stadt Wein, Inv. Nr. 96.021/30 *verso*, 34.8 × 21 cm, Ink on paper

Otto Wagner's work, although originating from a traditional education, anticipated the emergence of modern architecture. The innovative use of new technologies and materials (wrought iron, glass, and aluminum) found their way into his architecture. His buildings were often clad with decorative panels, as distinctive of the *Jugendstil*, or infused with historical expression. He influenced a generation of architects through his teaching and mentoring, such as Adolf Loos, Josef Hoffmann, and Josef Olbrich.

Born in Penzig, near Vienna, Wagner initially studied at the Polytechnic Institute in Vienna from 1857 to 1859. He enrolled at the Royal Academy of Building in Berlin for approximately one year before moving on to the Vienna Academy from 1861 to 1863. Wagner's earliest projects were apartment buildings in Vienna that depended on historical reference. Wagner's later projects, such as the Postal Savings Bank Office of 1904–1912, relied less on surface ornament and considered new technologies such as exposed structure. Other notable projects include the Neumann Department Store (1895), the Church of St. Leopold (1905–1907), Die Zeit Telegraph Office (1902), and the Lupus Sanatorium (1910–1913). He also designed many stations for the Stadtbahn System in Vienna and was advisor to the Commission for the Regulation of the Danube Canal (Geretsegger and Peintner, 1979).

Werner Oechslin, when discussing *raiment* as a theory to describe Wagner's architecture, compares the essence and appearance to the kernel and hull. In a reference to Gottfried Semper, he differentiates between the 'essential content' and the 'inessential cladding' (Oechslin, 2002, p. 86). Wagner believed that innovations in structure should be approached creatively, and he was dismayed with engineers that were predisposed to utilize concepts literally. He felt that structural elements should not intersect, but should stand independently to demonstrate their function (Geretsegger and Peintner, 1964).

Wagner's sketching style exhibits his control of fluid, expressive lines (inessential cladding). In ink or pencil, the quick lines show evidence of erasure but represent a remarkably clear image from his imagination (essential content). The fast, proportionally accurate, and beautiful sketches also reveal Wagner's comfort with his media, achieved with extensive practice. Many of his drawings and sketches were meant as preliminaries, for presentations or competitions. Framed with lines, they use a dramatic perspective angle and often include texture and value. Some even reveal the action of walking through a building with the drag of a pencil, while others exhibit the calculations and hesitation of a pondering mind.[1]

This sketch (Figure 5.2) represents an early design for a festival pavilion, built in celebration of the marriage of the Crown Prince Rudolf and the Belgian Princess Stephanie in 1881. Wagner proposed a lighted and decorated processional path (including the Elizabeth Bridge), grandstands, and a festival structure used to welcome Princess Stephanie into the city (Graf, 1985). The page shows an ink perspective of the pavilion which has been framed with single lines. Although a comprehensive view, it is a preliminary scheme since it describes different treatment of the columns. Lower on the page appears a blurred form, bleeding through the reverse side of the paper. On the reverse of this page, a dress design for Wagner's second wife Louise Stiffels has been sketched. Perhaps while designing the pavilion, his wife expressed concern about her attire for the celebration, since as 'honored citizens' they were undoubtedly attending the festivities (Mallgrave, 1993). With this interruption, Wagner may have turned the paper over and explored designs for her dress.

FIGURE 5.3

Gaudí, Antonio (1852–1926)

Colonia Güell church. Study for the nave of the church drawn on an inverted photograph of the funicular model, Catedra Gaudi, Cat. 48.7, Ink on inverted photograph

The architectural work of Antonio Gaudí sparks much controversy – numerous critics ascribe his imaginative buildings to gothic and Moorish tradition, or credit his fluid lines to the Art Nouveau movement (Sweeney and Sert, 1960; de Solà-Morales, 1984; Descharnes and Piévost, 1971). Much of this may be true; his beginnings took imagery from these styles and the look of his elegant forms appear similar to the contemporary Art Nouveau architects, but Gaudí cannot be classified easily and this may only be a partial view of a complex man. Deeply religious, Gaudí felt a strong affinity for the Catalan literary and artistic movement called *Renaixenca*, manifest in architecture as a revival of medieval archaeology (Collins, 1960). He was concerned with the unity of principle between construction and ornamentation, and he viewed beauty in classical terms of proportion and harmony (Crippa, 2002; Martinell, 1975). Finding beauty in truth, he felt that ornament was to 'contain nothing superfluous, but only the material conditions which make it useful; we must take into account both the material and the use which will be made of it …' (Martinell, 1975, p. 125). Thus, his architecture often reflected structural moment diagrams or found form in geometry such as parabolic arches. On top of this he placed decoration and sculptural imagery imbued with symbolism.

Born Antonio Gaudí y Cornet in Reus, Catalonia, he descended from a family of coppersmiths. He moved to Barcelona in 1869, enrolling in architecture at the Escola Superior d'Arquitectura in 1870. Upon finishing school, Gaudí immediately obtained his first commission for streetlights in the Placa Reial and Pla del Palau. Finding a wealthy patron, he built a palace for Eusebi Güell (1885–1893) followed by an urban park (1900–1914). He designed other projects such as Casa Milá and Casa Batlló, but the passion of his life was the design and construction of the Cathedral of the Sagrada Familia which he worked on until his death in 1926.

Gaudí explored structure and ornamentation using drawings and sketches, but the most unique and interesting method of his conception and testing of ideas was his use of models. His studio, in the basement of Sagrada Familia, was filled with plaster casts, ornament, and detail models. His search for beauty in the efficiency of structure led him to build polyfunicular models. Using strings or chains loaded with small weights, he replicated the stresses on arches.

This sketch (Figure 5.3) is one of the few remaining sketches by Gaudí, since many of his drawings, models, and personal records were destroyed by revolutionaries in 1936. A study for the Colonia Güell church, this image for the nave has been sketched on an inverted photograph of a funicular model. He understood the structural principles, but employed the photograph as a way to view the interior space. Needing to assign volume to the arches (missing in the cable arcs), he could sketch over them with the assurance that the structure and form would coincide. Without calculating a perspective, he could quickly view the interior space. Thin dark lines of the chains are covered with soft pencil or chalk shading, defining the vaults of the ceiling and the dimension of the columns and arches. Openings are articulated by darkening potential windows.

Here Gaudí was combining the media of model, photography, and sketching to gain the information he required. Although still a vague suggestion of the future space, he was able to see more than the thin wires afforded him. Similar to architects who use tracing paper over drawings as a foundation, Gaudí was using what he knew to find out what he did not.

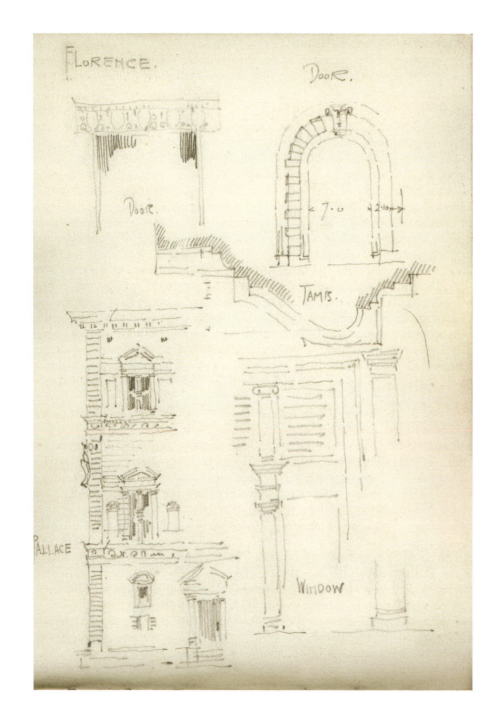

FIGURE 5.4

122

Mackintosh, Charles Rennie (1868–1928)

Sketch of doors for various palaces in Florence, (Contents: Florence, sketch u.l. shows door at the Palazzo della Zecca, Piazzale degli Uffizi, Florence. Sketch u.r. shows door of the Palazzo di Bianca Cappello, Via Maggio, Florence. Sketch l.l. shows the Palazzo Bartolini Salimbeni, Florence. Sketch l.r. shows trabeated forms of classical architecture), 1891, National Library of Ireland, PD 2009 TX 64, 17.4 × 12.6 cm, Pencil

Charles Rennie Mackintosh was born in Glasgow, Scotland. Although influenced by Art Nouveau, Arts and Crafts, and the Vienna Secession movements, his architecture was imbued with contextual aspects of Scottish vernacular tradition. Beginning his career as an apprentice to John Hutchison, Mackintosh easily moved between graphic design, interiors, and building construction throughout his life. While attending the Glasgow School of Art he won numerous honors and was a member of the group *The Four*, with Margaret and Frances Macdonald and Herbert MacNair. He joined the architectural firm of Honeyman and Keppie in 1889, and in 1891 he received an award to travel to Italy – his only travel outside the British Isles. He approached this visit with the same observational and analytical gravity as his sketching trips through Scotland (Grogan, 2002).

Mackintosh acquired the competition commission for the Glasgow School of Art for Honeyman and Keppie in 1897, his most celebrated project. With a small budget, on an awkward, sloping site, he designed a masonry exterior with asymmetrical façades. The relatively plain elevations reveal the simple massing, recognized by some as the first designed in the modern style (Cooper, 1978). A few of his other notable buildings include Hill House and the Cranston Tea Houses in Glasgow.

This illustration (Figure 5.4) is a page from one of Mackintosh's Italian sketchbooks. As a stipulation of the Thomson Traveling Studentship, Mackintosh was required to study classical architecture, record his findings, and present a lecture to the Glasgow School of Art upon his return. Although he rendered watercolors and completed larger drawings, the sketchbook is largely a collection of his architectural thoughts. The page displays several buildings in Florence, as if he was comparing their likenesses or differences. Very few of these sketches have been drawn in perspective; instead, he sketched parts of the building as if he was attempting to understand their nature. Analysis consists of study often involving the separation of a whole into its component parts for examination. Analysis also suggests drawing conclusions through manipulating or regrouping pertinent material and locating meaning in their relationships (OED, 1971).

Each sketch remains unfinished, as if Mackintosh was viewing the parts to comprehend the whole; or, once he understood their structure he could avoid repeating the details. Author of a collection of his sketches, Elaine Grogan explains that the Victorian sketchbook was used to understand nature, such as with a scientist's recordings (2002). Similarly, the sketchbook was a memory device for Mackintosh to record his thoughts, but it also provided an avenue for observation and analysis. He used this sketchbook to study how decoration was applied to structure.

Typical of Mackintosh's pencil technique, this sketch is executed with minimal lines. He used a slow hand with firm and definitive marks, accentuated by hesitation and emphasizing the line's end. Numerous slow, wavy lines show his concentration and desire to think as he was drawing. Much like his graphic work for paintings and posters, Mackintosh's single line accentuates edges and gives the image a flat quality reminiscent of Japanese paintings and Ukioye prints (popular at the time). The placement of objects in a field creates a solid/void relationship, further defining the sketch as a graphic statement.

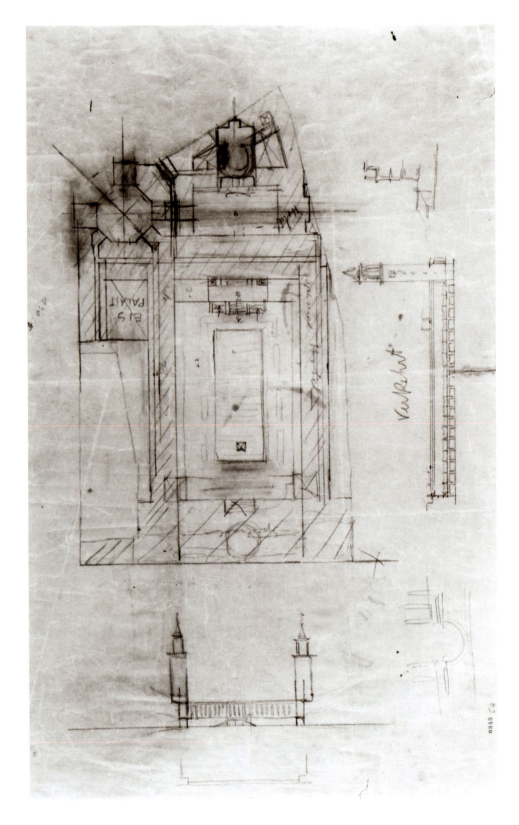

FIGURE 5.5

Loos, Adolf (1870–1933)

Modena park verbauung, Albertina, ALA 343 C4, Graphite on paper

The work of Adolf Loos exemplifies the contrasts and contradictions of the years leading toward modernism and the international style. Loos, who respected traditional architecture but experimented with sleek volumes, was actually better known for his writing. In his poignant and often ironic essays, Loos appraised contemporary culture and modern architecture, assuming the role of conscience for architects on the brink of a new modern style. He admonished the overly radical modernists in his article 'Poor Little Rich Man' and sarcastically entered Doric Column in the Chicago Tribune Competition.

Adolf Loos was born in Brünn (Brno), now the Czech Republic, in 1870. He was educated in architecture both at the State Technical School in Bohemia and later at the Dresden Polytechnic. He traveled throughout the United States between 1893 and 1896, attending the Columbia Exposition in Chicago and visiting New York, Philadelphia, and St. Louis. Upon his return, he wrote for the *Neue Freie Presse* until opening a practice in Vienna. Influenced by the architects Wagner, Semper, Schinkel, and Vitruvius, he felt a place in the evolution of architecture, which was based in tradition considering responsibility to contemporary functions.

Loos further critiqued the state of contemporary architecture through his built work. His belief that buildings should be plain on the exterior and reveal their complexity on the interior was seen with the Goldman and Salatsch store on Michaelerplatz (1910) (Gravagnuolo, 1982). Loos' relatively limited repertoire of building projects was primarily domestic, including the villas Steiner, Rufer, and Scheu, designed in the years before World War I.

Loos employed a formal approach to his design process initially drawing with ruled lines. On this page (Figure 5.5) it appears that he was attempting a final drawing and, during the process, became dissatisfied with its direction. Although begun with hard lines, the critique has been rendered freehand, and shows numerous lines that have been crossed out where they were deemed incorrect or unnecessary. Loos eliminated a stairway and in several instances added doors through the single line of walls. The diagrammatic layout of hard lines has been thickened with poché to better comprehend the positive space. The top left portion of the plan has been poorly erased, leaving a dark smudge. This entire area seems worked over with heavier marks and many alterations.

The elevation near the bottom of the page shows a formal and symmetrical façade flanked by oversized and exaggerated towers. The towers appear to be later additions, rendered freehand, in contrast to the limited articulation of the façade. They have been left unfinished to the ground, where the exaggeration in scale becomes obvious. When his attention shifted to the problem of the spires; he may have ignored their relationship to their context. Because of his satirical essays, Loos was familiar with the concept of caricature, and thus he may not have been disturbed by the variation in scale. The visual use of caricature often employs exaggeration to reveal a truth beneath outward appearances. The distortion is not meant to arbitrarily deform but rather to express a specific poignant feature (Gombrich and Kris, 1940; Kris, 1934). This caricature, not unlike the procedure of criticism, may not be intended to ridicule the look of the façade, but rather to more easily view the tower construction or to study the elements in isolation. Beginning the sketch with ruled lines may have reflected his interest to study simple geometries, but he may have also seen the definitive lines as a base for subsequent evaluation practiced in verbal criticism and irony, he may have purposefully put forth a visual hypothesis, expecting it to be altered through critical dialogue.

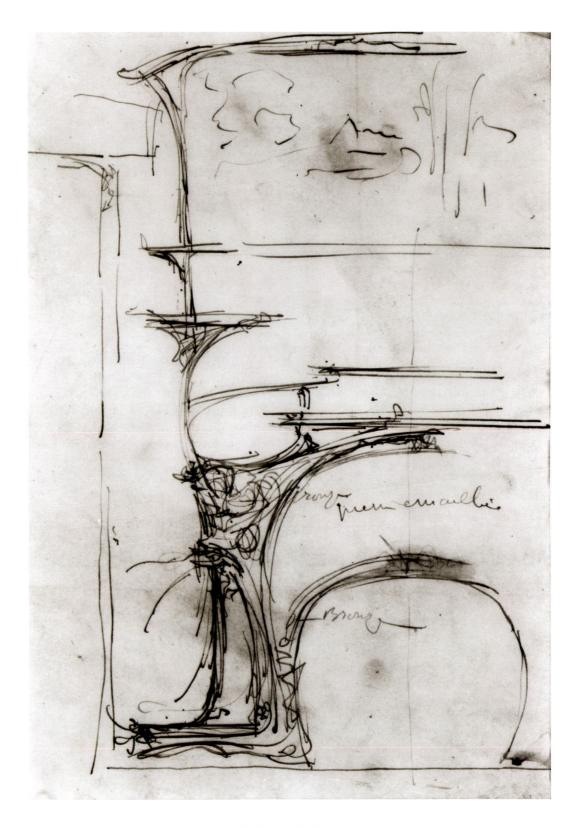

FIGURE 5.6

Guimard, Hector (1867–1942)

Design for a chimney (Cheminée et troumeau pour Castel-Beranger), c. 1897, Musée des Arts Décoratifs, INV.GP 508, Cl. 11438, 7 × 9.5 in.

Hector Guimard was born in Lyons and left at the early age of fifteen to study at the Ecole des Arts Décoratifs. He attended the Ecole des Beaux-Arts in Paris before building numerous houses in the Auteuil quarter of Paris. The project that launched his career was the apartment building Castel Béranger (1894–1898), featuring a façade of various materials and proficient use of ironwork. At this crucial point in his career (1894–1895) he traveled to England, obtaining extensive knowledge of the works of the English designers Voysey and Crane. He also visited Art Nouveau buildings in Belgium, met with Victor Horta, and viewed the Tassel House under construction. Guimard saw the Belgian architects' use of cast iron and how these techniques emphasized lightness and line (Dunster, 1978).

In step with other Art Nouveau artists, Guimard was interested in expressing the forces of nature with repetitive graceful lines, often replicating masks and seahorses (Van Vynckt, 1993). Although Guimard did not write extensively about his work, he adhered to three principles that guided his design: logic (the conditions), harmony (the context and requirements), and sentiment (combining logic and harmony to find expression) (Dunster, 1978). His architectural work has been most identified with the Metro Station entrances he designed for Paris, completed in 1901. Other projects of renown include the Ecole du Sacré-Coeur, finished in 1895, the Humbert de Romans Concert Hall, and numerous domestic projects.

Guimard's interpretation of Art Nouveau integrated decoration, structure, and form; he was particularly concerned with the qualities of line. The critic Henri Frantz wrote that Guimard's use of ornament avoided borrowing directly from natural forms but rather ' … he gets all his effects from the use of "line" or combinations of lines' (Dunster, 1978, p. 9). Consistent with this philosophy, this sketch for a chimney and pierglass for his office depended entirely on lines (Figure 5.6). It shows nervous parallel lines defining one half of the fireplace. Guimard used these lines to profile the form, concentrating on the edges, thus avoiding texture or massing. Sketched very quickly, the pen marks become squiggles or snap back on themselves – a sort of 'whiplash' ornamentation. These lines overlap and intersect as Guimard realized the curve imagined in his mind's eye, or refined the curve once viewed. Called by Ernst Gombrich 'making and matching,' this comparison causes the repetition of the parallel marks as he critically assesses one line and responded with another to correct it (1989, p. 29).

The inherent qualities of the media are united with Guimard's conceptual approach. The flowing veins of ink mimic the fluid movements of decoration, suggesting that the rendering technique itself may have informed the outcome of the architecture. The undulating movement of the strokes may have drawn themselves as much as being created by Guimard. Similar to a doodle, a line begun is easy to continue. The curved lines may reflect the gesture of his hands relying on the forms of nature to guide him. To the lower left of the sketch is a contorted face, giving this portion of the page an eerie, anthropomorphic quality. The abstraction of the wide mouth and large eye reveals how the Art Nouveau artists induced associative expression. The overall appearance of the sketch is sparse, providing only the necessary information. Considering the exuberance of ornament practiced by the Art Nouveau artists, this study maintains a noticeably more restrained attitude.

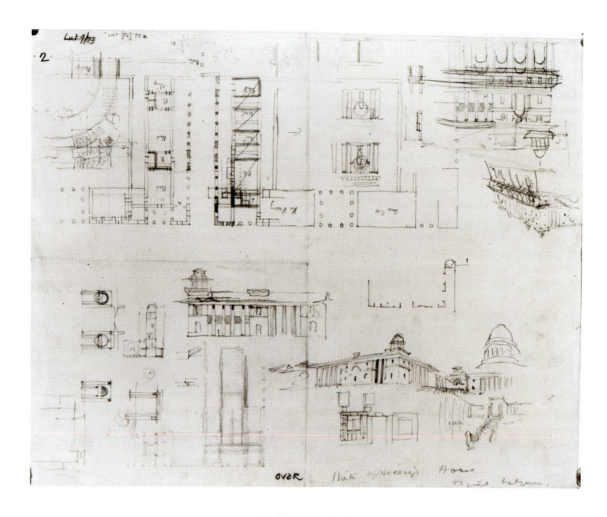

FIGURE 5.7

Lutyens, Edwin Landseer (1869–1944)

Design for Viceroy's House, RIBA, Lutyens [58] 73, Graphite on paper

Edwin Lutyens was born in London; his family moved to the countryside of Surrey when he was a child. After attending the South Kensington School of Art, with little education in architecture he began to work for the architect Ernst George in 1887. Leaving to start his own practice in 1889, he began with small domestic projects.

Peter Inskip, in David Dunster's collection of essays on Lutyens, writes that Lutyens' architecture, especially his country houses, replicated historical imagery and was influenced by the work of his contemporaries, including Richard Norman Shaw (1986). Incorporating elements of the vernacular, these domestic projects reflected the Tudor and classical baroque, some with castle-like romantic references. Building for newly rich Edwardians, Lutyens designed smaller estates that evoked manor houses of the previous century. Many of these houses displayed axial and processional siting, employing long drives and dramatic vistas. A distinctive feature included the extension of the house externally into baroque, geometrically organized gardens (Dunster, 1986). Some of his more celebrated house projects include Ednaston Manor, house and farm buildings for W. G. Player; Marshcourt, a house for Herbert Johnson, and Gledstone Hall, a house for Sir Amos Nelson.

Lutyens designed governmental projects in India between 1912 and 1939 and held the position of chief architect for the imperial capital at New Delhi, collaborating on the layout of the city with Herbert Baker. Concerning the design for the Viceroy's House in New Delhi, he felt it necessary to build with English classical proportions but adapted it to the regional climate (Irving, 1981).

These study sketches (Figure 5.7) for the Viceroy's House express techniques typical of Lutyen's design process. On folded grid paper, this page seems to have been approached from all sides, suggesting that he rotated the paper, looking for the next available space to continue his exploration. The page is comprised of partial plans, preliminary elevations, details and perspectives. Lutyen's pencil techniques reveal how he handled the various aspects of the building with a certain analytical evenness. Evidenced by the fact that each sketch has been studied with similar size and amount of detail. Lutyen's needed to quickly refer to a three-dimensional view; so fast, in fact, that the windows were rendered as thicker marks. Other parts, such as the plans, were slow and deliberate, as he made small changes in reaction to what he was perceiving. This displays both his comfort with the media and how easily the sketches conveyed necessary information. The graphite technique shows relatively small consistent lines delineating an amount of realism. It is as if he had much of the general form of the building in mind and was working out the specific look for the project. His sketching skills were highly developed, which is expected considering his father's occupation as an artist. His belief in the role of sketches surfaces as he delineates every aspect of the building, down to doorway details and connections. Without erasures, the pencil seems to be an extension of his hand as he moved easily between views. It appears that he sketched as fast as he could imagine or make decisions. The sketches represent the same stage of development and reference, both inside and out. They are executed with primarily the same line weight, since he did not stop to change media or test a finished solution. They reveal his concentration while drawing, evaluating what he imagined in three dimensions viewing the building in its totality. Not at all restrained, he was deeply engrossed in a dialogue with the sketches, pondering and reworking, while reacting to their communications.

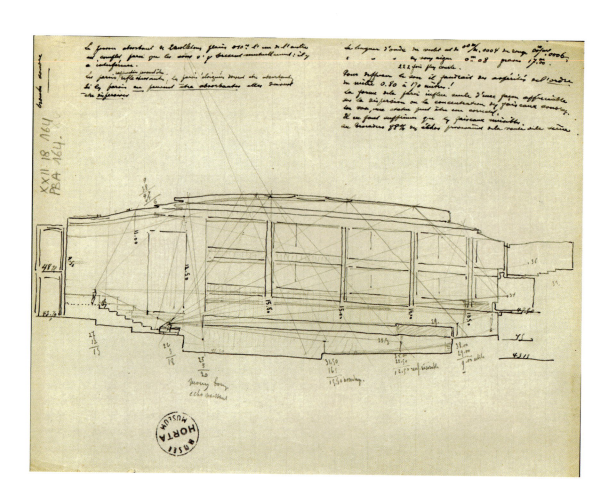

FIGURE 5.8

Horta, Victor (1861–1947)

Sketch of the main concert hall, SOFAM, XVIII. 15.24, 27.6 × 21.9 cm, Graphite and ink on paper

Victor Horta's architectural style characterizes the relatively short period of Art Nouveau, manifest primarily in Europe at the turn of the twentieth century. Although employing the sinuous lines of the style, 'Horta's vital imagery was inspired by nature but it never imitated natural shapes' (Borsi and Portoghesi, 1991, p. 13). Intent upon influencing behavior, his emotional freeform vines and floral shapes contain such elements as tangential connections, folding, rhythm, and a dialogue of contrasting materials such as glass and iron (Borsi and Portoghesi, 1991). Since the Art Nouveau movement intended to provide an 'introduction of feeling' to architecture, Horta also regarded comfort as an important aspect of civilization. He considered issues such as ventilation and central heating, all integrated into the flexible layout of rooms and the efficient and innovative use of materials (Borsi and Portoghesi, 1991).

Horta was born in Ghent, Belgium, in 1861. He began his education at the Ghent Academy and finished his studies at the Académie des Beaux Arts in Brussels, 1881. His office education included several years with the architect Jean Dubuysson in Paris. In addition to his private practice, Horta taught and administrated programs in architecture at the Université Libre in Brussels and the Académie des Beaux Arts in Brussels. The Tassel House launched his career, followed by such projects as the Autrique House (1893), the Hôtel Solvay (1900), the L'Innovation Department Store in Brussels, the Musée des Beaux Arts, Tournai, (1903–1928), the Halle Centrale which was the main railway station in Brussels, and his largest project, the Palais des Beaux Arts in Brussels (1920–1928).

Horta was first invited as a consultant for the Palais des Beaux Arts (Figure 5.8), an exhibition space and concert hall for the city of Brussels. He was eventually requested to provide a design for the project and finally was commissioned in 1919 for the construction of the building that began in 1922 (Aubry and Vandenbreeden, 1996). Horta had extensive knowledge of acoustics and an affinity for music. This attraction was evidenced by the strong rhythms of his architecture; in fact, he had attended the Académie de Musique prior to his interest in architecture (Aubry and Vandenbreeden, 1996). His concern for acoustics also showed in his design of the ceiling planes, and hidden lighting and ventilation systems.

This section shows how Horta visually studied the reverberation angles and distances of the concert hall. The freehand sketch consists of a simple outline describing the negative space of the hall. The structure and construction details have been eliminated in favor of the interior space necessary for acoustic control. The outline has been drawn in ink and the reverberation angles in graphite. Horta has placed a piano on the stage as the sound source and origin of the lines bouncing off various surfaces. Reacting to the calculated reflection of the sound, he was considering altering the bank of seating. A similar response, which led to the lowering of the ceiling over the stage, has also been presented in pencil. Despite its spare quality, the sketch provided sufficient information to assist in visualization. This concert hall, studied at a time before digital computing, required that the reverberation angles be comprehended visually; later in the history of acoustics, models have been used to mimic sound reflection with beams of light. He was able, using near ninety-degree angles, to provide the necessary information with accuracy. The sketched diagram supplied him the visual artifact to design a space primarily sound sensitive.

FIGURE 5.9

Ito, Chuta (1868–1954)

Sketch of gate of Shrine Shinobazu Bentendo Tenryumon, The University of Tokyo, Tokyo, Japan, Graphite on grid paper, 1914

Primarily an architectural historian, Chuta Ito is best known for his documentation of Japan's historical temples and monuments. Ironically, Ito was born the same year Japan established a parliament to initiate an open international policy. The Meiji reign led Japan to exchange culture and ideas that resulted in a style of architecture blending European aesthetics with Japanese construction and materials (Stewart, 1987).

Ito, originally from Yonezawa, Dewa Province (Yamagata Prefect), attended the School of Engineering at Tokyo Imperial University, completing in 1892. Upon finishing he entered graduate studies in architectural history, receiving a doctorate in 1901. Ito joined academia (School of Engineering) becoming a Full Professor in 1905. In the late 1890s, he prepared a survey of the buildings of Japan's oldest Temple, Horyuji at Nara. In 1898, he published the *Horyuji kenchikuron* 'Discourse on the architecture of Horiuji' discussing his findings of the construction, proportions and decoration of the temple (Turner, 2000). A member of Japan's Society for the Preservation of Ancient Shrines and Temples beginning in 1896, he also received the Cultural Medal of Japan in 1943. Additionally a practicing architect, his work includes Okura Shukokan Museum 1927; Memorial Hall for the Earthquake of 1923, 1930; and the Main Hall of the Temple Tsukiji Honganji, 1934, all located in Tokyo. Ito retired from academia in 1928 (Turner, 2000).

As an example of the careful recording of traditional monuments, this page (Figure 5.9) displays details of the gate of the shrine called Shinobazu Bentendo Tenryumon. An example of a series of studies this image was concerned with drawing as a means to observe and ultimately understand. Different than a design sketch to discover ideas and form though design, this sketch was used to uncover meaning. That meaning could have included historical analysis of materials, construction techniques, or symbolism.

This group of details has been studied on grid paper supposedly to comprehend and accurately record measurement, scale and proportions. The scale running up the left side of the paper has been divided into equal units and numbered to sixteen. The grid could also assist Ito to keep lines straight and to comparatively proportion objects, although these pieces were not sketched in the same scale. The roof exhibits decorative objects that have been sketched at a larger size to better understand their detail. To better understand its form the dragon/chimera was rendered three times, once in context, as a profile, and in three-quarters view.

The graphite technique used by Ito is meticulous, revealing fine detail and showing slight corrections to achieve the viewed angles and curves. The transfer from the three-dimensional object to the paper reveals a dedicated observer. This relocation has been accomplished entirely freehand but was facilitated by the grid lines.

The fastidious manner of the image suggests its importance as a device to hold a memory for posterity, an image to remain even if the original was damaged. Undoubtedly the sketch was also meant for study, to compare form and composition to other temples. Analysis often separates distinctive elements for individual inspection. Here the act of drawing helped him to thoroughly understand and the accuracy was vital for a scholarly discussion. As a sketch, this page was preparatory for something else, most likely the discourse of speculation. The study was intended for his own conclusions but it contained the added importance of helping to educate others. The sketch represented a phase in the process, one that could have sparked an unusual relationship between parts or stimulated an insightful discovery.

FIGURE 5.10

Hoffmann, Josef (1870–1956)
Synagogue in Galizien, Kupferstichkabinett der Akademie der bildenden Künste,
Inv.-Nr. 26.315, 1914, 15 × 26 cm, Pencil

A founding member of the Secessionist movement in Vienna, Josef Hoffmann exemplified the Austrian decorative style in both architecture and design. He was born in 1870 in Moravia (now the Czech Republic). Upon finishing his studies in architecture at the Academy of Art in Vienna he was awarded the Rome Prize in 1895. Subsequently, he began a long association with Otto Wagner, including sporadic employment in Wagner's office over the years. Hoffmann's most enduring legacy was his role in founding and supporting several artists' workshops, including the Wiener Werkstätte (1903), Kunstschau (1908–1909), Austrian Werkbund (1910) and the Künstlerwerkstätte (1943–1956).

Much of his architecture was designed for exhibitions, such as the Austrian pavilion Werkbund Exhibition (1913–1914). His early buildings include the Moser and Moll Houses (1901–1903) and the Palais Stoclet (1905–1911). Many of these homes were designed for wealthy clients, with interiors that exploited surface and ornament (Gresleri, 1981). Hoffmann abandoned traditional Austrian interiors and substituted a new style, although not the stark modernist compositions of the international style (Noever, 1992).

Associated with Olbrich and the artists of the Secession, Hoffmann's early work embraced the emerging movements of Art Nouveau and Jugendstil. Although his later work became more austere, Hoffmann continued to work on decorative designs when architects around the world had adopted the international style (Noever, 1992).

This sketch (Figure 5.10) is an outline of an elevation. It was a preliminary design for a 1914 competition, a synagogue in Sillein (Zilina). One of many alternatives in Hoffmann's search for form, the building has a steeply roofed dome surrounded by a vertically paneled wall.

In viewing many of Hoffmann's sketches, similarities surface. He often sketched on grid paper, supposedly to help with proportion, measuring, or the maintenance of straight lines. As an added effect of drawing on grid paper, most of his sketches have been composed in elevation. Small, precise alternatives had been drawn in successive rows, providing many possible combinations of form. Unsuccessful solutions were crossed out.

The technique of these sketches reveals lines that appear slow and deliberate; as a result, they become slightly wavy. Typical of Hoffmann's sketching style, this proposal reflects a lack of architectural materiality and is devoid of shading or detail. The exceptions are vertical lines on the roof and a few stippled marks on the walls. This purposeful sketching technique suggests a contemplative approach rather than an expressive exuberance. The implication is that Hoffmann was treating the sketch as if it was a work of art, or as a substitute for finished documentation. It may have been necessary to complete the sketch before he was able to evaluate its merit. This assumption is reinforced by the aforementioned preliminary sketches, also finished to this same degree. Other architects might reject an idea and proceed to another sketch, while Hoffmann was methodically pondering the whole before eliminating a solution. Since this sketch was not a commission but a competition, Hoffmann needed to see how it 'looked' before developing the scheme.

As an artist and designer of household objects, Josef Hoffmann was most likely accustomed to viewing the whole. A teapot, lamp, or chair could be precisely evaluated throughout the design process. Since architecture depends on drawing conventions, Hoffmann may have felt more comfortable bringing the idea to a relative conclusion. This reflective approach to sketching gave him time for consideration.

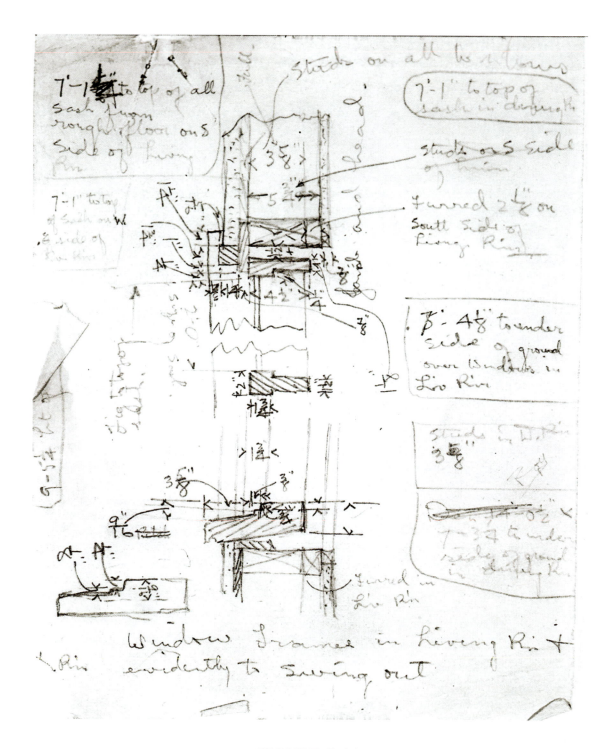

FIGURE 5.11

Greene, Charles Sumner (1868–1957)
Greene, Henry Mather (1870–1954)

Rough sketches of window details, G. Lawrence Stimson House, 1907, Avery Architectural and Fine Arts Library, NYDA.1960.001.03708, 12.4 × 10.2 cm, Pencil on paper

Buildings by the firm of Greene and Greene, Charles and Henry, are some of the best examples of Arts and Crafts architecture in the United States. Born outside of Cincinnati, the brothers' early education involved the crafts of woodworking, carpentry, metalwork, and tool-making at the Manual Training School of Washington University, St. Louis. After finishing a two-year course at Massachusetts Institute of Technology in 1891, they both entered architectural apprenticeships in Boston. Following their parents' move to California, they arrived in Pasadena in 1893. In the course of their trip across the United States, they attended the Columbia Exposition and saw the replica of the Ho-o-do of Byodo-in Temple at Uji (Current and Current, 1974; Makinson, 1977). This example of Japanese architecture would be later reflected in their use of woodwork joinery.

Their most celebrated project was a house for the David Gamble family (1907–1909). Completely designed and furnished by the architects, the house was constructed almost entirely of wood. The roof features shingle shakes and large eaves expressing exposed wood joists. The wood interior revealed the Greenes' concern for craftsmanship, with built-in cabinets and intricate joinery construction of the staircase.

Consistent with other architects of the Arts and Crafts, the Greenes worked closely with their craftsmen and builders. The abundance of forests and woodworking traditions in the United States facilitated their almost spiritual use of wood. The architectural theorist Reyner Banham stated that Greene and Greene represent craftsmanship to the extreme, considering every joint was articulated and the interior was 'like a cabin of a wooden ship' (Makinson, 1977, p. 22). Although suggesting an element of socialism, these houses were expensively crafted for the rich.

This page (Figure 5.11) demonstrates the Greenes concern for details and joinery. It is a series of studies for a window frame, sash and sill, where numerous section sketches explore the interrelationship of materials. Calculations have been scattered across the sheet, written from various sides of the page, and notes show down the margins. This may suggest that the sketch was passed between several people as a dialogue or the sketches were worked on intermittently. Most likely this sketch reflects Henry's hand, since he was the partner most interested in the tectonics of building. The crowding of the notes point to a search for an empty space in which to write, where the architect was concerned with the proximity to the visual description. Without the aid of a scale or straight edge, the specific numerical measurements imply a certain precision. This may suggest that the window detail could have been assembled from this sketch. A window frame was a common detail a contractor could have easily constructed but this study shows the Greenes' concern for design of the whole and control over the process.

With the extensive notes and measurements, this sketch may represent both a memory device and a medium to work through the construction of a detail. The sill has been rendered in the most pertinent place, where several different elements meet. The rest of the window frame uses cut lines only briefly to indicate the whole sash. The pieces have been identified by various methods in order to indicate their differences, some have been stippled or textured. The sketch, including both diagrams (the visual) and notes (the written), magnifies the idea that neither communication would suffice on its own. Together, they sufficiently describe the complex combination of pieces.

NOTES

1. Discussion with Dr. Renata Kassal-Mikula, Curator of the Historisches Museum, Vienna.

BIBLIOGRAPHY

Aubry, F. and Vandenbreeden, J. eds (1996). *Horta: Art Nouveau to Modernism*. Ludion.

Billcliffe, R. (1977). *Architectural Sketches and Flower Drawings by Charles Rennie Mackintosh*. Rizzoli/Academy Editions.

Billcliffe, R. (1978). *Mackintosh Watercolors*. Carter Nash Cameron.

Bliss, D.P. ed. (1979). *Charles Rennie Mackintosh and the Glasgow School of Art*. The Glasgow School of Art.

Borsi, F. and Portoghesi, P. (1991). *Victor Horta*. Rizzoli.

Brown, J. (1996). *Lutyens and the Edwardians: An English Architect and his Clients*. Viking.

Calvino, I. (1988). *Six Memos for the Next Millennium*. Harvard University Press.

Clark, R.J. (1974). *Joseph Maria Olbrich and Vienna*. Ph.D. Dissertation, Princeton University.

Collins, G.R. (1960). *Antonio Gaudí*. George Braziller.

Conrads, U. (1971). *Programs and Manifestoes on 20th-Century Architecture*. MIT Press.

Cooper, J. ed. (1978). *Mackintosh Architecture: The Complete Buildings and Selected Projects*. Academy Editions.

Crippa, M.A. (2002). *Living Gaudí: The Architect's Complete Vision*. Rizzoli.

Current, K. and Current, W.R. (1974). *Greene and Greene: Architects in the Residential Style*. Amon Carter Museum of Western Art.

de Solà-Morales, I. (1984). *Gaudí*. Rizzoli.

Descharnes, R. and Prévost, C. (1971). *Gaudí: The Visionary*. Viking Press.

Dunster, D. ed. (1978). *Hector Guimard*. Academy Editions.

Dunster, D. ed. (1986). *Edwin Lutyens*. Academy Editions.

Fergusson, Sir E. ed. (1997). *Secession: The Vienna Secession from Temple of Art to Exhibition Hall*. Verlag Gerd Hatje.

Geretsegger, H. and Peintner, M. (1964). *Otto Wagner 1841–1918. The Expanding City. The Beginning of Modern Architecture*. Praeger.

Gombrich, E.H. (1989). *Art and Illusion*. Princeton University Press.

Gombrich, E. and Kris, E. (1940). *Caricature*. Penguin Books.

Graf, O.A. (1985). *Otto Wagner, 1, Das Werk des Architekten, 1860–1902*. Herman Böhlaus Nachf.

Graf, O.A. (1985). *Otto Wagner, 2, Das Werk des Architekten, 1903–1918*. Herman Böhlaus Nachf.

Gravagnuolo, B. (1982). *Adolf Loos*. Rizzoli.

Gresleri, G. (1981). *Josef Hoffmann*. Rizzoli.

Grogan, E. (2002). *Beginnings: Charles Rennie Mackintosh's Early Sketches*. The Architectural Press, Elsevier and the National Library of Ireland.

Irving, R.G. (1981). *Indian Summer: Lutyens, Baker, and Imperial Delhi*. Yale University Press.

Janik, A. and Toulmin, S. (1973). *Wittgenstein's Vienna*. Touchstone.

Krimmel, B. ed. (1983). *Joseph M. Olbrich, 1867–1908*. Mathildenhöhe.

Kris, E. (1934). The Psychology of Caricature. *The International Journal of Psycho-Analysis*, 17, pp. 285–303.

Latham, I. (1980). *Joseph Maria Olbrich*. Rizzoli.

Loos, A. (1982). *Spoken into the Void: Collected Essays 1897–1900*. MIT Press.

Lustenberger, K. (1994). *Adolf Loos*. Artemis.

Lutyens, M. (1980). *Edwin Lutyens: A Memoir by his Daughter*. J. Murray.

Lyons, J.D. and Nichols, S.G. eds (1982). *Mimesis: From Mirror to Method, Augustine to Descartes*. Dartmouth College.

Macaulay, J. (1993). *Glasgow School of Art: Charles Rennie Mackintosh*. Phaidon Press.

Macaulay, J. (1994). *Hill House: Charles Rennie Mackintosh*. Phaidon Press.

Makinson, R.L. (1977). *Greene and Greene: Architecture as a Fine Art*. Peregrine Smith.

Mallgrave, H.F. ed. (1993). *Otto Wagner: Reflections on the Raiment of Modernity*. Getty Center for the History of Art and the Humanities.

Martinell, C. (1975). *Gaudí: His Life, His Theories, His Work*. MIT Press.

Massey, J. and Maxwell, S. (1995). *Arts and Crafts*. Abbeville Press.

Münz, L. and Künstler, G. (1966). *Adolf Loos: Pioneer of Modern Architecture*. Thames and Hudson.

Naylor, G. (1971). *The Arts and Crafts Movement: A Study of its Sources, Ideals and Influence on Design Theory*. MIT Press.

Noever, P. ed. (1992). *Josef Hoffmann Designs*. MAK, Austrian Museum of Applied Arts/Prestel-Verlag.

Nuttgens, P. ed. (1988). *Mackintosh and His Contemporaries in Europe and America*. Cameron Books.

OED (1971). *The Compact Edition of the Oxford English Dictionary*. Oxford University Press.

O'Neill, D. (1980). *Sir Edwin Lutyens: Country Houses*. Lund Humphries.

Oechslin, W. (2002). *Otto Wagner, Adolf Loos, and the Road to Modern Architecture*. Cambridge University Press.

Richardson, M. (1994). *Sketches by Edwin Lutyens*. Academy Editions.

Rukschcio, B and Schachel, R. (1982). *Adolf Loos: Leben and Werk*. Residenz Verlag.

Sekler, E.F. (1985). *Josef Hoffmann: The Architectural Work*. Princeton University Press.

Smith, B. and Vertikoff, A. (1998). *Greene and Greene: Masterworks*. Chronicle Books.

Stamp, G. (2001). *Edwin Lutyens: Country Houses from the Archives of Country Life*. Monacelli.

Stewart, D.B. (1987). *The Making of a Modern Japanese Architecture: 1868 to the Present*. Kodansha International.

Sweeney, J.J. and Sert, J.L. (1960). *Antoni Gaudí*. The Architectural Press.

Trachtenberg, M. and Hyman, I. (1986). *Architecture: From Prehistory to Post-Modernism*. Harry N. Abrams.

Triggs, O.L. (1902). *Chapters in the History of the Arts and Crafts Movement*. The Bohemia Guild of the Industrial Art League.

Turner, J.S. (2000). *Grove Dictionary of Art*. St. Martin's Press.

Van Vynckt, R.J. ed. (1993). *The International Dictionary of Architects and Architecture*. St. James Press.

CHAPTER 6

EARLY MODERN (1910–1930)

This period, approximately 1910 to 1930, was architecturally very fertile in anticipation of the modernist movement. The relatively small and localized movements of expressionism, futurism/*Nuove Tendenze*, the Amsterdam School and De Stijl, the Bauhaus, and constructivism each contributed to the roots of modernism in Europe. Although many of the included architects lived and practiced well into the twentieth century, their architectural legacies have been identified with this era and these movements. Their sketches are indicative of these associations, and more specifically the sketches' techniques were infused with ideology in anticipation of modernism. They advocated destruction of the ruling class and the tight control of the academy, as was evidenced by the Ecole des Beaux-Arts. The world was enjoying the benefits of the Industrial Revolution and found hope in the power of the machine. Early modern architects encouraged a departure from the past and traditional architecture, encouraging a near total abandonment of ornament. All were utopian and idealistic, promoting architecture as a vehicle to advance a new social agenda. Some may even be viewed as revolutionary, placing their faith in the worker and supporting the craftsman, and the replacement of established conventions. Whether because of ideology or political/economic circumstances, as a whole they built little. Each of these groups depended on visual communication to disseminate their movement's ideology. They used media to assist in the conception of new approaches to architectural design. These drawings and sketches could represent an idealistic future in the case of Antonio Sant'Elia's *Città Nuova*, whose sleek, dynamic images of industrial architecture spoke of a mechanized future. Sketches by Erich Mendelsohn embrace the fast lines and movement of the machine age by describing a plasticity of materials. Gustave Eiffel explored innovative uses for steel and glass, designing bridges and temporary structures. Michel de Klerk and Gerrit Rietveld, the most successful in seeing architecture through to construction, exercised extreme control over their images. Their sketches revealed the considered use of media to explore form and articulate details. El Lissitzky and Vladimir Tatlin moved easily between art and architecture, thereby enhancing their sketching skills. Julia Morgan, with her extensive practice, found the need to conceptualize through quick sketches and rely on her employees to translate her ideas into construction drawings. In contrast, Hermann Finsterlin chose sketches as a means to explore and disseminate theories of expressionism, using sketches as polemical dialogue. To elaborate on the uses of sketches by these architects it is important to place them in the context of their belief systems.

Expressionism in architecture grew out of the art movement of the same name in Germany. The major players included the architects Hans Poelzig, Peter Behrens, Max and Bruno Taut, Walter Gropius, and Hermann Finsterlin. Active in the years following World War I, they embraced utopian ideals with mysticism. They proposed architecture as 'a total work of art;' manipulating forms sculpturally and drawing upon human senses (Pehnt, 1973, p. 19). This reliance on emotions found metaphors in cave and mountain designs. Many of their beliefs were represented by a crystal; it was transparent and evoked concepts of stars and light. Accordingly, these architects began a series of communications and created a theoretical dialogue called the *Gläserne Kette*, or glass chain (Pehnt, 1973). They felt that expressionism was a new method of communication rather than a distinct style (Borsi and Konig, 1967). The economic depression following the war led to a period of limited construction. This situation, paired with a belief in the spiritual nature of the creative act, produced a large amount of theoretical images which might be referred to as *paper architecture* (Pehnt, 1985). This architecture, primarily 'built' on paper, was less concerned with function than with architectural form (Pehnt, 1985). These drawings and sketches often exhibited fluid expressions of amoebic shapes, as in the case of Finsterlin's abstract masses, and colorful emotional allusions by architects such as Poelzig and Bruno Taut.

Nuove Tendenze (heavily influenced by Austrian Secession) and futurism were primarily Italian movements that looked to industry and technology with an anti-historicist view. Visions of the machine age, with its electricity and new building materials, spurred an exploration of the city as a monumental and efficient social mechanism. The architectural sketches by Sant'Elia described a streamlined future of often molded forms, focusing less on specific materials and more on seamless elasticity. He was, in fact, visualizing prestressed concrete, and saw it as the material of the future (da Costa Meyer, 1995; Conrads, 1970). His architecture, with its flowing lines, expressed the speed of the machine metaphorically, but he also concentrated on architecture *for machines*, such as railway stations, power plants, and dams. These sketches used exaggerated and undefined scale to reinforce the monumentality of the speculative architecture. His stepped-back structures anticipate modernist skyscrapers and engage the observer's imagination (da Costa Meyer, 1995). Repetitive lines suggest buildings in motion and further the ideology of futurist architecture.

Two movements that evolved in a somewhat parallel fashion, and in close proximity to each other, were De Stijl and the Amsterdam School. Philosophically quite different, the architects of the Amsterdam School rejected classicism, concentrating instead on relationships between 'functionalism and beauty' (Bock, Johannisse and Stissi, 1997, p. 9). Beginning in the early 1900s, this movement stemmed from the common belief system of architects such as H. P. Berlage, J. M. van der May, M. de Klerk, and Piet Kramer. Fueled by political policy governing city expansion and mandates for workers' housing, these architects searched for sculptural forms that could be economically efficient and, thus, respond to social needs (Bock, Johannisse and Stissi, 1997; Casciato, 1996). Concerned with materials and construction methods, the architects of the Amsterdam School used sketches and drawings to envision building systems and massing. Not stylistically cohesive, the drawings and sketches by these architects were substantially diverse.

Many drawings (plans and elevations) of apartment buildings designed by de Klerk remain in archives. His sketches are characterized by combinations of selected ornament contrasted by building austerity. Drawn with a controlled hand, his sketches explore material intersections and the articulation of openings. His plans follow a trend in architectural drawing conventions by using symbols with legends and diagram techniques. The thickness of the walls was particularly important, considering he built almost exclusively with masonry. The De Stijl architects also built with masonry and explored massive geometric forms made from concrete. In contrast to the Amsterdam School, however, they eliminated decoration and most color, and assembled rectangular forms (de Wit, 1983). Naturally, their drawings and sketches had a minimal, abstract expression.

In nearby Germany, Gropius was transforming the former art school Staatliches Bauhaus in Weimar. (It is important to note that Gropius has been included in the modern chapter because of his significant influence on the style.) Based on the theory of the 'artist as exalted craftsman,' the Bauhaus attempted to unify the building and a whole, integrating its various elements (Conrads, 1970, p. 49). Gropius advocated bringing together sculpture, painting, and crafts into the design of the built environment. The masters of the Bauhaus were concerned with teaching craftsmanship in a workshop setting; besides craft, science, and theory, the school also provided instruction in drawing, painting, life drawing, composition, technical and perspective drawing, and ornament and industrial design (Conrads, 1970). These studios taught the techniques of sketching from memory and imagination (Conrads, 1970). Possibly stemming from a need to consider objects for domestic use, they also employed axonometric drawings. These two-dimensional projections showed three sides of the object or building equally, and were comprised of parallel lines which could be constructed with straight edges. They suggested the preciseness of the machine and reveled in the abstraction (Naylor, 1968).

First organized in Moscow in 1921, constructivism reconsidered the concept of creative activity. Its artists and architects promoted a post-revolutionary society of the working class, using modern construction materials instead of traditional modes of craft (Perloff and Reed, 2003). With this idea came the design not of aesthetic objects but of mass production. Advocating a functional and object-ive approach, they embraced the future of technology. With artists and architects such as Theo van Doesburg, Kasimir Malevich, Lissitzky, and Tatlin, constructivists sought expanded plasticity and spatial dynamics (Perloff and Reed, 2003). Disseminating their ideas through political posters and ideo-logical exhibitions, they found a unique style of spatial composition. Very linear and extending into all directions, the two-dimensional images advocated their three-dimensional concerns. Many of the sketches employed hard lines and solid planes of color using precision to emphasize ideas of solid and void. Both Lissitzky and Tatlin translated these conceptual explorations into physical constructions utilizing them as they would a sketch, making and remaking in quick succession.

SKETCHES

Architects of this period were building, but such tumultuous times saw an increase in the develop-ment of theory and the retention of sketches. Most of these architects obtained at least some training from art and architectural education institutions; most of them continued to associate with schools of architecture for a large part of their lives. Such relationships with education may have encouraged the archiving of their images, since students and colleagues recognized them as contributions to the his-tory of architecture. Part of the reason sketches remain from this period stems from the sketches as inherently imbued with ideological assertions. As with Boullée and Piranesi, the availability of pub-lication increased the collection and distribution of these artifacts. The remarkably attractive, fluid sketches by Mendelsohn and the painterly illustration sketches by Bruno Taut, for example, may have assured their preservation. Their dramatic perspective angles and fantastic architectural form con-tributed to capturing public imagination. In some cases, the sketches (especially by the expressionists and constructivists) were used in publication or were hung in exhibitions. The availability of tools may have contributed to the extensive existing design studies. The age of machines meant the manu-facture of drawing surfaces, and plentiful inexpensive instruments. Most likely the single feature that allowed the retention of architectural sketches from these movements pertains to the recognition and respect given to these sketches as remnants of creativity. A Renaissance of expression emerged from the rejection of tradition and the established academy, and encouraged a generation of prolific archi-tects who produced a spectrum of exciting sketches.

FIGURE 6.1

Sant'Elia, Antonio (1888–1916)
Study for a power station, 1913, Musei Civici di Como, 21 × 28 cm, Ink on paper

Antonio Sant'Elia was born in Como, Italy, 1888. He studied at the G. Castellini Arts and Crafts Institute, specializing in public works construction. After receiving his Master Builder Diploma in 1906, he joined the technical staff that was completing the Villoresi Canal. In 1913 Sant'Elia opened his own architectural practice in Milan, and he collaborated with the painter Dudreville on the national competition for the new headquarters of the Cassa di Risparmio, Piazza delle Erbe, in Verona. Sant'Elia joined the Volunteer Cyclists in World War I and died during the eighth battle of Isonzo in October 1916.

Although Sant'Elia's early influence was Art Nouveau, he was certainly aware of Frank Lloyd Wright, and much of his early work indicates that he looked to Otto Wagner and the Secessionists for inspiration (Caramel and Longatti, 1987). Sant'Elia was grounded in his knowledge of industrialization and changes in the contemporary city (Caramel and Longatti, 1987). He produced a series of drawings of his vision of the future city (the Città Nuova) and, with the *Nuove Tendenze* group, he exhibited these drawings along with his first version of the *Manifesto of Futurist Architecture*. As a result of this exhibition, he met members of the futurist movement, who embraced his vision; and his work thereafter became associated with this movement.

Sant'Elia's concern for a new city that embraced technology is evident in both the subjects and techniques of his sketches. Many of them are not connected to commissioned projects, but are explorations of the monumental qualities of the power of technology, with subjects such as railway and power stations. This sketch (Figure 6.1), dated 1913, shows just such a monumentally scaled building, given the title of power station. What makes this building seem so powerful is its lack of context. Its stark, dramatic view speaks of the building's function, not the human experience.

The straight, possibly ruled lines were reinforced through repetition, with lines drawn on top of each other. The overall effect accents the nervous vibrations of electricity which flows through the building. Another technique which adds to its monumental quality is the sharp angles of the perspective view. In most of Sant'Elia's sketches, he uses perspective instead of plans or elevations; he needed to envision the building as a whole impression and was not concerned with the nature of the interior spaces. He was representing the compelling expression of movement and 'swiftness' of the structure – terms he referred to in his *Manifesto*. He uses two-point perspective, with the points very close to each other, to increase the height of the building. He also employed a low horizon line to contribute to this impression.

The items that represent the power of electricity – the turbines – are prominently placed to the front of this station. They allow the building to speak about its function, proving that the architecture of the future has a role in creating a new society. The sketch lacks building details such as windows, doors, or material qualities, giving it a streamlined, machine-like feel. This 'machine aesthetic' was also mentioned in the tenets of the *Manifesto*: '[w]e have got to invent and remake the futurist city similar to an immense, tumultuous, agile, mobile building site, dynamic in every part, and the futurist building similar to a gigantic machine' (Caramel and Longatti, 1987, p. 302).

Sant'Elia likely had full knowledge that many of his designs would not be built. This is reflected in his connection with the expressionist movement of the period and the 'paper' architecture resulting from both the ideology of impending modernism or the general economic depression of the times that prevented much building.

FIGURE 6.2

de Klerk, Michel (1884–1923)

Sketch of design for a water tower with service buildings in reinforced concrete, 1912,
NAI, archive de Klerk 26.3/0321, 31.9 × 79.1 cm, Pencil on tracing paper

The recognized leader of the Amsterdam School, Michel de Klerk wrote little about his theories; he demonstrated his non-rationalist approach to architecture through his buildings. Born in an Amsterdam suburb in 1884, he demonstrated drawing skills from childhood. When he was fourteen, the architect Eduard Cuypers (*Cuijpers*) saw his drawings when visiting his school. Immediately, de Klerk began work in Cuypers' office, first as a clerk, then as a draughtsman, and finally as supervisor of works-in-progress (Frank, 1984). Employed there for twelve years, his first building opportunity came when he was hired by the architect H. A. J. Baanders to design the apartment house Johannes Vermeerplein (Frank, 1984). Soon after this project's completion, the client, Klaas Hille, asked de Klerk to design the first block on the Spaarndammerplantsoen, and it was during this time that he opened his own office.

The worker's housing, Spaarndammerbuurt, was tremendously influenced by the building codes for housing in Amsterdam at the time. Wolfgang Pehnt describes de Klerk's solution for the apartment building as basically the design of façades (1973). Over the next few years, de Klerk was involved with the design of the remaining two blocks, each with a slightly different approach. With windows flush to the façade, he employed various brick patterns; vertical to meet the street (and to demarcate the stories on the third block), horizontal string courses, some set in wave patterns, and others pulled away from the façade to articulate entrances.

Michel de Klerk's architecture was primarily constructed of brick using traditional construction methods. His mature work did not find any reference in history, although his influences included English Arts and Crafts, Scandinavian vernacular, and local Dutch models (de Wit, 1983). In addition to his concern for composition, Wim de Wit writes that: '[de Klerk's] work shows a search for an organically suggestive expression of life' (de Wit, 1983, p. 41). This expression was constructed with mass rather than planes and evoked a picturesque aesthetic (Frank, 1984).

Early in his career, de Klerk entered several competitions in order to expose his practice, taking second place in three contests. This sketch (Figure 6.2) shows design explorations for his entry in the 1912 Architectura et Amicita competition for a water tower with service buildings. His solution to the program was a tower made of exposed concrete (Bock, Johannisse and Stissi, 1997). The page has been covered with various elevations and perspectives, describing primarily the articulation of the shaft and top of the tower. The composition and 'look' of a cylindrical reservoir encased in a square structure was being explored. The numerous sketches study the relative expression of the structure in comparison to the container; in some cases the structure has been emphasized, while others accentuate the reservoir. Dotted site plans display alternative layouts for the juxtaposition of the tower and the service buildings.

de Klerk sketched with strong vertical lines, emphasizing the vertical feeling of the tower. Rendered primarily freehand with a few ruled guidelines, he used heavy lines to outline the forms, strengthening this verticality. The proposals appear surprisingly finished, which indicates that he was working out the design to some degree of completion in order to evaluate the alternate solutions. It was unnecessary to draw the whole tower, since a portion and the 'cap' conveyed most of the information. de Klerk was analyzing only the connection between the shaft and the top, purposefully ignoring the connection between the column and the ground. This sketch was mainly searching for a compositional appearance of the tower.

FIGURE 6.3

Eiffel, Gustave (1832–1923)

Eiffel Tower, detail of the opening of the arch, Réunion des Musées Nationaux/Art Resource; Musée d'Orsay, ARO 1981–1297 [53] (ART 177561), 27.5 × 42.5 cm, Graphite, pen and ink

Gustave Eiffel was born in 1832 in Dijon, France, where his parents owned a warehouse for the Epinac mines. With an interest in mechanical instruments and industry, Eiffel studied chemistry at the State School of Civil Engineering. In 1850, he found work as an apprentice in metallurgy in the Châtillon-sur-Seine foundry, learning the technical and financial dimensions of the industry. His experience with construction began when he started working with Charles Nepveu, the railway engineer. When Nepveu's business dwindled, Eiffel joined the Compagnie des chemins de fer de l'Ouest as a bridge designer (Loyrette, 1985).

Through a series of events, Eiffel later returned to Nepveu to work on a bridge for the Saint-Germain Railroad and, soon after, the Bordeaux Bridge (1858–1860) (Loyrette, 1985). He opened his own consulting firm in 1865, the Eiffel Company, with Maurice Koechlin as a collaborator, and designed portable bridges, some being sent as far as Manila and Saigon. Other large projects completed by the firm were the rail station at Pest in Hungary (1875) and the bridge over the Douro/Garabit viaduct that same year (Loyrette, 1985).

Eiffel is of course best known for the iconic tower of the 1889 Exhibition in Paris. In 1886, a call was made for an exhibition building possibly including a tower. Although an open competition, it was really directed to the Eiffel Company, who had been circulating a design for a tower since 1884 (Harriss, 1975). The idea for the design originated with Koechlin, but it was a Company collaboration. The exhibition tower stood approximately 300 meters tall and was constructed of wrought iron, chosen for its strength balanced by its weight (Harriss, 1975).

This sketch (Figure 6.3) has been attributed to Gustave Eiffel. There is convincing evidence that this sketch is from his hand: the page was included with papers acquired by the Musée d'Orsay from the Eiffel family. Eiffel was the managing partner in the firm and would have wanted to control such a high-profile project. He was also the engineer responsible for decisions in the firm, and his reputation for structural stability was essential. Considering what is known of Eiffel's sketching skills, comparison of this sketch to the initial drawing by Koechlin reveals disparate styles.

The page has six variations for the structure describing the base of the tower, all done with graphite and ink. Each one explores the bracing of the splayed base using single, double, cross-bracing, or circular reinforcing. The platform on the first level has been studied for thickness and function. One sketch shows a perfect circle inscribed between the legs, considering the efficient weight distribution and a concern for a geometric aesthetic. Eiffel was also contemplating the dimensions of the attachment to the ground with proportional measurement. One variation displays two sets of numbers divided by a centerline, which consider the width of the legs in comparison to the negative space.

These sketches describe the refinement of the bracing in regard to the aesthetic appearance of the base. Koechlin's early design drawing is of a tower that was far too light and flimsy to withstand the forces of the wind, a drawing that may have revealed his inexperience. Conversely, throughout his career Eiffel studied the wind's effect on his structures, even utilizing wind tunnels. His knowledge and experience show in his concern for the base; Eiffel was attempting to reconcile structural integrity with proportions and geometry. This sketch revealing a confident hand, suggests a vehicle to project thoughts pertaining to both the construction and appearance of the tower.

FIGURE 6.4

Lissitzky, Lazar Markovich (1890–1941)

Proun, study, *c*. 1920–1923, VanAbbemuseum, Inv.nr.244, 40.3 × 39 cm, Charcoal on paper

El Lissitzky, educated as an architect and engineer, is best known for his explorations of spatial construction and constructivist graphics. Born in the province of Smolensk, Russia, in 1890, he left for Germany in 1909 to study at the Technische Hochschüle in Darmstadt. With the advent of World War I, he returned to study engineering and architecture at the Riga Polytechnic Institute in Moscow. He was recruited by Marc Chagall to teach architecture and graphic arts at the Vitebsk Popular Art Institute, and began his association with Theo Van Doesburg, Kazimir Malevich, Hans Arp, Mart Stam, among others, and the contructivist and suprematist movements (Lissitzky, 1976; Perloff and Reed, 2003).

With little opportunity for work in architecture, Lissitzky found an artistic outlet in graphic design: books, Soviet propaganda posters, and photomontage. In 1919 he began a series of two- and three-dimensional projects he called *Prouns*. Lissitzky was experimenting with the 'problems of the perception of plastic elements in space' and the 'optimum harmony of very simple geometric forms in their dynamic and static relationships' (Lissitzky, 1976, p. 49). These geometric, spatial abstractions were titled for an acronym 'Project for the affirmation of the new' in art (Mansbach, 1987, p. 109; Perloff and Reed, 2003, p. 7).

Lissitsky had been searching for a venue beyond painting, one which extended to the creation of space (Mansbach, 1987). The *Prouns* questioned the tradition of perspective that used a single point by employing multiple visual points (Lissitzky, 1976). The resulting effect produced geometric compositions that seemed to float in space, with lines and planes extending in all directions. The *Prouns* took many forms, from prints and paintings to room-scale installations.

Both spatial and compositional, Lissitzky viewed the *Proun* constructions as sketches, since they referred to a beginning. They were explorations reaching toward perfection; continuously in process, they could never reach a state of completion (Mansbach, 1987). The opposite page (Figure 6.4) exhibits a graphite study for a *Proun*. The freehand techniques and scratchy pencil lines indicate its preliminary qualities. The sketch studies overlapping planes of various values on the left, balanced by open space on the right. Many lines appear to visually extend beyond the page connecting the *Proun* with the space beyond it. The composition emphasizes the correlation between the object and the ground surrounding it. More volumetrically complete, this sketch may have been the three-dimensional equivalent of the large-scale exploration. The image may represent a spatial construction that was abstracted for transfer to a lithograph.

Although Lissitzky maintained positive attitudes toward the machine aesthetic, it is not surprising that this *Proun* has been explored freehand. The manual, of the hand, was continually a concern for him, especially in relationship to vision. For him, the hand took a primary role in any creative activity (Perloff and Reed, 2003). Thus, the constructed installation *Prouns* consisted of the materials of the machine age, tempered by his concern for craftsmanship and tactility. This suggests that the starting point for all of his designs emerged from hand sketches.

Lissitzky used his *Prouns* to speculate on the construction of elements in space. Theoretical by nature, they inherently referred to an ideology rather than their objective qualities. Paradoxically, the action of hanging these images in galleries added to the perception of them as finished objects. If all of the *Prouns* completed by Lissitzky were intended to be preliminary, then this sketch may actually be a preliminary for a preliminary.

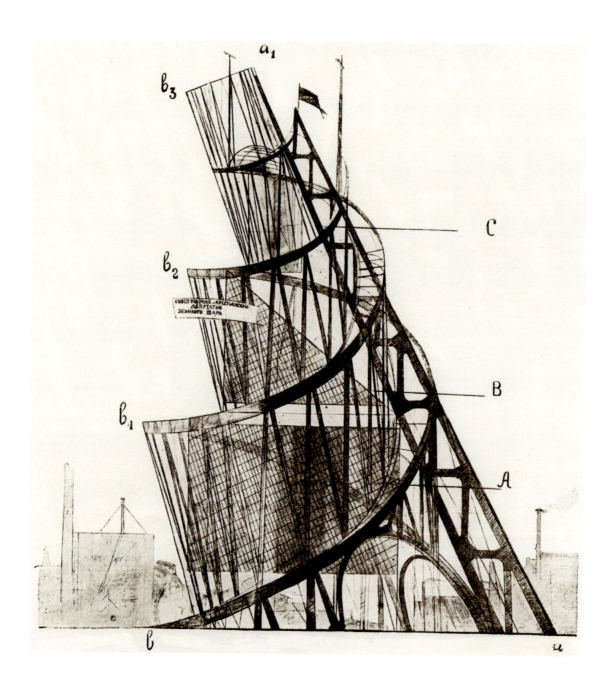

FIGURE 6.5

Tatlin, Vladimir Evgrafovich (1885–1953)

Sketch of the Monument to the Third International, *c.* 1919, Moderna Museet

Vladimir Tatlin was born in Moscow in 1885. He attended the Kharkov Technical High School and left soon after for the seaport of Odessa in 1902. There he found work on a ship that sailed the Black Sea and the Mediterranean. He studied at the I.D. Seliverstova School of Arts at Penza and the Moscow College of Painting, Sculpture and Architecture. It was through the painter Mikhail Larionov that he was introduced to artists and writers in Moscow and St. Petersburg (Milner, 1983; Zhadova, 1988). Around 1913, Tatlin began a career as a painter and became a member of the Union of Youth. His early work resembles impressionism and the paintings of the Kandinsky circle. In 1914, he visited Paris and was inspired by the work of the fauvists and French cubist painting. Although influenced by these groups, his work contained a vitality found in Russian art (Milner, 1983). During this period, he began the constructions he called 'painterly reliefs,' paintings with three-dimensional appliqué (Milner, 1983, pp. 92, 132).

An active artist throughout his life, Tatlin's repertoire was varied: drawing, painting, three-dimensional constructions, theater set design, clothing and costume design, furniture and domestic objects, architecture, and even a flying machine. Tatlin was continually interested in materiality, and especially exploring 'materials as language' (Milner, 1983, p. 94).

Talin's most influential and celebrated project was his proposal model for the Monument to the Third International, commissioned by the Department of Artistic Work of the People's Commissariat for Enlightenment in 1920. The project, although never realized as a building, was an icon for theoreticians that combined the social aspects of communism with constructivist art (Milner, 1983). The model displayed a series of leaning conical spirals meant to rotate at the various levels; the top portion was to contain a telegraph office speculatively intending to transmit images. Employing ruled lines and carefully constructed dimensions, this image (Figure 6.5) shows a diagrammatic elevation of the planned project. The page can be considered a sketch because it describes a preliminary or preparatory diagram, although it appears similar to an etching. This view of the monument reveals little context, consisting only of a few industrial buildings, either very distant or diminished in scale by the tower. Consistent with a diagram, Tatlin labeled the various levels of the tower in case the audience was not able to perceive his intent. The monument's structure and proportions are completely proposed, but as a building that was to house government offices, the sketch provided little explanation of mass or inhabitable volume.

Although the page's overall impression is not sketchy in technique, it reflects both the miniature model and the model as idea. The much-publicized design became an icon for the Soviet Revolution. It symbolized the forward-looking communist state, embracing a new ideology, and had far-reaching impact as a rallying point for an optimistic future. John Milner speculates that its form represents the 'progress of communism' and the leaning spirals mimic a step forward (1983, p. 156). They are also suggestive of Hermes or Mercury, and the stepped transition resembles a Ziggurat (Milner, 1983).

As a sketch, this image could be left unfinished and unresolved, since its purpose was ideological. The proposed monument speculated on a future and may have contributed to moving a political machine. It did not need to be fully resolved as architecture, instead it could suggest a belief system and through its vagueness, it could conjure and implore a whole country. Tatlin continued to alter and redesign the tower over the years. This continual manipulation resembles qualities of sketches as in process and the ambiguity of this image to be transformed. The Monument of the Third International acted as a social mechanism, the sketch and especially the model through their visual powers were able to help promote an ideological goal.

FIGURE 6.6

Mendelsohn, Erich (1887–1953)

Columbushaus exploratory sketches, 1931–1932, Staatliche Museen zu Berlin,
Hdz EM 192, 31.5 × 25.4 cm, Ink on paper

Erich Mendelsohn was born in 1887 in Allenstein, East Prussia, now Poland. He studied architecture at the Technische Hochschule of Berlin, and upon finishing his education he was introduced to expressionism and became associated with the Blaue Reiter group. After the Einstein Research Laboratory, his first commission, Mendelsohn obtained such urban architectural projects as the Schocken Department stores in Nuremberg and Chemnitz, and Columbushaus in Berlin. In 1933, he emigrated to England, keeping studios in both London and Jerusalem. He moved to the United States in 1941, taught at the University of California, Berkeley, and completed various projects, including synagogues, community centers and a hospital, until his death in 1953.

Throughout his career, Mendelsohn talked about his work in terms of 'dynamic functionalism,' which referred to feeling, imagination, and ' ... expression in movement of the forces inherent in building materials' (Pehnt, 1973, p. 125). He used these fluid qualities of the expressionist movement in his design for the Einstein Research Laboratory. It was intended to be built in the plastic material of concrete, but was eventually made of brick with a sculptural layer of concrete on top. Mendelsohn's architecture has been tied to expressionism and futurism and is often considered a precursor to modernism. His buildings, such as the Schocken Department stores, convey his concern for the strong horizontals of motion and the layering of transparency and solidity. His use of concrete, steel, and glass speaks of the human-made world of the machine. Mendelsohn had great interest in sketching throughout his lifetime; he would send sketches home from his post at the Russian front, writing that they were representative of a type of architecture he wanted to create. Some of these wartime sketches resemble flowing sand dunes and may have inspired his early architecture.

This is a page (Figure 6.6) of possibilities for the façade and volumetric massing of the Columbushaus project. All of the sketches contain strong horizontal lines, precursors for the repetitive ribbon windows. The lines, each representing one floor of the building, reveal Mendelsohn's concern for scale in these early attempts. The façade, with its curvature or straightness yet to be determined, considers its relationship to the urban edge of the street: some sketches include first floor shops. Although located on a busy street in Berlin, the building is sketched so as to ignore the context. The sketches that are circled or have an arced horizon may be acting as background or simply denoting the more promising proposals. The articulation and emphasis on the corner is seen in the finished building which is curved at one end. The final work of construction for the Columbushaus was to lift the top story, like a cap. In these sketches, the many alternatives for this accented upper floor can be seen.

Mendelsohn's technique is characterized by quickly drawn, confident, bold lines, which are straight and double back on themselves in their swiftness. He used ink to create these dark and definitive lines; this fluid media best represented his ideas for a fluid architecture. He wanted to analyze the entire building quickly and did not rework or erase a specific image, but continued to redraw the images until they matched the concept in his mind's eye. Two variations on a curved iteration and six variations on the straight proposal might explain a discrepancy in the techniques of the sketch.

The fact that Mendelsohn was not taking time to erase or cross out his sketches may indicate how he was thinking. Once an image reached a certain level of completion, he evaluated it and then moved on to the next. The wholeness of each sketch was necessary for its evaluation and critique.

FIGURE 6.7

Morgan, Julia (1872–1957)

Student rendering of a theater in a palace, Ecole des Beaux-Arts, 1902, Environmental
Design Archives, 8.75 × 13 in., Graphite, ink, watercolor and gouache on yellow
tracing paper, mounted on cream drawing paper

An architect practicing in the early twentieth century, Julia Morgan completed nearly seven hundred
buildings. Her work did not reflect a particular style, but responded to site conditions and client needs.
Designing with function as her priority, she also had a concern for details, light, color, and texture
(Boutelle, 1988). Many of her buildings displayed Renaissance, classical, vernacular, Arts and Crafts,
Spanish, and Native American references.

Born in San Francisco, Morgan began her architectural education at the University of California,
Berkeley, in 1890. While studying for an engineering degree, she met the architect/professor Bernard
Maybeck. He encouraged her interest in architecture, and she worked in his office for a year follow-
ing her graduation. She moved to Paris in 1896 and soon after she was admitted to the Ecole des
Beaux-Arts, becoming the first woman matriculated into the architecture program. She returned to
the United States in 1902 to begin her own practice.

As diverse as her architectural language, her repertoire of projects varied from domestic to institu-
tional to commercial. Her first projects included university commissions such as a bell tower and gymnasium for Mills College in Oakland, followed by a Sorority House and the Baptist Divinity School
for Berkeley. From churches such as the First Swedish Baptist Church and Saint John's Presbyterian
Church, to markets (Sacramento Public Market) and hospitals (Kings Daughters Home), she controlled the design of every project. Well known for her numerous buildings for the YWCA, the most
prominent are in Oakland (1913–1915), Honolulu (1926–1927) and San Francisco (1929–1930).

In her association with the Hearst family she produced two celebrated houses. Morgan first finished
the Hacienda del Pozo de Verona for Phoebe Hearst before designing a mansion complex on the
southern coast of California for media tycoon William Randolph Hearst. Named San Simeon, the cottages were completed in a style described by Hearst as 'Renaissance style from southern Spain'
(Boutelle, 1988, p. 177). The main building, fashioned after a church, was designed to display Hearst's
collection of paintings and art objects.

Most of Morgan's architectural drawings were destroyed when she closed her office in 1950,
although some of her sketches from the Ecole des Beaux-Arts still exist (Boutelle, 1988). This sketch
(Figure 6.7) dated December 3, 1901 was a preliminary design for her final Ecole competition. The
program called for a theater in a palace. Receiving a 'first mention' for the project, the sketch demonstrates tremendous skill in beaux-arts composition and decoration. It represents an artistic control
over ink and wash to achieve a complete impression. Details and ornament seem to have been thoroughly explored even though the swags and balustrades have been rendered as a series of squiggly
'w's.' It displays qualities that may be considered simultaneously precise and imprecise. Not necessarily a paradox, the sketch represents the beaux-arts technique of explaining the totality while providing minimal articulation of detail. From a distance, the sketch appears complete with shadow and
reflection. All parts have been included – even the draping of the doorway curtains. On closer
inspection, the doubled lines show the apparent search for the appropriate curve. These lines stop
short of intersection exhibiting the sketch's preparatory quality. The pilasters have been indicated by
simple horizontal and vertical marks and appear to list to the left showing her hurried lines. Being
both precise and imprecise, this sketch seeks interpretation.

FIGURE 6.8

Rietveld, Gerrit Thomas (1888–1964)

Rough draft variation of zigzag child's chair Jesse, July 13, 1950, RSA, 485 A 012, 20.5 × 15.7 cm, Crayon, ink on paper

Originally a furniture builder, Gerrit Rietveld was partially responsible for the architectural ideals of the De Stijl movement of the early 1920s. His Schröder House epitomized many of the movement's beliefs, including simplicity of form, verticals and horizontals that intersect and penetrate each other, primary colors, asymmetrical balance, and elements separated by space (Brown, 1958).

Born in Utrecht, Netherlands, Rietveld joined his father's furniture workshop at a young age. He attended evening classes in architecture, studying with the architect P. J. C. Klaarhamer. By 1917, he opened his own furniture workshop, and a year later he met various members of the newly formed group calling themselves De Stijl (Brown, 1958). Beginning his architectural practice in Utrecht he felt an affinity for the modern movement.

For several years, Rietveld exhibited his furniture across Europe, and even sent a chair to a Bauhaus show in Weimar in 1923 (Brown, 1958). Of all his well-known furniture designs, the Red Blue chair was the most exhibited and publicized. The chair was constructed of plywood planes, painted red and blue, floating through black vertical and horizontal sticks that overlapped each other. The compositionally elegant chair resembles a three-dimensional version of a Mondrian painting, although it was built prior to Mondrian's mature work.

Rietveld routinely destroyed many of his architectural drawings to make room for his latest projects; but with his prolific practice, evidence of his architectural drawing skills remains (Baroni, 1977; Vöge and Overy, 1993). These drawings demonstrate various stages in Rietveld's design process: construction diagrams, alterations and refinement, and ambiguous first proposals.

The sketch page (Figure 6.8) shows variations for a child's highchair studied from numerous angles. The sketches have been strewn across the page, with several of them overlapping and filling the available open space. The objects were sketched in ink then treated with colored pencil to provide texture and shading to several (possibly the most promising) renditions. Rietveld was using ink to outline the forms and emphasize the overall composition. The heavy, reinforced profiles suggest the construction of the chairs and the emphasis that Rietveld often put on the edges of his furniture. This technique darkened the profile and allowed for better viewing of the shape, and also accented the frequently used materials of plywood or planks of wood. The planar qualities of the chairs suggest the extension of these planes into space, reflecting some elements of De Stijl philosophy. For example, the ends of the black sticks supporting the planes of the Red Blue chair were painted a contrasting yellow. The repeated parallel lines were also necessary to imitate the thickness of the wood. Structurally, providing an approximation of the dimensions of the wood helped him to visualize the stability of the chair. Similar to the Zigzag chair, he was evaluating the balance and counterbalance that would provide steadiness.

This highchair appears to be based on the design of the Zigzag chair, designed approximately ten years earlier. Because the seat needed to be higher than the Zigzag chair Rietveld was evaluating alternatives for proportion – variations for the length of the base plane in relation to the taller 'leg.' In another attempt to visualize the completed chair, Rietveld used colored pencils to represent the shadows and tones of an anticipated red finish. These sketches allowed him to inspect the design three-dimensionally, prior to building a model or prototype.

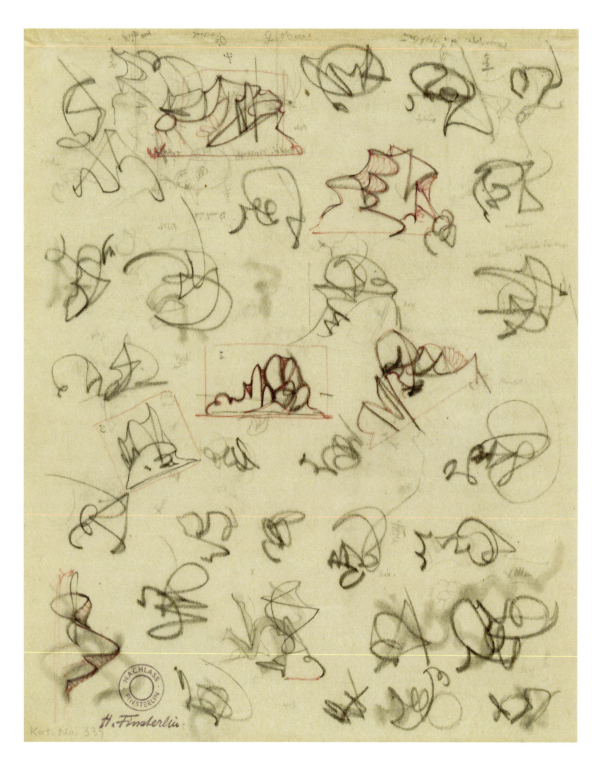

FIGURE 6.9

Finsterlin, Hermann (1887–1973)

Sketchbook page, *c.* 1920, Hamburger Kunsthalle/bpk, KH 11a, 31.9 × 25.8 cm,
Pencil and color pencil on transparent paper

An artist and fantasy architect of German expressionism, Hermann Finsterlin was born in Munich. After first studying the natural sciences and philosophy at Munich University, he redirected his studies to painting (Pehnt, 1973). In 1919, the architects of the Arbeitsrat group sponsored a competition inviting artists to show 'ideal projects' (Pehnt, 1973, p. 91). Entering the 'Exhibition for Unknown Architects,' Finsterlin thus began his association with these expressionist architects. (Pehnt, 1973).

This group of like-minded artists and architects, feeling somewhat isolated in their views, formed a community of correspondents called Die Gläserne Kette (The Glass Chain) which included Finsterlin, Bruno and Max Taut, Walter Gropius, Hans Hansen, and Hans Scharoun. In the early 1920s, Finsterlin attempted to build, but those projects were never realized and he dedicated himself to painting after 1924. This 'paper architecture' did not require a client or even a structure; rather, it encouraged fantasy and imagination and provided efficient dissemination of his beliefs. Always a theorist and idealist, Finsterlin was interested in theosophy and continued to study the 'biological creative urge in art which made use of the human medium' (Pehnt, 1973, p. 96).

Hermann Finsterlin speculated on the architecture of the future. Like Mendelsohn, his life-long friend, he was attracted to the abstraction of natural forms. His buildings often appear misshapen, conceived in a flowing elastic material that questions the tenets of architecture. Wolfgang Pehnt describes his paintings as 'exciting form-landscape in which interior and exterior are drawn together into continuous planes and spatial entities' (Pehnt, 1973, p. 97).

This page by Finsterlin (Figure 6.9) reveals a creative process searching for form. It appears that he sketched continuously, making a series of looped, abstract figures. Because of his use of translucent paper, many of the images have been framed and numbered from both sides. The squiggles are reminiscent of 'automatic writing' – seemingly made quickly, showing smooth lines in a frenzy of activity. With this deliberate technique, he chose to make curls rather than straight lines, providing him with results that anticipated the architecture he was envisioning. It appears he was attempting to instigate as much as possible accidentally into the process.

Consistent with expressionist ideology, sketches were generally valued for revealing creative inspiration (Pehnt, 1985). Edward Casey describes this as 'pure possibility,' a term used to explain a function of the imagination (Casey, 1976). Pure possibility suggests that all things are possible and at this early stage, for Finsterlin, no image was ruled out. Finsterlin put down what forms appeared in his head without judgment, and thus everything contained potential. Using the cognitive and visual techniques of resemblance and association, these images were so ambiguous that he could read anything into their vague form.

Once these sketches appeared on the paper, Finsterlin could, in a system of evaluation, highlight the forms he felt held the most promise. He framed several of these chosen sketches and, in pencil, began architectural articulation on others. The philosopher Richard Wollheim concerning translating abstract forms writes, 'Now my suggestion is that in so far as we see a drawing as a representation, instead of as a configuration of lines and strokes, the incongruity between what we draw and what we see disappears' (Wollheim, 1973, p. 22). These uncontrolled scribbles provided Finsterlin with images of 'pure possibility,' but the process required an evaluation phase to enable him to envision the sketches as future architecture.

161

BIBLIOGRAPHY

Andersson, H.O. and Bedoire, F. (1986). *Swedish Architecture Drawings 1940–1970*. Byggförlaget.

Baroni, D. (1977). *The Furniture of Gerrit Thomas Rietveld*. Barron's.

Benevolo, L. (1977). *History of Modern Architecture*. MIT Press.

Bock, M.S., Johannisse, S. and Stissi, V. (1997). *Michel de Klerk, Architect and Artist of the Amsterdam School, 1884–1923*. NAI Publishers.

Borsi, F. and Konig, G.K. (1967). *Architettura Dell'Espressionismo*. Vitali e Ghianda.

Boutelle, S.H. (1988). *Julia Morgan, Architect*. Abbeville Press.

Brown, T.M. (1958). *The Work of G. Rietveld, Architect*. MIT Press.

Caramel, L. and Longatti, A. (1987). *Antonio Sant'Elia: The Complete Works*. Arnoldo Mondadori.

Casciato, M. (1996). *The Amsterdam School*. 010 Publishers.

Casey, E.S. (1976). *Imagining: A Phenomenological Study*. Indiana University Press.

Conrads, U. ed. (1970). *Programs and Manifestoes in 20th-Century Architecture*. MIT Press.

Constant, C. (1994). *The Woodland Cemetery: Toward a Spiritual Landscape, Erik Gunnar Asplund and Sigurd Lewerentz 1915–61*. Byggförlager.

Cruickshank, D. ed. (1988). *Erik Gunnar Asplund*. The Architect's Journal.

da Costa Meyer, E. (1995). *The Work of Antonio Sant'Elia: Retreat into the Future*. Yale University Press.

de Wit, W. (1983). *The Amsterdam School: Dutch Expressionist Architecture, 1915–1930*. The Smithsonian Institution / MIT Press.

Drijver, P. (2001). *How to Construct Rietveld Furniture*. Bussum.

Droste, M. (1990). *Bauhaus 1919–1933*. Benedikt Taschen.

Frank, S.S. (1984). *Michel de Klerk, 1884–1923: An Architect of the Amsterdam School*. UMI Research Press.

Harriss, J. (1975). *The Tallest Tower: Eiffel and the Belle Epoque*. Houghton Mifflin.

Hochman, E.S. (1997). *Bauhaus: Crucible of Modernism*. Fromm International.

Holmdahl, G., Lind, S.I. and Ödeen, K. eds (1950). *Gunnar Asplund Architect 1885–1940: Plans Sketches and Photographs*. AB Tidskriften Byggmästaren.

James, C. (1990). *Julia Morgan*. Chelsea House.

James, K. (1997). *Erich Mendelsohn and the Architecture of German Modernism*. Cambridge University Press.

Küper, M. and von Zijl, I. (1992). *Gerrit Th. Rietveld: The Complete Works*. Centraal Museum.

Levin, M.R. (1989). *When the Eiffel Tower Was New: French Visions of Progress at the Centennial of the Revolution*. The Trustees of Mount Holyoke College.

Lissitzky, L.M. (1976). *El Lissitzky*. Galerie Gmurzynska.

Loyrette, H. (1985). *Gustave Eiffel*. Rizzoli.

Mansbach, S.A. (1978). *Visions of Totality: Laszlo Moholy-Nagy, Theo Van Doesburg, and El Lissitzky*. UMI Research Press.

Margolin, V. (1997). *The Struggle for Utopia: Rodchenko, Lissitzky, Moholy-Nagy, 1917–1946*. The University of Chicago Press.

Milner, J. (1983). *Vladimir Tatlin and the Russian Avant-Garde*. Yale University Press.

Naylor, G. (1968). *The Bauhaus*. Studio Vista.

Overy, P., Büller, L., Den Oudsten, F. and Mulder, B. (1988). *The Rietveld Schröder House*. MIT Press.

Pehnt, W. (1973). *Expressionist Architecture*. Praeger.

Pehnt, W. (1985). *Expressionist Architecture in Drawing*. Van Nostrand Reinhold.

Perloff, N. and Reed, B. eds (2003). *Situating El Lissitzky: Vitebsk, Berlin, Moscow*. Getty Research Institute.

Sharp, D. (1966). *Modern Architecture and Expressionism*. Braziller.

Smith, A.C. (2004). *Architectural Model as Machine*. The Architectural Press.

Vöge, P. and Overy, P. (1993). *The Complete Rietveld Furniture*. 010 Publishers.

Whitford, F. (1984). *Bauhaus*. Thames and Hudson.

Wingler, H.M. (1969). *The Bauhaus, Weimar Dessau Berlin Chicago*. MIT Press.

Wollheim, R. (1973). *On Art and the Mind*. Penguin Books.

Wrede, S. (1980). *The Architecture of Erik Gunnar Asplund*. MIT Press.

Zevi, B. (1985). *Erich Mendelsohn*. Rizzoli.

Zhadova, L.A. ed. (1988). *Tatlin*. Rizzoli.

CHAPTER 7

MODERN AND POSTMODERN (1930–1980)

It is difficult to summarize the numerous facets of modern architecture. Starting with the modern movement – whose primary figure was Le Corbusier with his social agenda – it evolved into an international style that affected architecture globally. As a movement spanning over forty years, it was not a unified style, but one filled with variations and contradictions. The concrete post and beam structures of the early years, the functionalist curtain walls of the 1950s, the exposed structure of shells and long spans all demonstrate the variety of buildings that fit under the title 'modern.' Many of the architects of this era were idealist, utopian, intuitive, functionalist, and interested in urban theory, prefabrication of building components, new technologies, and regional approaches. Charles Jencks insightfully calls this period a collection of modern movements rather than *the* modern movement (1973). However vast and diverse the architecture, the drawings and sketches by these architects reflect their belief systems, the questions they asked, the building materials they used, and the formal appearance of their buildings.

This period of modern movements extended over a large part of the twentieth century and was permeated with political and social movements, World War II, global migration, and tremendous advances in technology. The world had felt the effects of the Industrial Revolution, particularly machine age construction, materials, and transportation. These developments fascinated architects such as Le Corbusier, who found beauty in trains, cars, airplanes, and ships. Modern architects rejected the ornamental excesses of previous times and found clarity in primary forms and geometric shapes. With beliefs in simplicity, the spiritual implementation of structure, and clean lines, their architecture embraced an idealistic future (Trachtenberg and Hyman, 1986). The opportunities for construction in the postwar economy did much to encourage modern building (especially corporate construction) around the world.

Modernization greatly affected architects' education, practice, and prominence. Lacking an all-embracing theory, there was opportunity for cultural and regional variations within the international style (Jencks, 1973). Many architects were educated in technical schools or institutes for arts and crafts, such as the Bauhaus. Most of them visited famous sites, to learn from firsthand observation and sketching. As they experienced these monuments (both historic and contemporary), they took home their own interpretations. Many young architects found employment with the 'greats,' such as Le Corbusier and Walter Gropius, and used their experiences as a basis from which to develop their individual styles. This cross-fertilization created some interesting ancestry through offices and lineage of influence. This was part of the internationalization of the international style (named for an exhibition in New York), and part of its fallacy. Although sharing some of the same ideals, when these architects returned home they evolved their own attitudes reflecting local construction techniques, regional traditions, and individual modifications. The forms may have looked similar, but many of the social ideologies had changed.

MEDIA

Attitudes concerning practice affected the use of drawings and sketches. Since the turn of the century, architecture was gaining attention. The populations of major cities were aware of contemporary architecture and, in particular, urban renewal efforts. Buildings were viewed as isolated entities and were identified with their architects, becoming objects of personal ideology. The personalities (and egos) of many modern architects commanded headlines for their talents and their exploits. This changed the structure of architectural offices since they required larger numbers of draughts-people. Many factors were affected including who controlled design, the methods of presentation for commissions and competitions, and how drawings were used for publicity. The combination of firms, acquiring engineering departments, consulting, and providing planning services, all contributed to restructuring the profession. Most importantly, the changing role of architects in the design and construction process impacted both the amount and use of drawings and sketches.

Modern architects required more drawings than their predecessors, despite the assumption that simpler, prefabricated, or non-ornamented buildings would require fewer drawings.[1] Through history, architects were present on the site to supervise a building's assembly. They could immediately deal with problems and give counsel on material selection. By observing construction methods they could work with the craftsmen to achieve their intended effect. As 'master craftsmen,' these historic architects required fewer two-dimensional explanations since they could personally and verbally communicate design strategies. Modern architecture changed all that. Reasons for the architect's loss of control over the total process included a litigious society ('working drawings' changed to 'contract documents'), balancing many projects at the same time, and the division of responsibility in the stages of construction. As a result, drawings needed to be more thoroughly explanatory, describing connections and assemblies to insure the building was built as conceived. The traditions of construction had changed, and new materials, with their appropriate details, were unfamiliar to construction teams. The absence of the architect on site made communication that much more difficult; drawings became necessary as the primary mode of communication.

These more plentiful drawings of the modern age may have, in fact, been less informative. Comparatively speaking, sketches commanded more attention as the instruments to resolve construction details and their connections prior to construction drawings. They needed to be more clear and precise to imagine and anticipate the three-dimensional construction in two dimensions. Thus, these architects required more imagination to conceive of the entire project in abstraction before its manifestation. Sketches were a medium to explore the totality of the building, a method to understand proportions and regulating lines, a place to manipulate joints and material connections, and a way to calculate new structural systems. They also communicated information in an intra-office manner, conveying intent to those draughting the contract documents or to consultants outside the firm. Most importantly, drawings and sketches were vital to explaining and exploring the theoretical approaches of their creators.

The architects of the modern movements were very conscious of the revolutionary nature of their theories. They composed manifestos heralding a 'new' architecture, and with this change in attitudes, philosophies about the design process also changed. Often perceived as rejecting history, they did not, in fact, eliminate historical reference but interpreted it through a new idealism. These 'famous' architects were also concerned with their legacies: they retained sketches and drawings for posterity to make sure that future generations understood their philosophies and intentions. Their scientific and rational idiom was manifest in the quest for sincerity, order, logic, and clarity in their architecture (Richards, Pevsner and Sharp, 2000). These ideological goals showed in the forms of modern architecture, as it did in their two-dimensional representations. Often, this meant utilizing traditional drawing techniques but with new intention.

It was not necessary for these buildings to appear logical and rational, but they needed to be conceived through justifiable methods. Design processes *were* important to the architects of the modern movements. 'Universal space' was flexible space, used for various functions, conceived with rulers and right angles (Richards, Pevsner and Sharp, 2000). Partially emerging from post and beam construction, the 'squareness' of these spaces provided a direct relationship to grids and proportional geometries.

One of the most significant changes in drawing involved the use of orthographic projection to achieve these rational buildings. Still using plan, section, and elevation, these architects also employed axonometric drawings. Plans were the most dominant design tool, since they proved to demonstrate rational information. An easy way to view proportions, plans also helped to understand spatial relationships. They indicated rooms in relationship to each other and to the whole. They allowed architects to see the flow of space in an open plan, or to construct patterns of walls. Drawn with straight edges, plans could be based on grids and easily measured, and were used to explore the efficiency and function of the space. Equally rational was the axonometric drawing. Axonometrics were a mechanical version of a three-dimensional drawing where the object was viewed from a corner, and the sides receded most commonly at forty-five, thirty-three, or thirty-sixty degrees from a baseline. These drawings placed *all* lines parallel and could be easily constructed by moving triangles along a straight-edged base. The axonometric drawings placed the object at a distance from the viewer. Unlike a perspective construction, where the space surrounded or passed the viewer's peripheral vision, an axonometric drawing took an overhead or bird's-eye view. It did not command a one-point view location but gave each side an equal emphasis. The observer was no longer part of the space, but viewed the object in isolation. This distancing presented an unemotional stance, objectifying the subject rather than enticing the viewer's participation. Axonometric drawings can be constructed in less time (with a less complicated process) and still provide a volumetric view. They are more rational because they do not distort proportions, and measurements on the XYZ axis are true. Both plan and axonometric drawings can be constructed with straight-edged instruments, leaving little imperfection or subjective qualities.

Sketches were often freehand replicas of these orthographic drawings. The modernist architects were accustomed to drawing in plan, section, elevation, and perspective/axonometric, so they easily continued this practice when sketching. Freehand explorations were obviously less precise and often became combinations of several types of drawings. Architects did not need to take the time to be entirely accurate, since the sketches functioned as a personal dialogue. The fact that sketches were freehand did not necessary preclude them from being proportionally precise. As with descriptive geometry, a method using dividers and proportional systems can be more precise than using measurement.[2] Modern architects had methods to find and record proportions, such as x's to indicate the squaring of a space, or symmetry, designating equality. A sketched plan could ignore the thickness/poché of walls without losing its communicative abilities. Likewise, doors and windows added into walls at a later time still indicated openings.

Although still using sketches for recording, evaluating, designing and communicating, the media they employed reflected their architectural approach. Using various types of paper, graphite, ink, and colored pencils, modern architects also added newly refined and precise media and instruments such as rapidiograph pens and felt tip markers. Although used for many years, tracing paper experienced a resurgence and was the surface of choice for design. Although less durable, it was plentiful and facilitated the easy and exact transfer of images. This was important – part of the design could be retained while troublesome aspects were altered. This was substantially more efficient than redrawing and also saved common details that were reused or prefabricated. The medium also allowed minor changes to simple, geometrically conceived designs. The fixed parallel bar of the *paraline* system assisted rational architecture. Its quick manipulation of horizontals and verticals perpetuated right-angled architecture and made sketching with tools much more attractive. Moving from inches and feet to the metric system also replaced concentration on the human body in architecture with rational proportion, reflecting the modernist concern with the functional over the experiential. Meters demonstrate an abstract idea, while inches and feet encourage comparison to the human body; again, a distancing architecture. Sketches and drawings were seen as a means to an end, rather than an embodiment of architectural thinking or something infused with the essence of experience. Surprisingly, there was still a remarkable amount of very expressive sketches.

The disparagement of drawing did not necessarily stop architects from sketching. The sketches by the 'strict modernists' (in the functional/rational sense) such as Le Corbusier, Ludwig Mies van der Rohe, and Walter Gropius are as minimal and functional as their architecture. Later architects imbued their architecture, and similarly their sketches, with regional and expressive elements, including Alvar Aalto, Togo Murano, Luis Barragan, Eero Saarinen, and Louis Kahn. These architects included memory and experience in their architecture and were apt to make more fluid and emotive sketches. Alison and Peter Smithson used ideograms, Aldo Rossi considered multiple views in his sketches, Kunio Maekawa utilized strong horizontal lines and, of course, Frank Lloyd Wright claimed not to have sketched at all. Many of these architects also participated in the construction process, such as Felix Candela, who built full-scale mock-ups of concrete shell structural systems. Architects such as Eero Saarinen relied heavily on models and full-scale prototypes to evaluate and visualize complex building systems and structure.

As unique as their buildings, modern architects used vastly different sketching styles. They responded uniquely to the questions they asked themselves. Since querying the sketch about the relationships between adjoining rooms, an architect may have responded with a plan. Where an architect asked about regulating lines, a diagram in elevation would have been the best method for study. Since there were few rules that guided the techniques of sketches, each architect found unique approaches to their relationships with visual design media. The most striking are sketches by Aalto, where his overlapping wavy lines have been exhibited in nearly all of his sketches. These architects implemented individual conventions and the results reflected their personalities. The variations might suggest signatures that varied from bold lines to delicate tracings. As the art historian Giovanni Morelli found prominent painters from the Renaissance each had a 'language' in the way they formed ears or hands, similarly modern architects can be distinguished and identified by specific traits (Fernie, 1995). The period of modern architecture has been massively generalized. Although as the name the 'international style' suggests many factions and interpretations were entertained around the world with generally similar ideals.

FIGURE 7.1

Asplund, Erik Gunnar (1885–1940)

Architect Competition proposal 'Tallum'; 'Study of the Chapel Basin' sketch of the 'Toward the Crypt' series, 1915, Swedish Museum of Architecture, 25 × 25 cm, Thick paper

Influenced by the classicism of Italy, Gunnar Asplund blended Swedish national romanticism with the geometric forms of early modernism (Wrede, 1980). His sketches and drawings display an integration of architecture with nature, a distinctive aspect of his work. Born in Stockholm, nearly all of his projects were built in Sweden. He first studied architecture at the Royal Institute of Technology, Stockholm, from 1905 to 1909 (Cruickshank, 1988). After traveling to Germany on a scholarship, he interned for a short time with I. G. Clason.

His early independent projects were primarily houses, but in 1915 he and Sigurd Lewerentz won the competition to design burial grounds at the Woodland Cemetery. Although a relatively small project they successfully incorporated the natural features the site. Having returned from a trip to Italy in 1913–1914, Asplund's chapel in the Woodland Cemetery revealed his interests in both classicism and romanticism (Constant, 1994). For this chapel, a processional walk through the woods culminated in a columned portico with a steeply angled shingled roof. For a short time (1917–1920), additional buildings completed during his career include the Bredenberg Department Store, Stockholm, 1933–1935, and the Woodland Crematorium, Göteborg, 1936–1940. His much publicized City Library in Stockholm, 1920–1928, exhibits a stark cylinder referencing the classical form of the Pantheon and uses a circle in a square motif throughout. Asplund's later work continued to employ vernacular and Nordic references but acquired symbolic qualities (Wrede, 1980).

This sketch (Figure 7.1) was one of a series that Asplund and Lewerentz included in their submission for the Woodland Cemetery competition. The series of perspectives describes their design of various aspects of the cemetery, gardens and burial sites. They named the perspectives in association with the experiential characteristics of the views, such as Urn Walk (Constant, 1994).

The sketch attributed to Asplund, describes a view of a sunken garden. It has been labeled 'Study of a chapel basin (toward the crypt).' The crypt in the center of the sketch has been designed as a smooth façade. Around the façade are placed smaller monuments on terraced slopes. To each side of the pool low thick trees have been planted. The sketch shows diagonal striated lines giving it volume. The value (a function of dark and light areas) provides depth and contrast to the perspective, allowing a three-dimensional interpretation. Although the crypt has been situated to the rear, it is understood as being behind the trees. The texture of the trees accents the light façade to make it both a focal point and a destination. The one point perspective has been sketched symmetrically suggesting a certain balance and calmness. Although the parallel strokes might indicate a nervousness, the texture grounds the image.

Caroline Constant describes the design of the cemetery as presenting a ritual procession. She speculates that the architecture allows the visitor to move from dark to light, possibly symbolizing a life after death (Constant, 1994). Asplund's sketch similarly layers the scene with dark and light areas. The open front of the space has been contrasted by the restricted space between the row of trees behind. The dense rendering of the foliage creates a layer in front of the façade, separating one area from the other. The sequence of spaces helps to indicate how Asplund used nature and natural materials to mold and define architectural space, not differentiating interior from exterior volume.

FIGURE 7.2

Terragni, Giuseppe (1904–1943)

Monumento ai Caduit, Erba, preliminary perspective sketches, 1928–1932,
Centro Studi Giuseppe Terragni, Ink and graphite

Giuseppe Terragni was a leader in the Italian rationalist movement in the early part of the twentieth century. With tremendous energy and devotion to architecture, he built a large repertoire of modernist constructions in his short life. His sketches used firm lines that accentuated the edges and defined the box-like forms of his architecture.

Born in Meda (near Milan, Italy), Terragni studied at the Milan Polytechnic School of Architecture between the years 1921 and 1926. Upon leaving school he opened a practice in Como in 1927. He collaborated extensively with his brother Attilio and his longtime friend Pietro Lingeri. His architectural style was influenced by Russian constructivism and later the work of Le Corbusier and Mies van der Rohe (Pevesner, Richards and Sharp, 2000). In 1928, he joined the National Fascist Party, an event that shaped much of his career.

In 1932 he began work on a building for the Fascist Federation called the Fascio House. As a building for a new political system, Terragni was searching for an equally new architectural language. The project was a headquarters for the party organizers and had to reflect Mussolini's ideas of fascism by evoking the transparency of the party (Schumacher, 1991). An open grid filled with glass dominated the front façade, which was compositionally organized by the golden section and regulating lines (Pevesner, Richards and Sharp, 2000). A few of Terragni's other projects include the Casa Giuliani-Frigerio in Como (1938–1938), Novocomum Apartment Building (1928), the Kindergarten Antonio Sant'Elia (1936), and the Palazzo dei Congressi (1942).

This page of sketches (Figure 7.2) exhibits early studies for the Monumento ai Caduti in Erba from approximately 1928. This monument for World War I veterans reflects Terragni interests in nationalistic architecture. To remember fallen soldiers, the monument was placed at the crest of a hill. A long set of stairs encouraged the visitor to ascend to a compositional structure of convex and concave arcs. On this page, Terragni was concentrating on the configuration of the splayed, and almost baroque, stairs at the bottom of the hill. This sketch was not concerned with locating conceptual ideas but rather the refinement of an earlier, determined form. Here, he was studying the relationship of this base to the retaining wall, and the most appropriate look for a niche and urn. Sketched mainly from the same perspective angle, he was comparing the alternatives three-dimensionally. Using both ink and graphite as media, some of the sketches have been rendered smaller and some larger, scattered across the page. In his hurry, various sets of stairs have been sketched as abstracted arcs, where in other instances, he detailed the rise and tread.

Terragni sketched the stair primarily from one angle, knowing it would be constructed symmetrically. He was most likely right handed, since the forms have been viewed from the left, indicating how he started drawing with the uppermost curved steps, left to right. As bird's-eye perspectives, he was looking down on the scene rather than viewing it from a human's experience. This distancing may suggest his theoretical or ideological attitude toward the project. To support this assertion, it can be noted that he included little contextual information.

Throughout Terragni's architectural career, he designed many monuments. This building type may have allowed him to experiment with his rationalist position by designing structures that did not always require functional space. His theoretical position affected what he sketched and also the techniques he utilized.

FIGURE 7.3

Yasui, Takeo (1884–1955) Japanese

Nihonbashi Nomura Building, Yasui Architecture & Engineers, Osaka, Japan

Takeo Yasui began his career in architecture in Manchuria, where he was recognized for his style that infused Japanese architecture with elements from China and the West. Following this experience, he relocated to the city of Kansai in the western part of Japan. There he worked on several office buildings in art deco and modernist style. Returning to Japan, he graduated in architecture from the Imperial University of Tokyo in 1910. At this time, he joined a railway company in southern Manchuria. Again relocating to Japan in 1919, Yasui established private architectural practice in 1924.[3]

Involved in education during his practice, Yasui taught at Waseda University from 1925 to 1935, and the Kyoto Imperial University from 1933 to 1946. With his active practice, in 1936 he held the prestigious position of Vice-President of the Architectural Association of Japan.

The series of studies on the opposite page (Figure 7.3) concern interior details for a special dining room. The elevation, joint sections and corner explorations have been sketched on grid paper. In units of ten, the grid has been articulated in 100 square components. As a guide, the grid regulates lines and calculates measurement without a ruler. The outlined elevation, although unfinished, shows the primary features of an interior wall. The lines are very straight, both following the grid lines and some so straight they appear to be drawn with a guide. Faintly in the center of the window can be seen markings to tick off measurements. Although the information presented by the elevation is minimal, it does provide proportional organization.

The sketches located lower on the page are variations of a detail that connects beams with a column. They are less rigid in their construction showing the freehand technique. They do not all adhere to the grid and are not necessarily drawn to scale. Yasui did use the grid to guide the vertical lines of the column. The sketches have been strewn across the page not all completed to the same extent. The joint appears to have been expressed by building up layers of wood to celebrate a meeting of horizontal and vertical elements. Yasui has combined small pieces to create many horizontals and verticals where their repetition resembles ornament.

Decoration can be viewed as application of unnecessary elements, where ornament may be considered the expression of a material, detail, or connection. Modernist architects would condemn the use of unnecessary elements, reveling in the function of the structure. Here Yasui, does not strip down the point of connection but emphasizes the joining of two materials. Here he was celebrating the exposed beams and the point of their intersection rather than hiding their relationship.

Concerned with how the pieces fit together Yasui has also studied the joint in section. One can also see numerous beginnings sketched around the borders of the page. These half thoughts most likely represent tests, rejected intentions, and new directions in his thought process. These beginnings have been sketched with pencil, and some lines are reinforced with double strokes. The joint studies use a combination of perspective and axonometric, allowing Yasui to view in three dimensions.

The theme of the architecture blends traditional methods of woodworking with contemporary space. It is easy to view where the Arts and Crafts movement found their origins. These details strongly resemble the work of Frank Lloyd Wright, as he is known to have studied Japanese architecture.

This sketch emphasizes the span of Yasui's life and how he bridged into modernist style. The sketch also conveys the move from traditional understanding of construction and joinery to a period where the sketch could facilitate the design of new paradigms.

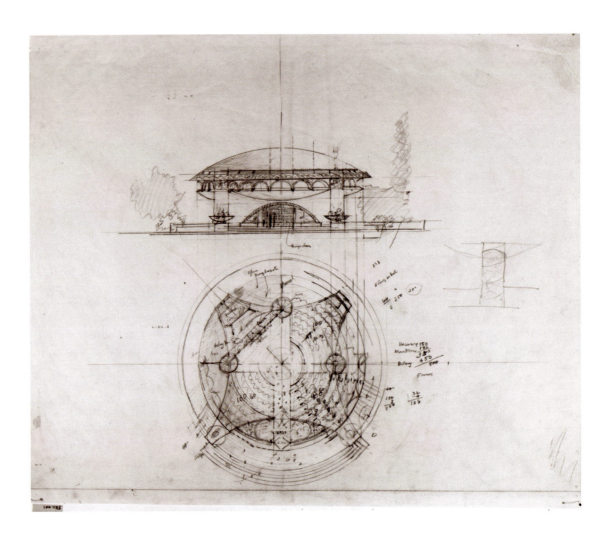

FIGURE 7.4

Wright, Frank Lloyd (1867–1959)

Annunciation Greek Orthodox Church, Wauwatosa, Wisconsin, 1956, The Frank Lloyd Wright Foundation, FLLW 5611.001, 37 × 30 in., Graphite pencil and color pencil on white tracing paper

A true icon of the twentieth century, Frank Lloyd Wright's work has been honored around the world. In reference to his design process, he claimed to bypass conceptual sketches entirely, progressing directly to a finished drawing stage (Hewitt, 1985). Although no one can doubt the tremendous imagination of Wright, there remains evidence of his use of sketches. Many of these images were a combination of ruled and freehand drawings indicating the semblance of a sketch.

Born in the upper Midwestern United States, Wright's family settled in Spring Green, Wisconsin, an area of the country which proved to be important to his work. Its gently rolling hills provided the impetus for his Prairie-style houses. He initially studied civil engineering. Eager to learn about architecture, Wright moved to Chicago and found work with the office of Adler and Sullivan in 1888. He learned from (and greatly respected) Louis Sullivan, and after several years was responsible for the firm's domestic commissions (Kaufmann and Raeburn, 1960). Wright established his own office in 1893, primarily designing houses. Speculating on new spatial qualities for domestic life, the Usonian Houses relied on simple massing, with flat roofs accenting their horizontality (Roth, 1979). The Prairie Houses integrated architecture with the landscape and featured cantilever roofs and open plans containing large central hearths (Kaufmann and Raeburn, 1960; Roth, 1979). Always concerned with his interpretation of the *Organic* (the relationship of parts to each other and an analogy to the growth of organic plant life). Several of his more celebrated projects were the Robie House (1906–1909); Imperial Hotel in Japan (1915–1922); Johnson Wax Administration Building (1936–1939); the Guggenheim Museum (1956–1959); and especially Taliesin in Spring Green, his home and studio, and Taliesin West in Arizona (Roth, 1979).

This page (Figure 7.4) describes Wright's typical sketching technique. In this design for the Annunciation Greek Church in Milwaukee, the patina of his process shows as he layers guidelines, ruled lines, erasures, shading, and notes. The sketch displays a front elevation and a circular plan; they correspond to each other so that Wright could easily transfer measurements. With this technique, he could also study how the decisions made in plan affected the elevation and vice versa. To relate these drawings to each other, he used ruled guidelines for accuracy. Onto this drawing he sketched freehand details and changes reflecting his design exploration. The page indicates notes identifying the bronze doors and numbers in the margins of the plan. The seats for the sanctuary show as wavy lines. Stairs and planters have been sketched over structure, and ornament on the dome above has been indicated on the edges of the outer circle in plan. The drawing has been worked over with erasures, shading, layers of guidelines, and moved walls.

The patina indicates the method he used for development of the project. Patina is the oxidation on the surface of bronze. This concept of the transformation of a surface can be extended to other materials, and might involve wear or discoloration. In this sketch, the marks left by Wright's hands express his absorption while contemplating the interior spaces. This can be evidenced by erasures that smear and change the surface of the paper.

Although Wright may have drawn schemes directly from his imagination, he still relied on sketches to visually develop the details and spatial relationships. This page also suggests that his early images were not considered sacred. He felt comfortable writing notes and calculations, and sketching alterations onto an initial idea.

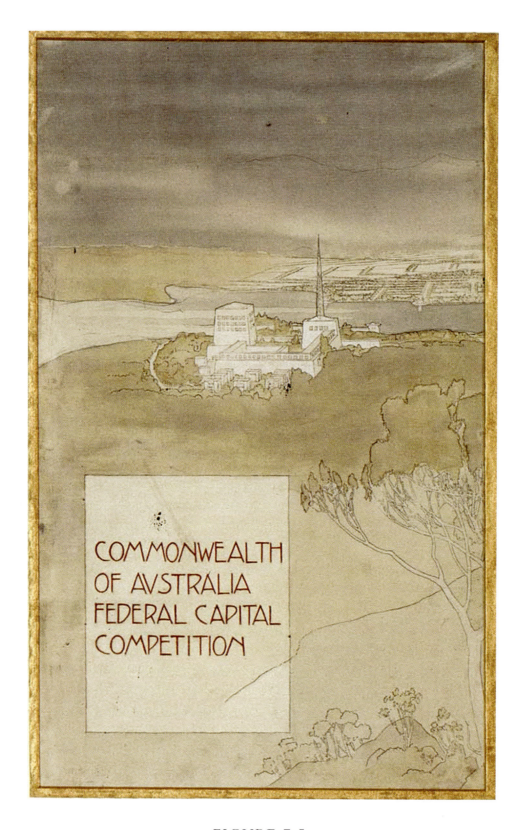

COMMONWEALTH
OF AVSTRALIA
FEDERAL CAPITAL
COMPETITION

FIGURE 7.5

176

Griffin, Marion Mahony (1871–1961)

Federal Capital competition, left panel, view from summit of Mount Ainslie (Part A), 1911–1912, National Archives of Australia, Series #41854 38, Accession #A710/1, 63.2 × 232.7cm (A, B, and C panels), Watercolor

Australia's first internationally recognized architects are best known for their winning plan for the capital city of Canberra. Although the work of their architecture firm displayed the name of Walter Burley Griffin only, it is recognized that Marion Mahony Griffin was his partner, collaborator, and an architect in her own right. They jointly designed the competition plan of 1911, and Marion has been credited with the large watercolor perspective illustrated on the opposite page (Figure 7.5) (Turnbull and Navaretti, 1998).[4]

Marion graduated from Massachusetts Institute of Technology in 1894, and she immediately accepted employment with her cousin Dwight Perkins in Chicago. Walter attended school at the University of Illinois, Urbana-Champaign, from 1895 to 1899. It was in the office of Frank Lloyd Wright where they met. Walter left Wright's office to enter private practice in the Chicago School, primarily designing houses of the 'Prairie' style. While with Wright, Marion held a position that may be likened to head designer and was responsible for many of the presentation renderings of the office (Turnbull and Navaretti, 1998).

After their winning entry, the pair moved to Australia where Walter accepted the position of Federal Capital Director of Design and Construction. During this time, they designed and built projects such as the Capital Theater in Melbourne (1924); Incinerators in Willoughby and Pyrmont (1934); and the subdivision development at Castlecrag/Haven Estate (Turnbull and Navaretti, 1998). Their architecture took on an Australian character by integrating the architecture into the site, contrasting heavy masonry with delicate appendages, and incorporating indigenous plants (Turnbull and Navaretti, 1998).

This watercolor from their Canberra competition entry provides a persuasive view of the grand layout for the city. It may be considered a sketch because, as a competition entry, it is a brief indication of an idea. This sketch is the left panel of Marion Griffin's watercolor triptych. It shows a view not from directly overhead, but a dramatic approach to the city. Entitled 'view from the summit of Mount Ainslie,' it was sketched from site information provided in the competition package, with the hill described as being 800 feet above the plain on the outskirts of the proposed site. The watercolor image has been rendered in muted shades of green, gray, and blue, using typical techniques of Art Nouveau or the Arts and Crafts graphic imagery prevalent at the time. The metropolis fades beyond the lakes, helping to articulate the great scale of the project using a *sfumato* technique. The atmospheric, cloudy sky has been broken by the sun shining directly over the capital building.

This view of the proposed city helps to understand the purpose of a competition entry. Without a commission, an entry hopes to persuade a jury through the use of imagination; the submittal must attract attention over the other contestants. Its purpose is to seduce the viewers with the ideas of the project, since the scheme has not yet been fully resolved. It must provide sufficient information without the detail necessary for construction drawings. Without a firm building in mind, such a sketch can be the medium to envision the future in compelling terms.

Marion Griffin, having rendered drawings for F. L. Wright, was certainly familiar with techniques of seduction through images. Wright's architecture was presented from dramatic perspective angles with pastel colors, presenting an atmospheric totality of the building incorporated into its site.

FIGURE 7.6

Saarinen, Eero (1910–1961)

David Ingalls Rink perspective study, *c.* 1953, Yale University Library Archives, #5081, 8.5 × 11 in., Dark pencil on yellow notebook paper

Although it is difficult to label his architectural style, Eero Saarinen approached modernism by considering the design of each project from its unique context and program, some with dramatic sculptural and structural expression (Saarinen, 1962; Román, 2003). Most interesting about Saarinen was his distinctive design process that involved the extensive use of sketches and models.

Saarinen was born in Finland where his father was the prominent architect Eliel Saarinen. The family emigrated to the United States in 1923, when the elder Saarinen accepted a position at the University of Michigan. Eero Saarinen studied sculpture at the Académie de la Grande Chaumière in Paris in 1929 and the Graduate Program of Fine Arts at Yale University to study architecture. In 1938, he worked briefly for the designer Norman Bel Geddes and then returned to Michigan to begin work with his father. They collaborated on many architectural projects until Eliel Saarinen's death in 1950. With his own practice, Eero Saarinen designed projects such as the Jefferson National Expansion Memorial in St. Louis (1948–1964); Kresge Auditorium and Chapel on MIT campus (1953–1956); the United States Embassy, London (1955–1960); Trans World Airlines Terminal, New York (1956–1962); and Dulles International Airport in Virginia (1958–1962). Constantly exploring new materials and technologies for building, Saarinen experimented with shell structures and tension construction in such projects as TWA, Ingalls Hockey Rink, and Dulles Airport.

Such structurally innovative constructions were difficult to imagine, and also challenging to envision through drawings. Using models, Saarinen and his office were able to comprehend and explore complex forms (Román, 2003). The projects were often first imagined as two-dimensional sketches. They were then modeled to analyze form, connections, and structural integrity. The final part of the process was to translate the project into construction drawings. This process allowed Saarinen to visually understand the form of the buildings and suggests that the use of models allowed him to easily keep track of the progress of projects in his office. This page (Figure 7.6) shows a perspective sketch from the design phase of the Ingalls Hockey Rink in New Haven, Connecticut. On first observation, this sketch appears to have a definitive look that might imply it was rendered after the completion of the building. Comparison to the finished structure, however, indicates the sketch was employed earlier in the process.

Sketched on yellow notebook paper with soft graphite pencil, the image is fluid, as the smooth line of the arched spine has been sketched in a continuous stroke. Shadows, foliage, and texture enrich the three-dimensional illusion and contextual qualities. One aspect that feels unresolved is the connection of the spine to the ground in front of the entry doors. Here the graphite appears darker, possibly because Saarinen reworked the terminus, hoping to find a solution with the perspective.

It would be difficult to visualize the fluid deformation roof without first having studied the structure of the arc. It is likely that Saarinen sketched this image as a reflection of a model. The ridge is dominant, but in the finished building, the ends have been turned up toward the sky and one end was finished with a sculptural piece. The entrances have also been altered from this early sketch. In the built version, the roof extends to become an overhang and the curve frames the doors. Saarinen's design process assisted him to understand complex forms, as is evidenced by this beautiful and confident sketch.

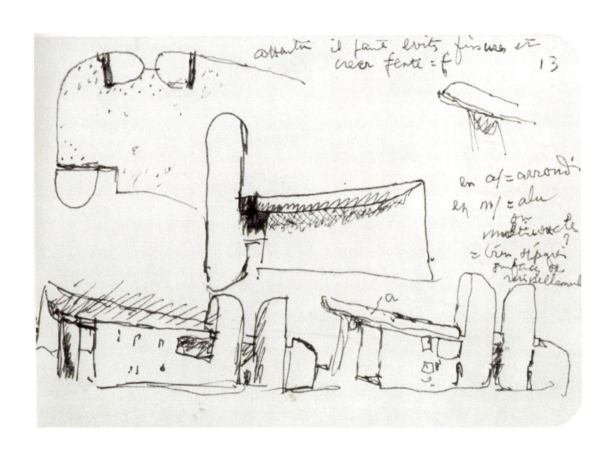

FIGURE 7.7

Le Corbusier (1887–1965)

Plate #322, Sketchbook 18, Volume 2, sketch of Notre-Dame-du-Haut, Ronchamp, February 1951, Le Corbusier Foundation/ARS, Carnet E18, 15 × 10 cm, Ink on sketchbook paper

Charles-Edouard Jenneret, better known as Le Corbusier, needs little introduction. He was the prominent figure in modernist architecture and crucial in the development of the international style. Although sketches remain from specific projects he designed, recently four volumes of his sketchbooks have been published. These sketchbooks were specifically saved and numbered by him, and were found (after his death) carefully stacked in a closet (Le Corbusier, 1981). They include travel and conceptual sketches, distinct from sketches in his office for specific buildings.

Le Corbusier was born at La Chaux-de-Fonds, Neuchâtel, Switzerland, in 1887. His early education included vocational school at the Ecole d'Art. Encouraged by a teacher, Charles L'Eplattenier, he left to study architecture. In 1907, he embarked on an extended visit to Italy; upon his return, he found work with the architect Auguste Perret. In 1913 he opened his own firm and began experimenting with ideas for the Dom-ino House. Conceptually, this building system consisted of a rectangular 'skeleton' made of reinforced concrete (Tzonis, 2001). In 1917, Le Corbusier moved to Paris, further exploring the building technology of concrete.

Around the time he entered practice with his cousin Pierre Jeanneret in 1922, Le Corbusier began to combine the elements that defined his rational and functional approach to architecture. Le Corbusier's large body of built work includes the Unité d'Habitation, Marseille (1949), and the Dominican Monastery of Sainte-Marie-de-la-Tourette (1952).

The published sketchbooks provide rich insight into Le Corbusier's thought processes and sketching techniques. Undoubtedly, the travel sketches were used to remember visual information, as sights could be noted and retained for further use. Other types of notations occur in his sketchbooks, such as codes for colors, train reservations, recordings of types of trees, hand and sun symbols, and written analysis and evaluation (Le Corbusier, 1981). Some of the sketches show a firm and definitive pencil technique, while others have a wavering, slow deliberation.

This sketch (Figure 7.7) shows early ideas for the non-rational Chapel Notre-Dame-du-Haut, Ronchamp (1955). Uneven and scratchy lines were used to explore the chapel in plan and elevation. A single line gestured the arc of the chapel on what appears to be a roof plan. The rounded light wells have been roughly shaded and appear lumpy. Le Corbusier is studying the relationship between the massing of the roof and the vertical towers. The two lower elevations, which resemble perspectives, show variations for the shape and volume of the roof. Indicating his concern for this roof/wall proportion, he minimized the window openings to simple parallel lines. The roof to the right has been identified with the letter 'a.' On the legend which describes his symbols, 'a' has been translated as *arrondi*, 'round.'

Given the abstract qualities of the sketch, Le Corbusier may not have trusted his memory. He needed a written note to remind him of that moment in the process when he was thinking about the curve of the eave. He also made notes of his personal dialogue, writing 'attention' to remind himself about fissuring. This may indicate something vital to the design and construction of the roof that required subsequent examination. Considering the briefness of the sketch, it is clear that Le Corbusier depended upon additional written messages to later recall his design intention. The sketchbooks were for him a discussion about design and also represented memory devices.

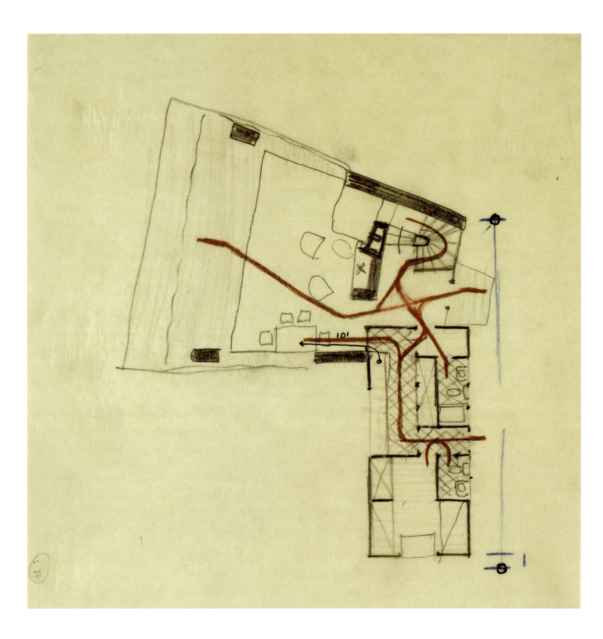

FIGURE 7.8

Gropius, Walter (1883–1969)

Lorant Residence, Arlington, VT; sketch of plan with circulation routes, 1942, Busch-Reisinger Museum, Harvard University Art Museums, BRGA.95.2, 22.9 × 22.8 cm, Graphite and colored pencil on paper

Emerging from his role as an educator at the Bauhaus, Walter Gropius had tremendous influence on generations of students and was a profound figure in the modern movement. A consummate collaborator, his rational architecture was less about the object and more about social responsibilities and industrial standardization.

Starting his life in Germany, Gropius studied architecture at the Technische Hochschule in Berlin and Munich, finishing in 1907. That same year he began working for Peter Behrens, and three years later he left to start his own practice. His first significant commission, assisted by Adolf Meyer, was the façade for the Fagus factory in 1911. Predating many modernist buildings, the factory found an appropriate industrial vocabulary with clear modern intentions. Various house projects followed, along with the design of the industrial buildings for the Cologne Exhibition of the Deutsche Werkbund Congress.

Combining the Higher Institute of Fine Arts and the School of Applied Arts, the Bauhaus was formed in 1919 with Gropius as its director. He emigrated to Britain and then the United States in the mid-1930s, when he was summoned to head the Graduate School of Architecture at Harvard. His architectural practice often collaborated with Marcel Breuer and he was a founding member of the firm The Architect's Collaborative (TAC). Other projects of note, in which he had primary responsibility, include the United States Embassy in Athens (1956) and a skyscraper for Grand Central Station, New York City (1960) (Berdini, 1985; Fitch, 1960; Isaacs, 1991).

Drawings by Gropius reveal the rational clarity and functionalist approach of modernism (Tzonis and Nerdinger, 1990). His drawings and sketches were most often graphite on paper, primarily employing the conventions of plan, section, elevation, and axonometric. This sketch (Figure 7.8) is a design for the Lovant Residence in Arlington, Vermont (1942). Although the project was never constructed, the program specified a small house equipped with viewing windows on a ninety-acre site (Tzonis and Nerdinger, 1990).

This plan shows circulation paths sketched in red. Obviously concerned about the material thickness of walls, Gropius used poché to add weight to structural walls. He also differentiated the floor surfaces by shading certain areas and crosshatching others. These visual indicators help to emphasize that the house was to be built using local materials, fieldstone, and wood. The careful control of proportion and the consideration for spatial relationships indicate that Gropius used this sketch for concentrated and deliberate thinking.

The red paths are the most distinctive part of this sketch. Gropius was visually 'walking' his pencil through the house, checking the efficiency and flow of the circulation. The circulation in this small house seems particularly chaotic in the entry vestibule, where all of the paths intersect. In later versions of the house, Gropius eliminated the 'L' of the kitchen and designed it as a galley space, thus simplifying the options for circulation. The patterns of movement have been separated between public and private. For example, the lines from the maid's room through the kitchen to the dining table are separated from the entry, living, and guest toilet. To further support this interpretation, a thin line starts on the kitchen counter and ends with an arrow on the dining table (additionally indicated by the only measurement on the sketch, ten feet). Most lines consist of single weight; conversely, the circulation paths have been sketched over as if he was walking the possible routes several times. Gropius' reputation for efficiency would support a theory that he was concerned with the economical delivery of food and the distances of travel through the space.

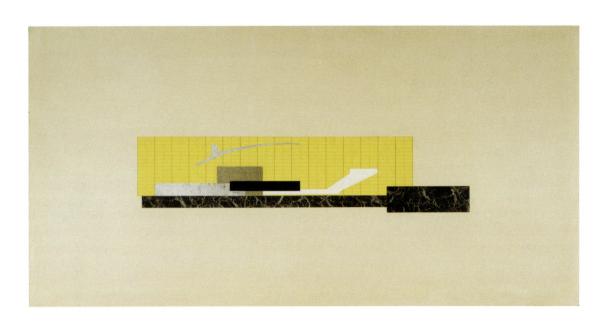

FIGURE 7.9

Mies van der Rohe, Ludwig (1886–1969)

Theater project combined elevation and section, May 1909, The Museum of
Modern Art/SCALA/ARS/Art Resource, #717.1963, 121.9 × 243.8 cm,
Graphite, ink, and cut and pasted papers

The architecture of Ludwig Mies van der Rohe was based on the ideology of a new technology, manifest in steel and glass. As an accomplished rationalist, he was objectively interested in the efficiency of construction as well as the expressive qualities of structure (Blaser, 1997). Mies also used a formal, geometric, and proportional system to order space according to its function.

The son of a builder and stonemason, Mies was born in Aachen, Germany. He was schooled in Berlin at the School of the Museum of Arts and Crafts and the Institute of Fine Arts. In 1905 he entered the profession of architecture, working with Bruno Paul in Berlin, and then Peter Behrens in Neubabelsberg. In 1924, he founded the group called *The Ring* in rebellion against the conservative establishment of architects in Germany. Becoming involved in the education of architects, Mies took the position as the director of the Bauhaus (1930–1932). Prior to World War II, in 1938 he immigrated to the United States to direct the future architecture program at the Illinois Institute of Technology in Chicago. Building his practice in Chicago, he completed projects such as the Crown Hall on the campus of IIT (1950–1956); Farnsworth House (1945–1951); the Seagram Building, New York City (1954–1958); and the Toronto-Dominion Center (1963–1969) (Blaser, 1997; Cohen, 1996; Drexler, 1960; Schulze, 1985).

Mies had begun his career with theoretical projects of houses and glass skyscrapers, but his first prominent project was the Barcelona Pavilion (the German Pavilion at the International Exhibition in Barcelona in 1928–1929). A building without a program, the Pavilion was an open plan of glass and green marble with slender columns clad in chrome. Its ambiguous enclosure of horizontal and vertical slabs found its ornament in the rich materials.

At the Bauhaus, Mies encouraged his students to develop their projects with vast numbers of sketches before committing to final drawings (Cohen, 1996). Mies' sketches, from the collection at the Museum of Modern Art, show mostly plans accompanied by interior perspectives and elaborate construction details that show connections (Drexler, 1986).

An unusual technique Mies employed was that of collage. These paper constructions were abstractions, not intended to portray spatial qualities. They may be considered sketches since they present a basic outline, pertain to conceptual thinking and provide little pictorial orientation. Pieces of cut paper were pasted in juxtaposition so as to make a semblance of a *parti*. The constructions were often combinations of elevation and section, in order to study the compositional proportions that expressed the essence of the project. This image (Figure 7.9) represents such an example. Using five or six pieces of colored paper, Mies has carefully cut rectangles to place in comparative positions on the page. He used bright yellow paper drawn over with a grid, resembling fenestration or an abstract pattern. In the center has been placed a very dark rectangle surrounded with light gray, tan, and white pieces.

This collaged sketch is really about precise and imprecise. The paper has been cut very neatly and shows exact proportions. The forms reflect Mies' bold and simple rectangles which act as planes slicing through space. In contrast, the composition of pieces is simultaneously imprecise. These cutouts are not plan, section, or elevation; they suggest building blocks and are therefore alluding to spatial relationships and construction. Without a ground line, the assembly provides little orientation. The proportions may be valid from any direction. This collage from 1909, early in his career as an architect, reveals Mies' penchant for the De Stijl-like juxtaposition of horizontals and verticals.

FIGURE 7.10

Kahn, Louis (1901–1974)

President's Estate, the First Capital of Pakistan, March 23, 1965, University of Pennsylvania and the Pennsylvania Historical and Museum Commission, #675.108.23, 30.5 × 61 cm, Graphite and charcoal on white trace

As a departure from the strict functionalism of modernism, Louis Kahn spoke in terms of the poetics of architecture. His passion showed not only in his buildings, but in his devotion to the dialogue of sketching.

Born in Estonia, Kahn immigrated with his family to the United States when he was very young. He studied architecture at the University of Pennsylvania, Philadelphia, from the years 1920 to 1924. After graduation, he worked with John Molitor, the city architect; William H. Lee, architect; Paul P. Cret, architect; and the firm of Zantzinger, Borie, and Medary Architects in Philadelphia. Kahn began independent practice in 1935. His first high profile building came with the commission for the Art Gallery at Yale University (1951–1953). Other projects in his prolific career include: Richards Medical Research Building, University of Pennsylvania (1957–1964); Salk Institute Laboratory Building, California (1959–1965); Sher-E-Banglanagar National Assembly, Dacca, Bangladesh (1962–1974); Kimball Art Museum, Texas (1966–1972); Library, Phillips Exeter Academy, New Hampshire (1967–1972); and the Center for British Art and Studies, Yale University (1969–1974). A critic in architecture at Yale for several years, he also taught at the University of Pennsylvania from 1957 to 1974 (Yoshida, 1983).

Kahn promoted a turn from functionally social architecture to the *experience* of architecture. This spiritual approach took a new look at materials and texture, and especially the effects of light. His massive walls articulated architectural space, and his juxtaposition of materials such as concrete, steel, and wood presented a strong sense of materiality in construction (Yoshida, 1983).

Marshall Meyers, a designer in the office, writes that Kahn's early design process always started with notebook sketches (playing with the program) and progressed to analysis and critique to determine if the idea was viable. Kahn would rework and refine the project continuously through to construction drawings. He would sketch fervently as he described his ideas to his employees (Yoshida, 1983). In his lectures on drawing and sketching, he spoke about how one should not imitate exactly, but be critical about the conceived image and find significance in it. He spoke of his love of beginnings and enjoyment in learning (Latour, 1991).

Kahn's sketches show a bold hand, as he often used charcoal or a soft pencil, altering, reworking, and emphasizing different aspects of the sketch. This sketch for the President's Estate, the First Capital of Pakistan (Figure 7.10), displays his enthusiastic dialogue with his sketches. Done with charcoal and graphite on tracing paper, the plan shows large forms contrasted by a few delicate diagrams. It is likely that where he drew lines over and over on a circle, he was not attempting to achieve the perfect curve but to emphasize the power of the shape. The fluid and expressive strokes suggest a passion that involved his entire body. The large circles on this sketch necessitated a full sweep of his arm on the relatively large sheet of paper, 30.5 × 61 cm (approximately 12 × 24 in.). With this much charcoal it was doubtful he could have kept his hand or arms clean. He was intellectually, emotionally, and physically interacting with the sketch. Immersed in the making, he had rubbed out, crossed out, and drawn over many aspects in the sketch as if it spoke to him. This discourse, and his absorption with the visual media, suggests an intense concentration that engaged his whole being in the process.

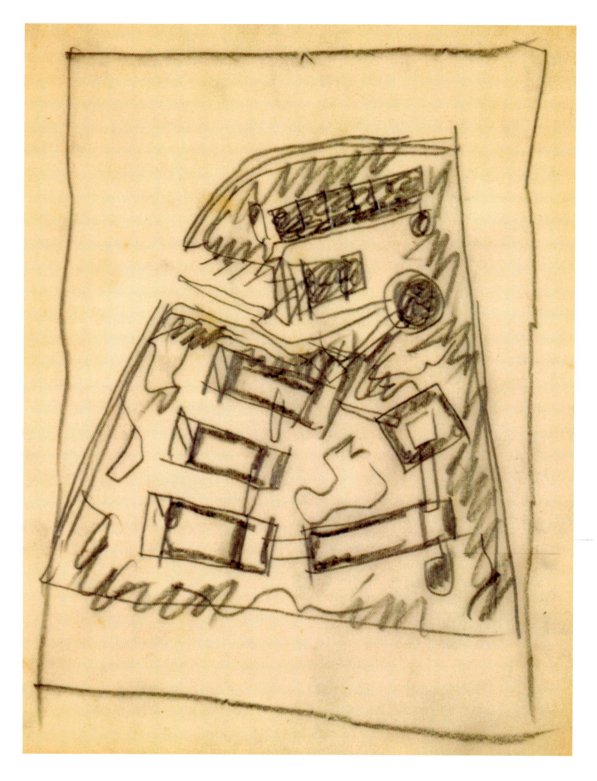

FIGURE 7.11

Villanueva, Carlos Raúl (1900–1975)

Museo Soto sketch, *c.* 1969, Fundación Villanueva Caracas, #3219r, 21 × 18 cm, Graphite on sketch paper

Known for his urban renewal projects in Venezuela and for organizing professional architecture and planning associations, Carlos Raúl Villanueva promoted a modern architecture balanced by respect for the preservation of the colonial architecture of Latin America.

The son of a Venezuelan diplomat, Villanueva was born in Croydon, England. He studied at the Ecole des Beaux-Arts and received a diploma in 1928. Relocating to Caracas, he began private practice the following year. Although beaux-arts trained, Villanueva led the modern movement in Venezuela, reflecting his contemporaries' work in Europe. He successfully integrated art into his architecture and translated modernist concrete forms to the sunlight of the tropics, using screens, reflection, and shading devices. One of his most celebrated projects was the elementary school Escuela Gran Colombia (1939). A building to attain the social ideals of modernism, it rejected historical precedent. Other buildings designed by Villanueva include the Olympic Stadium (1950–1952), El Paraiso Housing Development (1954), and the University City projects, School of Architecture and Urbanism, Pharmacy Building, and the Olympic Swimming Stadium (1957), all in Caracas (Van Vynckt, 1993; Villanueva and Pintó, 2000).

Paulina Villanueva explains that her father had a distinct method of using sketching during his design process. He sketched with 'strong yet precise strokes that enabled him to compose complex ideas with few lines' (Villanueva and Pintó, 2000, pp. 9–10). She recalls that he would sketch many small images to reach a design solution and continually revisit those first sketches. To achieve these bold and efficient sketches he used a blunt pencil. The resulting heavy line provided a concise outline. Although he destroyed many of his drawings and sketches, considering them as only part of the process, a few of these graphically robust images remain, primarily from his final projects.

Villanueva's sketches appear consistent with his architecture. The straightforward expression of edges, abstract shape, and precise proportion reflects his use of bold modernist forms. This page (Figure 7.11) presents a preliminary study for the Jesús Soto Museum of Modern Art in Bolivar City, Venezuela. The sketch, dating from the late 1960s, shows a site plan of the museum and describes the juxtaposition of the various buildings. At this early stage in conceptual design, he was not concerned with straight lines or details. This shows in the minimal forms that describe buildings, some with only four lines. Several of the buildings have been roughly darkened and others appear unfinished, such as the overhangs/porches on the galleries. The sketch is an attempt to quickly comprehend the whole site. Concerned with contrast that could help him visualize the context, he shaded the ground with bold texture using a continuous zigzag stroke.

Considering the series of sketches that exist for this project, the design evolved as to location of the parking, placement of the irregular central plaza, and shape of several buildings. The three rectangular gallery spaces that face the curved street remained consistent throughout the process. Here he held fast to the bold and strong forms, using them to anchor the site.[5]

Villanueva utilized an economy of lines for these first studies. He was recording forms as they presented themselves, not eliminating their potential. This is evidenced by the fact that he did not take the time to erase and redraw shapes. Villanueva was comfortable visualizing a spatial organization from a small sketch, then critiquing its qualities for the evolution of the scheme. The abstraction of the small sketches did not hinder the early development of the design. Most importantly, he was able to 'read' these partial forms to translate them into architectural form.

FIGURE 7.12

Aalto, Alvar (1898–1976)

Preliminary studies for Finlandia Hall, Helsinki, 1962/1967–1971, 1973–1975, The Alvar Aalto Museum/Drawing Collection, 30 × 75 cm, Pencil on tracing paper

Alvar Aalto, a Finnish architect first influenced by the international style, created an architecture combining modern and vernacular. Interpreting Aalto's approach, Winfried Nerdinger describes his architecture in terms of 'human functionalism', where the work was less about 'formal, economic or constructional constraints' and more concerned with human purposes (Nerdinger, 1999, p. 15). Much of this approach integrated Finnish cultural identity, and acquired undulating, fluid forms, particularly when viewed in plan.

Aalto began his architectural observations in the small town of Jyväskylä. He completed his formal education in architecture at the Helsinki Technical University in 1921. Initially traveling to Stockholm, he began his internship with Arvid Bjerke in Gothenberg. His first major commission came when he won first prize for the Southwestern Agricultural Co-operative Multiuse Building Competition. The Co-operative was constructed between 1927 and 1929, and another important competition success followed in 1929 with the Tuberculosis Sanatorium in Paimio. He became known in the international arena through his design of the Finnish Pavilion at the World Exposition in Paris (1937) and the Finnish Pavilion at the New York World's Fair (1939) (Pearson, 1978; Schildt, 1989; Nerdinger, 1999). Other important projects include: Villa Mairea (1938–1939); Baker House, Senior Dormitory at MIT (1946–1949); Säynätsalo Town Hall (1951–1952); University of Technology in Otaniem (1955–1964); Opera House at Essen (1959–1961); and Finlandia Hall, Helsinki (1967–1971).

The extensive archive of Aalto's drawings and sketches reveals his unique hand. Besides the light touch and fluid lines, these lines show strong ending points, as if he was hesitating before removing the pencil from the surface or was reinforcing prominent edges. He entered a dialogue with the images, as they contain notes, calculations, and, in many instances, have been oriented from numerous directions. This immersion in the conversation through the sketch also shows marks where he rested the pencil or prodded the sketch for emphasis. Aalto frequently strengthened important walls or boundaries by continually drawing over his lines. The sketches suggest that he held the drawing instrument so loosely that the image appeared to be articulated independent of his hand. This technique gives the sketches a lively, pulsating quality, that could be compared to a Ouija board, where the light touch enables the line to take on a life of its own.

This early sketch for Finlandia Hall (Figure 7.12) demonstrates Aalto's design process, describing the indirect flow of spaces and the non-geometric theme of his mature work (Fleig and Aalto, 1995; Schildt, 1989). Alternating between section and plan, this sketch has been crowded with calculations and partially complete forms. The lower section drawing addresses Aalto's concern for the acoustic qualities of the auditorium in profile. The undulating form of the ceiling also anticipates construction issues. The remainder of the page has been strewn with partial design beginnings, possibly rejected as unpromising directions. The intensely worked plan and section indicate Aalto's absorption in his design process. To animate is to inspire or endow with life. It can also mean to breathe life into or put into motion. Aalto's repeated lines tend to give his sketches a nervous animation suggesting his interaction with the project as a living being. Its liveliness reflects the constant motion of his hand and also breathes life into the future building.

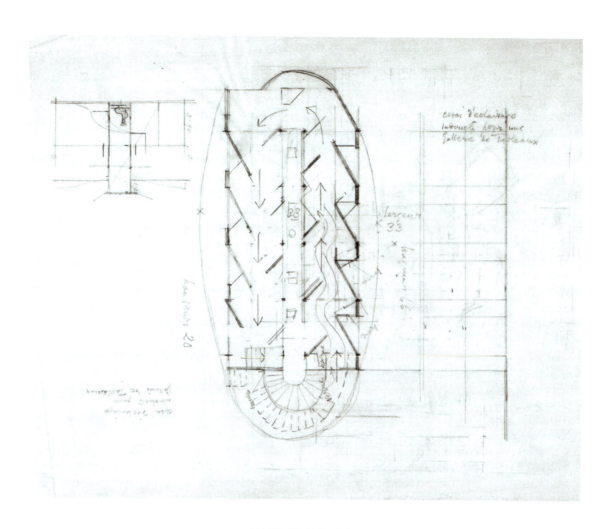

FIGURE 7.13

Gray, Eileen (1879–1976)

Plan, section and elevation, V&A Picture Library, AAD/1980/9/16, 10 × 8 in., Pencil on paper

Best known for her lacquer work, carpet weaving, and interior design, Eileen Gray built several architectural projects in the early years of the twentieth century. Despite her lack of a formal architectural education, her sketches and drawings show an understanding of architectural space, and her buildings, a sensitivity for materials.

Gray was born in Ireland as Kathleen Eileen Moray Smith. Her higher education began at the Slade School of Fine Arts in London. In 1902, she moved to Paris to study drawing, and the same year encountered the restoration of antique lacquer with D. Charles in London. Having inherited sufficient wealth to be independent, in 1907 she returned to Paris to work with the Japanese lacquer master, Seizo Sugawara. By 1910, Gray established a lacquer workshop and a weaving atelier. She opened a decorating shop called Jean Désert in 1922, receiving commissions for interior design. Near this time, she met Jean Badovici, an architectural critic and editor who had received formal education in architecture. He encouraged her talents in architecture and between 1926 and 1929 she built a house for herself and Badovici in the south of France at Roquebrune. Literature establishes that they collaborated on this house, but that Gray designed the project and Badovici's role was that of critic (Constant and Wang, 1996). The house was titled E. 1027 *Maison en bord de mer*. Located on the shore, the design reflected Le Corbusier's tenets of modern architecture. The house was set on *piloti*, organized in an open plan with a terrace overlooking the sea. Gray designed the furniture, successfully integrating it with the architecture. Her architectural work includes another house for herself, the *Tempe à pailla* in Castellar, several apartment renovations in Paris, and numerous unbuilt projects (Hecker and Müller, 1993; Constant, 2000; Constant and Wang, 1996).

This sketch page (Figure 7.13) dates approximately from the 1930s and presents a plan for an art gallery (Constant and Wang, 1996). It references alterations made for her Vacation and Leisure Center (Exhibition Pavilion) in Le Corbusier's Pavilion des Temps Nouveaux. The pencil sketch shows a ruled floor plan with a small section to the right and a faint elevation on the left. The page contains several notes, dimensions, proportional guidelines, and an outlined lozenge shape. This approximate ellipse constitutes the spatial theme of the project, and reflects her concept for circulation through the space. In a fairly small room, Gray was studying sophisticated solutions to lighting the surfaces of the exhibition. The section shows a diagram for light to be emitted from a clerestory. The skylights, situated directly above the sculptures in the center, provide an additional source of illumination. The openings in the walls have been set at forty-five degree angles to experiment with reflected light bouncing off diagonal surfaces.

Gray was walking through the experience of the space with her pencil. She used arrows for the intended direction of the visitors' movement. She also employed wavy parallel lines to express the width of the flow around and between the display panels. In this way, she was visually questioning the scale of the spaces. This also provided an indication of the way observers would perceive the exhibition panels. This zigzag path was a method to move people through the gallery and to provide as much wall area for artwork as possible. Understanding how artwork requires indirect illumination, Gray could envision the light permeating the space from behind the visitors by inhabiting the sketch herself. Sketched lightly in the center she even locates the placement of these objects. The development and evaluation of the project occurred as she sketched and allowed her to project herself into the proposed interior space.

FIGURE 7.14

Barrágan, Luis (1902–1988)

Lomas Verdes, Mexico City, 1964–1973, color marker, Barragán Foundation/ARS

Winner of the prestigious Pritzker Prize in architecture (1980), Luis Barrágan is known for his bold use of color in the design of Mexican regionalism with Mediterranean flavor. He was particularly adept with the integration of landscape and architecture that responded to the environment of his native Mexico (Van Vynckt, 1993).

Born in Guadalajara, he received an engineering diploma with some experience in architectural studies. Aware of the modernist initiatives surfacing in Europe, he traveled to Paris to attend lectures by Le Corbusier. His year in Paris was part of a lifetime of travels, especially to Europe (the Mediterranean coast) and North Africa. The simple forms he observed in North Africa influenced his use of clean shapes constructed in concrete. He built small projects between 1927 and 1936 before starting speculative housing projects in 1936. Founder and director of the Jardines del Pedregal de San Angel, Mexico City (1945–1952), Barrágan opened private practice with Raul Ferrera (Júlbez, Palomar and Eguiarte, 1996; Smith, 1967).

After the early 1940s, his projects were concerned with a blend of vernacular and international styles. He designed several churches such as the Convent of the Capuchinas Sacramentarias (1952–1955), but the buildings most representative of his work were the San Cristobal Stable and the Egerstrom House completed in 1967. This building complex makes use of his skill in landscape design and of massive walls of color. The large flat planes, in a shade of bright pink, have been contrasted by geometric fountains and pools.

Barrágan often sketched using color media. Many of his sketches are bold and abstract, where he employs a blunt lead for a heavy line or chooses media that will give him bright colors. Some of these sketches appear surprisingly minimal, using the fewest lines possible. This sketch (Figure 7.14) represents a study for the Lomas Verdes Project. Beginning approximately 1965, Barrágan and Sordo Madaleno collaborated on various dwelling types and monumental entrances for the subdivision Lomas Verdes. In the early 1970s, streets were laid out and building sites were sold, although in the end little infrastructure was actually constructed (Zanco, 2001). Barrágan and Madaleno had planned for extensive gardens and landscaping, which has been reflected in this sketch.

The sketch exhibits bold vertical lines, accented by equally bold wavy ones. Sketched with a felt tipped pen, the image has been rendered in bright colors – blue for the sky, red and orange for the buildings, yellow and brown for the hillside in the foreground, and green abstractions to represent trees. The streaky lines have been drawn quickly, evidenced by the transparency and very straight strokes of the felt marker. The white showing through behind the color reveals how the ink skipped across the paper. This is unlike the dense saturation of color that happens when the marker rests on the surface. The buildings were drawn first and the sky later, giving the image background and context. The buildings have been set atop a mound, making them seem as though they have grown out of the hills. Each structure has been given a few strokes of the marker for windows. Without these indications of openings, the shards of buildings could have been interpreted as sheer-faced rock. Interestingly, the buildings have been treated very similarly to the background of the sky. This could be a factor of the medium's properties or an intentional tactic to avoid differentiation between building and landscape. Barrágan's architecture, although rectangular and regular, had a unique ability to appear integrated into the landscape. Considering the use of bold color in his architecture, it is fitting that the sketched with bright colors.

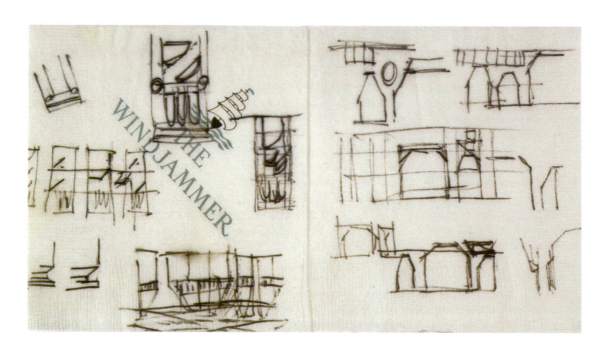

FIGURE 7.15

Moore, Charles Willard (1925–1993)

Elevation studies for campanile and arcade, 1975–1978, The Charles Moore Foundation
for the Study of Place, 5 × 10 in., Ink on paper napkin

An eclectic and playful architect, Charles Moore was an early critic of modernism. Advocating a humanist approach, he often designed colorful buildings evoking historical precedent. Moore sketched constantly using any media at hand, as seen by his many paper napkin sketches. Very facile with pencil and paper, he would sketch to illustrate even non-architectural dialogue (Johnson, 1986). He attended Princeton to earn both a Masters in Fine Arts and a Ph.D., in 1957. He started his practice with private homes, building numerous houses, including eight for himself, over the course of his life (Johnson, 1986).

A dedicated educator, Moore taught and administrated architectural programs in several universities, including Berkeley, Yale and University of California. Some of his best known projects include; Sea Ranch, California (1960s), Kresge College and Faculty Club, University of California, Santa Cruz (1966–1973), St. Matthew's Episcopal Church in California (1979–1983), and Beverly Hills, Civic Center (1982) (Johnson, 1986).

Moore had great talent for working collaboratively with clients and community groups (Johnson, 1986). His architectural projects primarily consisted of simple geometric shapes using compositional balance. Moore's work found distinction in its playful treatment of colors, cutouts, and graphics, and the symbolism was often humorous. The Piazza d'Italia (1975–1978), a small downtown park sandwiched between buildings in central New Orleans, exemplifies this light attitude. The small plaza features water surrounding an island formed in the shape of Italy, with an arcade of columns that has been painted in shades of red and ochre.

The varied and plentiful sketches by Moore express the enthusiasm of his architecture. He often used color and whimsical features in his drawings. Seldom erasing an image, he sketched quickly, dancing between thoughts. The gesture of his body and this continuous dialogue create a narrative of his thinking. Illustrated by this sketch (Figure 7.15) on a paper napkin, one can view evidence of his intense vision. The napkin has been imprinted with the words 'The Windjammer,' the name of a restaurant. It is possible to imagine a scenario that puts Moore in the restaurant awaiting his meal and entering into a conversation about the Piazza d'Italia in New Orleans. Choosing the nearest drawing materials, he began to explore the form of the campanile and arcade. The two sides of the napkin show that he sketched from opposite directions. The reversal may have also derived from the presence of another person. To show the napkin and continue the conversation could have changed the direction of his groundlines. Moore was exploring the proportions and composition of the series of arches with very small sketches, since the cocktail napkin was only five inches square.

Moore's design sketch includes the campanile, with its simple geometric forms, and arches viewed through the exposed structure. Accenting the joints, he drew circles at crucial intersections. He was also trying variations and testing the composition of the three separate pieces that made the vertical tower. On the right half of the napkin he was concentrating on the arcade, where he was grouping various sized arches. The little sketches, some only an inch high, allowed him to view a comparison between forms very quickly.

Moore understood that the physical sketch was no longer valuable after the thinking process was complete. It was more important to sketch at the moment, rather than wait for an appropriate piece of paper. He found the closest and most convenient media at the time, afraid that his ideas would escape him. Since the sketch has been retained and published, he must have put it in his pocket for further reference.

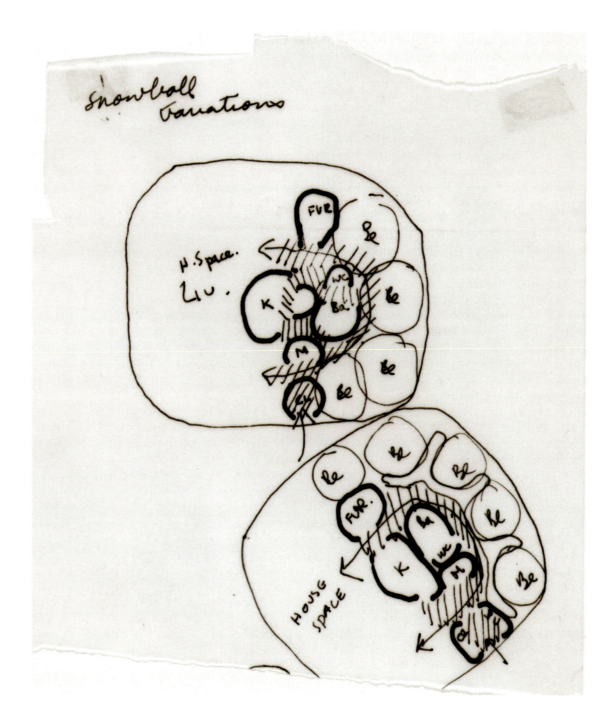

FIGURE 7.16

Smithson, Alison (1928–1993)

Sketch plans for two Snowball Appliance Houses, 1957, Canadian Centre for Architecture,
DR 1995:0052, 12 × 11.5 cm, Pen and black ink on tracing paper

The Smithson's greatest influence on the architectural world came through their writing, teaching, and competition entries. Although devoted to professional practice, they balanced building with theory, disseminating their ideas concerning social issues of housing.

British by nationality, Alison was born in Yorkshire and Peter in County Durham. They met while studying in the Department of Architecture at the University of Durham, Newcastle. Marrying in 1949, they won the commission to design the Hunstanton Secondary Modern School. Active in CIAM, the Smithson's organization of the 1953 conference earned them the adage *Team X*. Their colleague Reyner Banham described their work as brutalist, with dominant use of concrete structures and rationalist form. The Smithson's writings challenged architects to re-examine basic tenets about housing and urban theory. They designed the prototype House of the Future (1956); headquarters for *The Economist* magazine in St. James' Piccadilly (1964); British Embassy in Brasilia (1964) (unbuilt); Garden Building at St. Hilda's College, Oxford (1967–1970); Robin Hood Gardens apartment complex (1966–1972); and buildings at Bath University starting in 1978.

Interested in social aspects of living, the Smithson's most prominent housing project was the Robin Hood Gardens. They designed rows of apartments in linear buildings dispersed with plazas. Eventually unsuccessful because of crime, their sensitive architecture could not keep the complex from falling into social disarray.

Constantly exploring theoretical ideas, the Smithsons used sketches extensively. Many of these sketches take the form of diagrams that they called *ideograms* (Smithson, 2001). These simple images were often very small, using few lines. With these sketches the Smithsons were critically reviewing conceptual theories (analysis) while demonstrating a visual communication between the two of them. With their precise qualities, the sketches feel cartoon-like, having firm, unbroken lines and act very much like a *parti*. This sketch by Alison (Figure 7.16) is a diagram for an *appliance house*. Iterated in black ink on tracing paper, the lines are single thickness, some showing heavier and others lighter, as if two pens were used. Soon after the prototype for the House of the Future, the appliance houses were based on the concept of prefabricated housing. This intention was not so much concerned with the manufacture of these units but with the spaces necessary for the inhabitants. The Smithson's had been conceiving of two different organizations, one linear and the other clustered like a snowball.[6] This small sketch shows numerous circular shapes within a larger enclosure of the snowball *parti*. The notion of this house was to gather all of the 'appliances' or functional aspects of the house (on one side) leaving a large area for family living.

These very concise sketches reveal Alison Smithson's thinking. The bedrooms remain circles in each iteration, possibly because circles are faster to draw than squares and these sketches were not concerned with the bedrooms but rather the 'appliance' spaces. With this example, Alison Smithson was rendering the functional spaces of most concern to her, abstracting the rooms less important at the moment. More time has been taken to sketch the kitchen, for example, although it takes on an amoeba shape. This sketch emphasizes the popularity of 'bubble' diagrams. A technique to study only one aspect of a project, bubble diagrams are not plans in a strict sense, but show adjacencies. Here the 'bubbles' inflluenced the shape of the rooms in this early stage of the process.

FIGURE 7.17

Candela, Felix (1910–1997)

Paragnas en San Jeromino, 1960, Avery Architectural and Fine Arts Library, DR 69-12,
Approx. 12 × 16 in., Marker sketch with shadows

From an early fascination with mathematics and structural shell construction, Felix Candela designed many innovative buildings, primarily in Mexico. He received an engineering education at the Escuela Superior de Arquitectura in the city of his birth, Madrid (1927–1935). As a result of his military service he emigrated to Mexico as a refugee. Newly settled in Mexico, Candela teamed with his brother Antonio to start the construction company Cubiertas Ala. The Cosmic Ray Pavilion for the University City, Mexico City (1952), provided one of his first opportunities to experiment with shell construction. This building gave him international attention and other projects followed such as the Church of San Antonio de las Huertas, Mexico City (1956), and the 'umbrella' structures used in warehouses. In 1971, he emigrated to the United States and he continued to provide services as a structural and construction consultant, architect, and university professor in Mexico and the United States until his death in 1997 (Smith, 1967; Van Vynckt, 1993).

Depending on intuition and experimentation balanced with calculation, Candela, although often an architectural consultant, was able to influence design through the requirements of the structure. His attitude emphasized economic and material efficiency, and the inherent strength of concrete reinforced with steel mesh. Many of his shell structures were remarkably thin where he was able to find strength in such shapes as warped hyperbolic paraboloids (Smith, 1967; Van Vynckt, 1993). The graceful shapes were particularly appropriate for ecclesiastical architecture, and he collaborated on projects such as the Church of San José Obrero in Monterrey (1959) and the Chapel of San Vicente de Paul, Coyoacan (1960).

This sketch (Figure 7.17) is a study of a concrete shell structure. It was sketched on tracing paper, first outlined with pencil guidelines and then reinforced with a felt pen. The left side of the sketch has more guidelines and appears more controlled. The right contains fewer pencil lines and more corrections occur with the ink lines. This may stem from his eagerness to see the whole impression quickly, before he constructed all the guidelines. Or perhaps he was impatient to view the whole and, having understood its shape, could quickly finish the right half less carefully (particularly true if Candela was right handed).

With brief guidelines to follow, the sketch shows firm, definitive lines. Most of them have been rendered as a single mark, but a few have been corrected to refine an angle. With the shape mind one could speculate that he was concerned with the look of the entire shape since he used an elevation view. He may have needed to comprehend its totality, because it had been studied previously in diagrams. Because of his extensive experience with concrete shell structures, he may have intuitively understood the structure once it emerged on the page.

Candela's primary concerns are revealed in what he sketched and what he left out. The dimensions of the folded plates were important as he tried to show depth through shadows. He was obviously concerned with the structure over contextual issues, since the sketch sits alone on the page. One may speculate that the building was either a prototype, or that he was comfortable in allowing the primary architect to be worried about the concerns of the site and program.

This sketch may have been used to comprehend proportions. Candela may have needed to view the folds in relationship to the height and angles of the incline. He was also studying the contrasting texture of materials. Most likely, he was anticipating glass on the inside of the peaked arches because these areas have been rendered differently than the concrete.

FIGURE 7.18

Rossi, Aldo (1931–1997)

Perspective sketches, sketch plans, and detail sketches for the Centro Direzionale, Florence, 1977, Canadian Centre for Architecture, DR 1987; 0152, 29.7 × 21 cm, Blue ballpoint pen and black felt tip marker on glossy white paper

Aldo Rossi left a tremendous amount of thought-provoking sketches representing his design process. These playful sketches were part of intense research and also served as a method to facilitate his imagination (Rossi, 2000).

Rossi was born in Milan and attended the Milan Polytechnic, graduating in 1959. Upon leaving school, he became an assistant to Ludovico Quaroni at the School of Urban Studies in Arezzo. Also in 1959, Rossi joined the *Il Contemporanco* editorial staff, becoming editor of *Casabella* in 1964. Beginning his architectural career with competitions, theoretical, and small projects, he also held positions in academia – professor at the Milan Polytechnic, the Federal Polytechnic of Zurich, and the University of Venice. Serving as visiting professor in such schools as Cornell, Cooper Union, Yale, and Harvard, Rossi questioned paradigms of architecture and the city. He published his first book, *The Architecture of the City*, in 1966 (Rossi, 1981).

Rossi's architecture references recurring themes of ritual and memory. He felt strongly about place as a regional, cultural, and yet global concept (Rossi, 1981). Rossi received the Pritzker prize for architecture in 1990 in consideration of his body of work, including the Cemetery of San Cataldo, Modena, Italy (1971); Teatro del Mondo, Venice (1979); Civic Center, Perugia, Italy (1982); Carlo Felice Theater, Genoa (1983); and Center for Contemporary Art, Vassiviére, France (1988).

Rossi's vast number of published sketches demonstrate how he utilized images in the process of design and as a dialogue between the past and the future. These pages are layered with elevations, bird's-eye axonometric views, and distorted perspectives, constantly utilizing the sketch to enforce multiple viewpoints (Rossi, 2000). Many of the sketches, as part of complete pages, intersect and overlap with these views. Rendered in color with active, fast lines, the sketches often include full context and become dense conglomerations of cities. Paolo Portoghesi writes that Rossi's interest in viewing a design from many angles stems from an idea of *torsione*, or twisting. This use of *torsione*, was 'a means of maintaining contact with memories without abandoning them' (Rossi, 2000, p. 13).

This sketch (Figure 7.18) reflects the playful nature of Rossi's design process. The page contains axonometric, plan, and plan/oblique sketches, all oriented to provide multiple views. The images show two types of pen, one lighter in tone, and the other facilitating a free flow of ink and rendering a darker line. Here, a second layer refined his first thoughts and acted as guidelines, encouraging a level of critique. Several of the brief plans have been dimensioned or reinforced to show he studied them more thoroughly than others. At the bottom of the page has been placed three slender towers topped with fully extended flags and a door piercing a crenellated wall. The largest axonometric, describing two adjacent buildings, has been flanked by a yard appearing to contain a giraffe or a horse.

The cube-shaped plan/oblique to the upper left has been detailed with a pediment over the door, a cut corner, and a long walkway. The building appears surprisingly like an animal, especially since it was given two blue ink eyes. The remainder of the page has been left relatively monochromatic, accenting the eyes. Perhaps as Rossi was sketching the small structure, with its corner cut ears and the pediment nose, he could not resist adding a circle to enhance the nose and two blue eyes. This page reflects Rossi's strong sense of architecture as being permeated with memories and evoking associations.

NOTES

1. Suggested by Dr. Marco Frascari in a seminar at Georgia Institute of Technology, Atlanta, Georgia, USA, in the late 1980s.
2. Another example of a theoretical concept introduced by Dr. Marco Frascari.
3. Biographical information on Takeo Yasui provided by So Hatano, Researcher at the Tokyo Institute of Technology, Japan.
4. Information provided by The National Archives of Australia.
5. Paulina Villanueva kindly sent me a series of sketches describing the early phases of this project. She explained that Villanueva considered proportions at this early stage. Since she was given the task to translate the sketched thought into a drawing, she questioned the preciseness of his sketch. Paulina writes that he took out a wooden ruler and showed her the precise measurements of the sketch.
6. Background information about this sketch provided by the archives of the Canadian Centre for Architecture, Montreal.

BIBLIOGRAPHY

Allen, G. (1980). *Charles Moore*. Whitney Library of Design.

Altherr, A. (1968). *Three Japanese Architects, Mayekawa, Tange, Sakakura*. Verlag Arthur Niggli AG/ Teufen.

Andersson, H.O. and Bedoire, F. (1986). *Swedish Architecture Drawings 1940–1970*. Byggförlaget.

Baker, G.H. (1996). *Le Corbusier: The Creative Search*. Spon.

Berdini, P. (1985). *Walter Gropius*. Nicola Zanichelli Editore.

Blaser, W. (1965). *Mies van der Rohe*. Praeger.

Blaser, W. (1997). *Mies van der Rohe*. Birkhäuser Verlag.

Bognar, B. (1996). *Togo Murano: Master Architect of Japan*. Rizzoli.

Busignani, A. (1973). *Gropius*. Hamlyn.

Cohen, J-L. (1996). *Mies van der Rohe*. E & FN Spon.

Constant, C. (1994). *The Woodland Cemetery: Toward a Spiritual Landscape, Erik Gunnar Asplund and Sigurd Lewerentz 1915–61*. Byggförlager.

Constant, C. (2000). *Eileen Gray*. Phaidon.

Constant, C. and Wang, W. eds (1996). *Eileen Gray: An Architecture for all Senses*. Deutsches Architecktur Museum/Harvard University Press.

Cook, J.W. and Klotz, H. (1973). *Conversations with Architects*. Praeger.

Cruickshank, D. ed. (1988). *Erik Gunnar Asplund*. The Architect's Journal.

De Long, D.G. ed. (1996). *Frank Lloyd Wright: Designs for an American Landscape, 1922–32*. Harry N. Abrams/ Canadian Centre for Architecture/Library of Congress/Frank Lloyd Wright Foundation.

De Long, D.G. ed. (1998). *Frank Lloyd Wright and the Living City*. Vitra Design Museum/Skira Editore.

Drexler, A. (1960). *Ludwig Mies van der Rohe*. George Braziller.

Drexler, A. ed. (1986). *An Illustrated Catalogue of the Mies van der Rohe Drawings in the Museum of Modern Art*. Garland Series.

Eisenman, P. (2003). *Giuseppe Terragni: Transformations Decompositions Critiques*. Monacelli Press.

Fernie, E.C. (1995). *Art History and Its Method: A Critical Anthology*. Phaiden Press.

Fitch, J.M. (1960). *Walter Gropius*. George Braziller.

Fleig, K. and Aalto, E. (1995). *Alvar Aalto, Volumes 1–3*. Birkhäuser.

Frampton, K. and Futagawa, Y. (1983). *Modern Architecture 1851–1945*. Rizzoli.

Giurgola, R. and Mehta, J. (1975). *Louis I. Kahn*. Westview Press.

Hecker, S. and Müller, C.F. (1993). *Eileen Gray: Works and Projects*. Editorial Gustavo Gill.

Hewitt, M. (1985). Representational Forms and Modes of Conception. *Journal of Architectural Education*, 39/2.

Holmdahl, G., Lind, S.I. and Ödeen, K. eds (1950). *Gunnar Asplund Architect 1885–1940: Plans Sketches and Photographs*. AB Tidskriften Byggmästaren.

Isaacs, R. (1991). *Gropius*. Little, Brown and Co.

Izzo, A. and Gugbitosi, C. (1981). *Frank Lloyd Wright: Three-quarters of a Century in Drawings*. Horizon Press.

Jencks, C. (1973a). *Le Corbusier and the Tragic View of Architecture*. Harvard University Press.

Jencks, C. (1973b). *Modern Movements in Architecture*. Anchor Books.

Johnson, E.J. ed. (1986). *Charles Moore: Buildings and Projects 1949–1986*. Rizzoli.

Júlbez, J.M.B., Palomar, J. and Eguiarte, G. (1996). *The Life and Work of Luis Barrágan*. Rizzoli.

Kahn, L.I. (1975). *Light is the Theme: Louis I. Kahn and the Kimbell Art Museum*. Kimbell Art Foundation.

Kahn, L.I. (1981). *Drawings/Louis I. Kahn*. Access Press/Max Protetch Gallery.

Kahn, L.I. (1987). *The Louis I. Kahn Archive. Personal Drawings: The Complete Illustrated Catalogue of the Drawings of Louis I. Kahn*. University of Pennsylvania/Pennsylvania Historical and Museum Commission.

Kahn, L.I., Scully, V.J. and Holman, W.G. (1978). *The Travel Sketches of Louis I. Kahn*. The Academy.

Kaufmann, E. and Raeburn, B. (1960). *Frank Lloyd Wright: Writings and Buildings*. Frank Lloyd Wright Foundation/Meridian.

Keim, K. ed. (1996). *An Architectural Life: Memoirs and Memories of Charles W. Moore*. Little, Brown and Co.

Kultermann, U. (1960). *New Japanese Architecture*. Praeger.

Latour, A. ed. (1991). *Louis I. Kahn: Writings, Lectures, Interviews*. Rizzoli.

Le Corbusier (1981). *Le Corbusier Sketchbooks, Volumes 1–4*. The Architectural History Foundation, MIT Press and Foundation Le Corbusier.

Littlejohn, D. (1984). *Architect: The Life and Work of Charles W. Moore*. Holt, Rinehart and Winston.

Lobel, J. (1979). *Between Silence and Light: Spirit in the Architecture of Louis I Kahn*. Shambhala.

Lyndon, D. (1994). *Chambers for a Memory Place*. MIT Press.

Reynolds, J.M. (2001). *Maekawa, Kunio and the Emergence of Japanese Modernist Architecture*. University of California Press.

Nerdinger, W. (1985). *Walter Gropius*. Bauhaus-Archiv/Busch-Reisinger Museum.

Nerdinger, W. ed. (1999). *Alvar Aalto: Toward a Human Modernism*. Prestel Verlag.

Pearson, P.D. (1978). *Alvar Aalto and the International Style*. Whitney Library of Design.

Pevesner, N., Richards, J.M. and Sharp, D. (2000). *The Anti-Rationalists and the Rationalists*. The Architectural Press.

Quantrill, M. (1983). *Alvar Aalto: A Critical Study*. Schocken Books.

Richards, J.M., Pevsner, N. and Sharp, D. eds (2000). *The Anti-Rationalists and the Rationalists*. The Architectural Press.

Román, A. (2003). *Eero Saarinen: An Architecture of Multiplicity*. Princeton Architectural Press.

Rossi, A. (1981). *A Scientific Autobiography*. Oppositions Books/MIT Press.

Rossi, A. (2000). *Aldo Rossi: The Sketchbooks, 1990–1997*. Thames and Hudson.

Rossi, A. edited by Adjmi, M. (1991). *Aldo Rossi: Architecture, 1981–1991*. Princeton Architectural Press.

Roth, L.M. (1979). *A Concise History of American Architecture*. Harper and Row.

Ruusuvuori, A. ed. (1981). *Alvar Aalto, 1998–1976*. Museum of Finnish Architecture.

Saarinen, E. edited by Saarinen, A. (1962). *Eero Saarinen on His Work*. Yale University Press.

Schildt, G. (1989). *Alvar Aalto: The Mature Years*. Rizzoli.

Schulze, F. (1985). *Mies van der Rohe: A Critical Biography*. The University of Chicago Press.

Schulze, F. ed. (1989). *Mies van der Rohe: Critical Essays*. The Museum of Modern Art.

Schumacher, T.L. (1991). *Surface and Symbol: Giuseppe Terragni and the Architecture of Italian Rationalism*. Princeton Architectural Press.

Smith, C.B. (1967). *Builders in the Sun: Five Mexican Architects*. Architectural Book Publishing.

Smithson, A. and P. (2001). *The Charged Void: Architecture*. Monacelli Press.

Stewart, D.B. (1987). *The Making of a Modern Japanese Architecture, 1868 to the Present*. Kodansha.

Suzuki, H., Banham, R. and Kobayashi, K. (1985). *Contemporary Architecture of Japan, 1958–1984*. Rizzoli.

Trachtenberg, M. and Hyman, I. (1986). *Architecture: From Prehistory to Post-Modernism*. Abrams.

Turnbull, J. and Navaretti, P.Y. (1998). *The Griffins in Australia and India: The Complete Works and Projects of Walter Burley Griffin and Marion Mahony Griffin*. The Miegunyah Press.

Turner, J. ed. (1996). *The Dictionary of Art*. Grove.

Tyng, A. (1984). *Beginnings: Louis I. Kahn's Philosophy of Architecture*. Wiley.

Tzonis, A. (2001). *Le Corbusier: The Poetics of Machine and Metaphor*. Universe.

Tzonis, A. gen. ed., Nerdinger, W. ed. (1990). *The Walter Gropius Archive, Volumes 1–4*. Garland Publishing/ Harvard University Art Museums.

Van Vynckt, R. ed. (1993). *International Dictionary of Architects and Architecture*. St. James Press.

Villanueva, P. and Pintó, M. (2000). *Carlos Raúl Villanueva*. Princeton Architectural Press.

Walden, R. ed. (1997). *The Open Hand: Essays on Le Corbusier*. MIT Press.

Wrede, S. (1980). *The Architecture of Erik Gunnar Asplund*. MIT Press.

Wright, F.L. (1953). *The Future of Architecture*. Horizon Press.

Yoshida, Y. ed. (1983). *Louis I. Kahn: Conception and Meaning*. A+U, Architecture and Urbanism.

Zanco, F. ed. (2001). *Luis Barrágan: The Quiet Revolution*. Skira, Barragan Foundation/Vitra Design Museum.

Zevi, B. (1980). *Giuseppe Terragni*. Zanichelli Editore.

CHAPTER 8

CONTEMPORARY (1980–)

In a different approach from the previous chapters, selected prominent designers who are currently practicing were asked to submit a sketch of their choice for inclusion in this book. They were also requested to send a brief biography and a short description of their thoughts while completing the sketch. In most cases, the architects sent biographical materials and a paragraph or two describing the architecture or the impetus for its design. Very few replied with discussion of their thoughts concerning the sketch during the design process. It may have been difficult to remember specific processes; or, perhaps this activity was hard to translate into words, and thus the process remains elusive even to those who constantly use sketches.

It is always challenging to distance oneself to assess a current condition; this is the case with architectural sketches and likewise with architectural style. Viewing contemporary conditions echo this concern. Without the advantage of historical perspective, there are several trends and movements at the turn of the twenty-first century that elucidate a discussion of architectural sketches.

Contemporary architecture is as diverse as the architects practicing. Architects such as Frank Gehry have been building signature buildings around the world, while Daniel Libeskind was recently awarded the re-construction of the World Trade Center site. Japanese architects, such as Kazuyo Sejima, have been designing minimalist architecture with ephemeral and illusionary materials. Elizabeth Diller and Ricardo Scofidio question the built environment with their thought-provoking and theoretical installations. Many architects have been exploring newly developed building materials to be more energy efficient, create diverse visual expression, and lighting effects. Still other practitioners have been exploring the design and fabrication of buildings through use of digital media. One development common to all these contemporary architects concerns the question of how digital technology influences their practice and the buildings they construct.

SKETCHES; DIGITAL MEDIA

Computers are a vital component of contemporary architectural practice, and very few firms can successfully build without their use. Digital representations are employed in all phases of architectural production, from early conceptual ideas to construction management. They are particularly effective for contract documents, as details can easily be carried between drawings. They are vital to structural analysis, tracking the performance and integration of building systems, and presentation renderings, to name a few. For many years the contribution of the computer was limited to CAD documents, but the digital world has expanded to infiltrate every aspect of the building process.

One of the last areas to embrace the computer has been the conceptual stages of the project – the initial sketches. Hand sketches, so representative of the intent and personality of architects, have long been considered sacred. Recently, new digital programs have become available to facilitate this intimate thinking process. Digital sketching programs such as Sketch-Up have attempted to imitate conceptual thinking. If a sketch is defined as being preparatory to something else, and also consists of simple forms similar to an outline, then these digital images may indeed be viewed as architectural sketches. The digital medium easily and quickly forms primary geometric shapes, similar to architects' hand-constructed diagrams. The shapes, devoid of detail, could also be considered preliminary because they provide basic conceptual information prior to design development. The more these programs increase their speed and ability to manipulate (form and deform) shapes, the more they replicate the creative impulses of hand sketches. Whether they are truly as effective, only their extensive use will determine.

It is obvious, however, that computer sketches of even simple shapes can be limiting. In most cases, it takes substantially more time to render details digitally, especially perspectives. Digital programs tend to create straight-sided objects more easily than rounded, although this problem is quickly being rectified. A digital program that will stretch the shapes and then allow them to be viewed from numerous perspectives certainly has advantages. In many cases, the 'true' look of the image depends upon the needs and intent of each architect. In some situations, the more ambiguous object encourages architects to derive inspiration from the undefined form.

The interpretive qualities of the imagination sort the undefined as the human mind wishes to make sense of the fragments. The philosopher and psychologist James Gibson found that 'a picture cannot at the same time possess high fidelity for something concrete and high univocality for something abstract' (1982, p. 248). In the same line of thinking, but in different words, Richard Wollheim supports this theory: 'we cannot, at one and the same moment, see a picture as configuration and as *trompe l'oeil*' (1974, p. 29). Providing absolute clarity early in the process may not always be possible or even desirable. Similar to a caricature, the deformation or exaggeration might prove to be more insightful. The use of the computer for sketching may therefore suggest an inherent conflict between precision and imprecision.

The digital image can be seen but not felt. The direct relationship between the pen/pencil and the paper may, for some architects, provide an intimate connection to the object of their creation. The hand gestures of the drawing instrument add expression to their sketches. Although technology has replaced keyed coordinates with the stylus and more responsive mouse controls, the human body is still separated from the image emerging on the screen. The immediacy and personal control of the hand sketch may encourage thinking in a way that digital technology cannot.

The advantages and disadvantages of both media are numerous and the success of each of these forms of sketches may be determined by their time, place, and intention. As mentioned earlier, when solicited for sketches to be included in this volume, nearly all of the contemporary architects contacted sent in hand sketches. This is surprising, since they were given the opportunity to send either digital or hand sketches. This may be particularly revealing, since many of these architects use computers extensively in their design process and throughout the development of the project. Either they still use hand sketches for initial design thoughts, or when a 'sketch' was requested they thought first of one completed by hand. Very few of the architects sent a statement explaining what they were thinking when sketching. This brought to light several issues in the making of sketches. First, these prominent and busy architects had little time to explain their design thinking. Second, it meant that remembering or writing down a visual thought process was difficult for them, considering the time that has passed.

Whatever their form, sketches take other roles in the design and construction process besides conceptual discovery. As suggested in the general Introduction, architects additionally use them for recording impressions, evaluating and communicating ideas, as a way to facilitate observation, and because they enjoy the activity and learning that comes from sketching. Architects also employ sketches in various stages of process, such as exploring details, making changes during construction, or during intra-office visual communication.

Architects such as Greg Lynn utilize advanced technologies to invent fluid, amorphous forms. These abstract forms can be more easily viewed in perspective and analyzed (such as a section cut) with computer rendering. Frank Gehry, although using sketches extensively for early ideas, relies heavily on the computer to develop and visualize his complex shapes. Zaha Hadid provokes theoretical constructs with paintings and digital images as a starting point to locate form.

THEORETICAL EXPLORATIONS

Postmodern philosophy has influenced the drawings and sketches used by contemporary architects. The investigation of process is being explored as the item in constant flux, and as a factor of transition. This constantly evolving mode of communication leaves open the opportunity for translation and interpretation. A movement called *genetic criticism* is exemplary of this thought (Jenny, 1989; De Biasi, 1989; Robinson-Valery, 1989). Investigating the *rough draft* as a process is not easily compared to the final product, the genetic critic must interpret the transformation of the text through stages of editing and revising. This method finds value in the unfinished remnants of the thought process caused by refinement and development. Not necessarily a linear process, this study is interested in the fluid, interpretive state of the text. Recent interest in the concept of the grotesque stresses similar ideas such as transitory and constantly moving meaning, the object of the grotesque as hovering between the known and the unknown, and the paradoxical qualities that elude interpretation (Harpham, 1982). Writings by philosophers concerning deconstruction and the constantly interpretable text can view the image as fluctuating in meaning (Hans, 1980, 1981; Kearney, 1988).

Architects have always been curious about process. The transformation of conceptual inspiration into form (a building) is both elusive and magical. Difficult to define, creativity seems to appear at random in certain people. The ability to sketch and to visually represent concepts is a coveted skill. Humans are not impressed by the ability to speak, but the ability to draw may be compared to the talents of writing poetry or charismatic public speaking (Eco, 1976). From the Renaissance, prominent architects' and artists' skills were assigned mythical proportions. They appeared to have superhuman talents and became Godlike in their reputations (Kris and Kurz, 1979). Their 'divine' abilities were considered magic.

Several contemporary architects have gained a reputation through theoretical investigations. Architects such as Daniel Libeskind began his career disseminating his beliefs through drawings. These fragmented and complex drawings became visual debate. Upon becoming a common name in the architectural realm, he began to receive commissions for buildings. Architects such as Aldo Rossi and Massimo Scolari have published fantasy drawings as a way to purport theoretical investigations. The question of the text, again referencing postmodern philosophy, may suggest the blurring of the terms *architecture* and *architectural*. The question arises whether a drawing that is architectural can be considered architecture. Since drawings and sketches can represent theory and themselves be an act of theory, it would be consistent to conclude they are representative comparable to the representational qualities of architecture (buildings).

Contemporary architects are exploring the design process and conceptual thinking, utilizing new media to manipulate images in new ways. Regardless of the medium used, architects still rely on the *image* to evoke a dialogue. This book has explored the media techniques, uses, and meaning behind the images architects use in the process of design. Not surprisingly, the freehand examples from Renaissance architects differ little in technique with those from contemporary architects. This is primarily because most architects, contemporary and historic, use graphite pencils and ink pens to explore their thoughts. Far more differences begin to surface when comparing various movements and the architects' educations or styles. It may be argued that the greatest development in the evolution of sketches has been the emergence of the computer. This is not necessarily true, however, since the sketches' intentions remain constant, although the media has changed. Sketches have been and will continue to be conduits of dialogue.

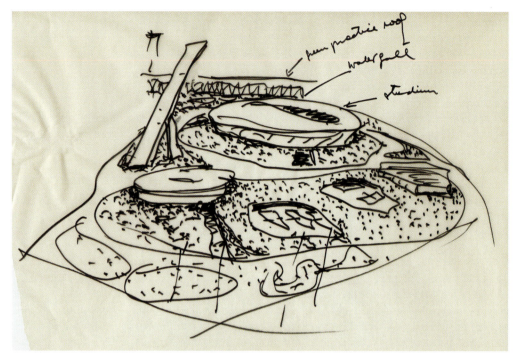

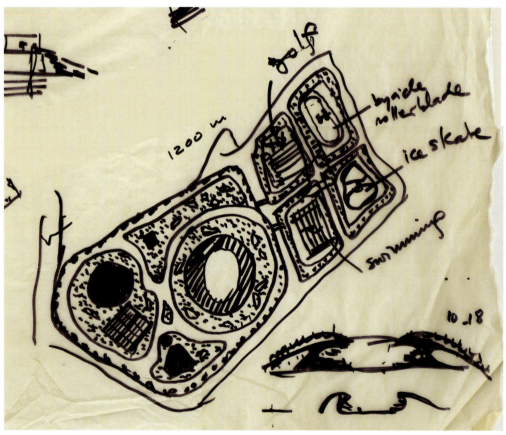

FIGURE 8.1

Agrest, Diana (1945)

Sport City, Design process: plan study, overall view, October 18, 2003, Sport City, Shanghai, China, Aerial view: 13 × 9.5 in., Plan: 13 × 10.5 in., Black ink on trace paper

An educator and theorist in addition to her practice, Diana Agrest has studied semiotics and film as ways to question the ability of architecture to represent. She has worked extensively with urban issues winning the competition for a Master Plan and Urban Design Proposal for five square miles in the center of Shanghai, China, and was a Fellow at the Institute for Architecture and Urban Studies in New York where she was also the Director of the Advanced Workshop in Architecture and Urban Form.

Argentine born, Agrest graduated in architecture from the University of Buenos Aires in 1967. She continued her studies in Paris at the Ecole Pratique des Hautes Etudes and the Centre du Recherche d'Urbanisme. A Professor of Architecture at the Cooper Union in New York City, she has also taught at Columbia, Princeton, and Yale Universities and the UP 8, Paris, France. She is a principal of Agrest and Gandelsonas, founded in 1980 and of Diana Agrest Architect in New York City. A few of their most recent projects include the Melrose Community Center, South Bronx, New York (1998–2000) and the Breukelen Community Center, New York (2002–2005), and urban master plans such as the Vision Plan for Red Bank, New York (1992–1997).

Using the tools of a theorist, Agrest has published numerous books and articles. Her books include *The Sex of Architecture* (editors, Agrest/Conway/Weisman), *Agrest and Gandelsonas, Works,* and *Architecture from Without: Theoretical Framings for a Critical Practice.*[1]

Incredibly facile with ink, this pair of sketches (Figure 8.1) conveys Agrest's exploration of the design for Sport City, located in Shanghai, China. The black ink is bold and expressive. As a result of its heaviness, she needed to further intensify the contrast between the buildings and their surroundings by solidly filling in the buildings in the plan. Devoid of erasures, the confident lines narrate the entire story of the project with efficiency. The site has been rendered with paths and stippling most likely replicating grass. The marks giving texture to the grass have been placed hurriedly as they become commas. Out of scale, certainly they were not to represent grass but instead to provide an alternative texture to the buildings to make the sketch easier to comprehend. The textured articulation ends at the boundaries of the project, without providing context. On the plan Agrest has identified portions of the program with words, such as golf, swimming, and roller-blades. The buildings were easy to distinguish by their shapes but in the abstraction of the small sketch it would have been difficult to render the swimming pool so that it was recognizable in plan. Thus, the notations clarified the details less easy to recognize.

The sketches in plan and overall view intensify the relationship between forms on the site. The white of the paths surrounding the buildings help them to appear as floating islands. The three-dimensional view shows the negative space between the structures in a very different way. Here the foreshortening of the space suggests the dynamic nature of the cylinders as growing out of the landscape. Possibly used for comparison or in reference to each other, both sketches have been viewed from a corner. This may indicate that Agrest found significance in the orientation, either a reference to north or viewed from a point of distinction.

This design sketch appears both vague and precise simultaneously. The simple geometric shapes act as placeholders in the master plan, whereas Agrest did not want to forget the sports aspect of this complex.

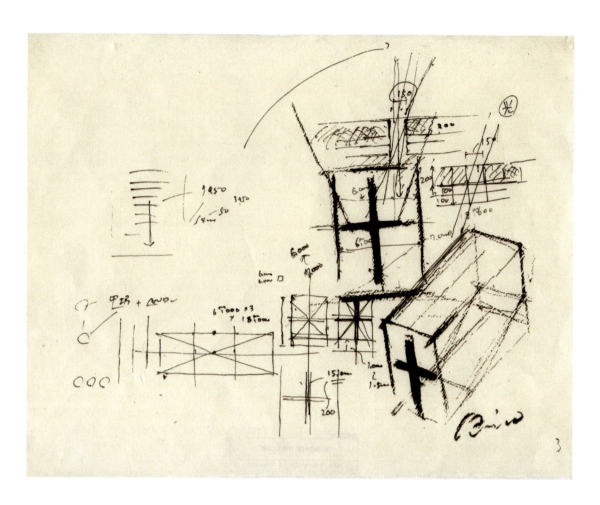

FIGURE 8.2

Ando, Tadao (1941)

Preliminary design sketch, light slit on the altar, 1987, Church of the Light, Ibaraki, Osaka, Japan, 11.7 × 8.5 in., Felt pen on Japanese paper (*washi*)

Self-educated, Tadao Ando is one of the most widely regarded architects currently working in Japan. He was born in Osaka, Japan, in 1941, where he established his architectural office, Tadao Ando Architect & Associates. Through his career he has won numerous awards for design, including the Pritzker Architecture Prize (1995), the Royal Gold Medal from the Royal Institute of British Architects (1997), and the Person of Cultural Merit (2003). He has taught in several universities including visiting at Yale University, Columbia University, and Harvard University, and he holds a professorship at Tokyo University. A few of his best known works include: Rokko Housing I, Kobe (1983); Water Temple, Awaji Island (1991); FABRICA Benetton Communications Research Center, Treviso (2000); and Sayamaike Historical Museum, Osaka (2001).[2]

This page (Figure 8.2) displays preliminary sketches for the Church of the Light in Ibaraki, Osaka, Japan. It was designed in 1987–1988, and underwent construction during 1988–1989.

> It consists of a rectangular volume sliced through at a fifteen-degree angle by a completely freestanding wall that separates the entrance from the chapel. Light penetrates the profound darkness of this box through a cross which is cut out of the altar wall. The floor and pews are made of rough scaffolding planks, which are low cost and also ultimately suited to the character of the space. I have always used natural materials for parts of a building that come into contact with people's hands or feet, as I am convinced that materials having substance, such as wood or concrete, are invaluable for building, and that it is essentially through our senses that we become aware of architecture. … [O]penings have been limited in this space, for light shows its brilliance only against a backdrop of darkness. Nature's presence is also limited to the element of light and is rendered exceedingly abstract. In responding to such an abstraction, the architecture grows continually purer. The linear pattern formed on the floor by rays from the sun and a migrating cross of light expresses with purity man's relationship with nature.

The sketch has been rendered with black ink on heavy (Japanese) paper. The black ink is very dense in places (such as the crosses), while in other areas it skips off of the heavy paper in haste. The ink shows strong contrast to the white paper and is very definitive. Architects, artists, and authors have feared the blank page because the first stroke sets the stage for what comes after: the entirely white paper can be intimidating. The blank sheet expects something profound, and any marks stand out strongly in the vast whiteness. Ando does not erase or scratch out any images, but he finds a blank space in which to draw. He sketches confidently, allowing the forms to overlap as his ideas flow.

The page contains several sketches in plan and axonometric. One small sketch appears to be a plan for the organization of the pews in the chapel or the processional movement, a rectangle with many horizontals. The shaded sketches are details showing the thickness of the walls and how the light would glow through the cross opening. The ink used to make the crosses creates a reversal; the wall was meant to be dark and the cross glowing with light.

The minimal forms tell the story of a conceptually strong approach to the light in a small chapel. In writing about the importance of sketches in design process, Ando writes: 'my sketch[es] usually help me to clear and refine the initial image and to integrate it with architectural space and details.'

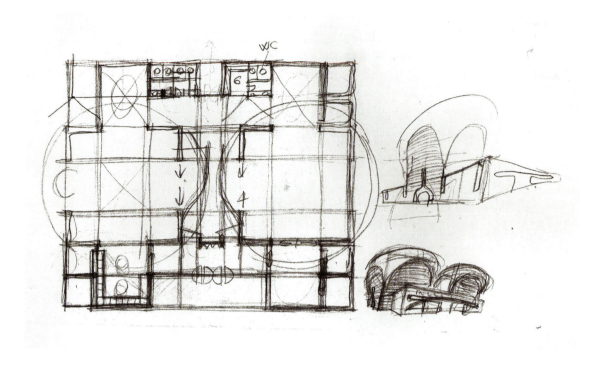

FIGURE 8.3

Botta, Mario (1943)

Studies for the ground floor plan and verifications of the building's volume and shape, 1996,
The Cymbalista Synagogue and Jewish Heritage Centre in Tel Aviv, Israel, 1998,
31 × 50 cm, Pencil on white sketching paper

Mario Botta's reputation is international, his architecture is both modern and contemporary. Christian Norberg-Schultz writes that he infuses his buildings with a strong sense of place and meaning (Botta, 1984).

Born in an area of Switzerland near the Italian border (Mendrisio, Ticino), Botta's first experience with architecture was an apprenticeship in the architectural firm of Carloni and Camenisch in Lugano. He left this office to attain further education at the Art College in Milan and the University Institute of Architecture in Venice. He was directed in his studies by Carlo Scarpa and Giuseppe Mazzariol, and had the opportunity to meet and work with Le Corbusier and Louis I. Kahn.[3]

Beginning his own private practice in 1970, Botta found distinction with his designs for houses, museums, and churches near Ticino. Several of his most recent and celebrated projects include: Theatre and Cultural Center André Malraux, Chambéry, France (1987); SFMOMA Museum of Modern Art, San Francisco (1995); Kyobo Tower, Seoul (2003); and Office building Tata CS, New Delhi (2003). Botta has been honored with awards such as the Merit Award for Excellence in Design by the American Institute of Architects.

Botta likens his sketches to fragments of a large mosaic of possible designs, from early concepts to the final details. They are the notes throughout the process, traces of particular solutions, and messages to help find conclusions. For Botta, sketches are the memories involving intuitions and alterations behind a definitive design.[4]

Botta clearly maintains a constant dialogue with his sketches. This image (Figure 8.3) is a sketch for the Cymbalista Synagogue and Jewish Heritage Centre in Tel Aviv. The organization of the project was to consider two spaces of equal size and importance, a synagogue and a lecture hall. On the campus of Tel Aviv University, these two spaces, expressed on the exterior by two towers, speak of a combination of the religious and the secular. On the plan are many changes and corrections that reveal how Botta responded to the information the sketch provided. The rectangular shape has been divided into symmetrical spaces. Many faint lines extend across the plan to indicate either elements above or guidelines for the proportions of the *parti*. One can imagine how he visualized the space as he walked through the sketch. Doors have been indicated with arrows for their movement, and walls are given their thickness through many parallel marks. As he drew the plan, Botta was acutely aware of the towers and their placement above, sketching them lightly over their locations.

The two perspectives to the right of the page demonstrate how easily Botta moved between the plan and the rendering of volume. As variations for the exterior, the three-dimensional sketches illustrate how a plan can be interpreted in different ways. He recognized the need to move between the two types of drawing conventions. It also shows how he was thinking, trying something in plan and evaluating the ramifications with perspectives.

This sketch represents not the first thoughts, but the development of an idea. Beginning with the clear program of two towers, Botta was able to refine and visualize the design with this sketch. Although not an exact replica of the finished building, the concept developed here shows through in the final outcome.

FIGURE 8.4

Calatrava, Santiago (1951)

Sketch plan (05), 1999, Tenerife Concert Hall, Santa Cruz de Tenerife,
Canary Islands, Spain, 30 × 40cm, Watercolor

An architect and engineer known for his anthropomorphic structural systems, Santiago Calatrava designs pavilions, bridges, and canopies that are both elegant and efficient. Calatrava was born in Spain in 1951, traveling to Paris and Switzerland as an exchange student in his youth. Intending to study at the Ecole des Beaux-Arts, he instead enrolled in the Escuela Tecnica Superoir de Arquitectura in Valencia. Finding an interest in the mathematical rigor of certain great works of architecture, he pursued post-graduate studies in civil engineering at the Federal Institute of Technology in Zurich. He began his career by winning the design and construction of the Stadelhofen Railway Station in Zurich in 1983. Other notable projects are the Bach de Roda Bridge, commissioned for the Olympic Games in Barcelona; the Alamillo Bridge and viaduct (1987–1992); Campo Volantin Footbridge in Bilbao (1990–1997); and the Alameda Bridge and underground station in Valencia (1991–1995). A few recent projects by Calatrava include the expansion of the Milwaukee Art Museum (2001); Athens Olympic Sports Complex (2004); and the Palacio de las Artes in Valencia (2004). He has received numerous honors and awards such as the Gold Medal of the Institute of Structural Engineers, London, and the Gold Medal of Merit in the Fine Arts, Ministry of Culture, Spain.

This sketch (Figure 8.4) is from a series of design sketches for the Tenerife Concert Hall. The 'Concert Hall is the gateway to a new park in the western part of Santa Cruz, designed to help revitalize a coastal strip that had been the site of industrial plants and oil refineries. The building is the result of a specified desire for a dynamic, monumental building that would not only be a place for music and culture but would create a focal point for the area.'[5]

'The all-concrete building is characterized by the dramatic sweep of its roof. Rising off the base like a crashing wave, the roof soars to a height of 58 meters over the main auditorium before curving downward and narrowing to a point. The building's plinth forms a public plaza covering the site and allows for differences in grade between the different levels of the adjacent roads. ... Geometrically, the roof is constructed from two intersecting cone segments. By contrast, the symmetrical inner shell of the concert hall, which is 50 meters high, is a rotational body, generated by rotating a curve to describe an ellipse.'

The plan, section, and elevation sketches for this Concert Hall have been explored with graphite and watercolor in hues of blue and yellow. The plan sketch on the opposite page is not a typical floor plan that could be used for construction, but rather an instrument for design. Without the written explanation of the building, it would be difficult to understand the abstraction of the plan. It appears to show several levels and the exterior of the structure all at the same time.

The graphite under the watercolor has been sketched freehand. The form being slightly asymmetrical did not prevent the sketch from assisting Calatrava in visualizing the building's organization. The slow, careful, and controlled strokes of the pencil imply a sketch in the development stage, rather than the first fleeting concepts. The specifications for the project list white concrete and broken ceramic tiles among the building materials.

For the interior, the principal materials include platinum blue granite and structural wood. Although the sketch appears to illustrate the refinement of form, Calatrava was also employing color to help him imagine the space and, possibly, represent the building materials.

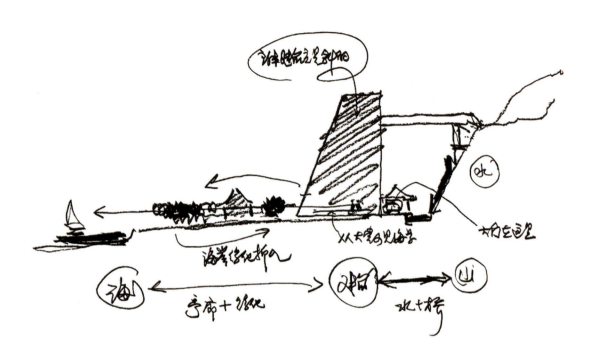

FIGURE 8.5

Chen, Shi Min (1935)

Section sketch, October 24, 1982, Nan Hai Hotel, SheKou, ShenZhen, China,
8.3 × 11.7 in., Pencil on tracing paper

Chinese architect Chen Shi Min has completed many celebrated large-scale commercial projects. The firm that carries his name has offices in ShenZhen and Hong Kong. He was born in Ya-An town of Sichuan Province in 1935. He attended Chongqing Institute of Architecture and Engineering, graduating in 1954. Chen has had two books published about his work, *Era and Space* (1996) and *Chen Shi Min* (1997). A few of his more renowned projects, all in China, include: Hongji Commercial Center, Tianjin (1994–1999); Daxin Building, Chongqing (1997–2000); New Downtown, Shenzhen (1996); Shenzhen Railway Station (1989–1992); Architectural Cultural Centre, Beijing (1995–1999); and the China Construction Corporation Complex, Chongqing (1996–1999).[6]

This sketch (Figure 8.5) shows early explorations for the Nanhai Hotel in Shekou, ShenZhen, China. Chen writes that the project was being designed during a period when China was moving towards modernization. At this time, most buildings were of high-rise construction; this was a low-rise design, with respect for environmental resources and its site features. The organization presents five volumes, spread along a curve, to form the complex – referencing Chinese traditional architecture by linking volumes. Inside the hotel, the space is organized in a fan shape, in accordance with the curved enclosure resulting from the composition.

Chen describes the site as having a backdrop of hills and facing the open sea, as the Nanhai Hotel is located away from the city's busy traffic. The priority of the design was to ensure harmony between the hotel and its beautiful environment. The master plan of the project was formed by five rectangular building blocks, evenly distributed along a curved line that echoes the lines of the seashore and the hills. The main feature of the hotel buildings is their terraced forms. This not only maximizes natural light and fresh air to the hotel rooms, but also harmonizes with the outline of the hill. The green space of the hotel blends with the foreshore vegetation to form a single open space. To gain the full benefit of the location, the ground level has been raised so that visitors can enjoy the ocean view (with Hong Kong visible in the distance) from the lobby, café, restaurant, and other public areas.

The sketches show a perspective view from the water and a diagram section through the site. As Chen has described it, one can see the connected volumes in the minimal sketch. Done by a controlled hand, the small sketch is composed of few lines representing the salient features of the hotel. In many cases, an architect's hand does not waver in the distance of a short line and the gesture is within the size of a hand stroke. Both sketches appear to envision the whole project in relation to its parts to visualize the look of the complex and the volume relationships through the site. Many of the lines have been left gaped since they need not cross each other to achieve the intended effect. This ambiguity helps to understand the totality of the project in its early stages, before final details have been determined. In like manner, the windows and roof have not been completely rendered, giving a brief impression of openings and the shape of the roof.

The section diagram identifies important features and specific views with arrows. Chen has used written notes to comment on these design factors for spatial relationships or identifying elements. The two sketches communicate a thinking that requires visual notes.

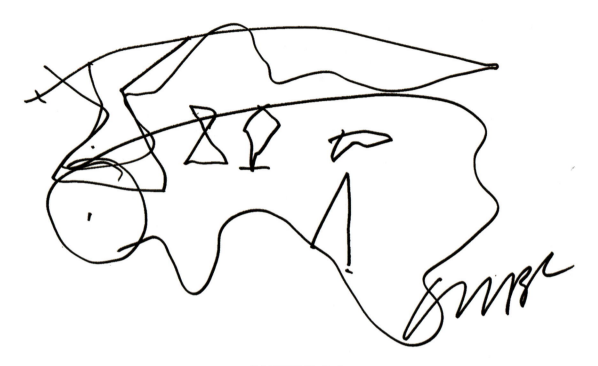

FIGURE 8.6

COOP HIMMELB(L)AU
Prix, Wolf D. (1942) and Swiczinsky, Helmut (1944)
Untitled sketch, 2001, BMW Welt, Munich, Germany, 29.7 × 21 cm, Black felt pen

Wolf Prix and Helmut Swiczinsky co-founded the practice COOP HIMMELB(L)AU in 1968. First based in Vienna, Austria, they have opened offices in Los Angles, United States of America (1988), and Guadalajara, Mexico (2000). Known for their innovative juxtaposition of forms and materials, they have a substantial repertoire of built work.

Prix was born in Vienna and educated at the Technical University. He also studied at the Architectural Association in London and Southern California Institute of Architecture in Los Angeles. Swiczinsky was born in Poznan, Poland, and also attended the Technical University. Like Prix, he went to the Architectural Association in London to study architecture.

Highly sought after critics, Prix has been the Professor of the Architecture 3 Masterclass at the University of Applied Arts in Vienna since 1993. They have taught as visiting critics at many schools in Argentina, Great Britain and the United States. They are both members of the European Academy of Sciences and Arts, headquartered in Vienna. Working together for many years their work has received awards such as the Erich Schelling Architecture Prize (1992), the European Steel Design Award (2001), and the Gold Medal for merits to the federal state of Vienna (2002). A few of their most recent commissions include the Groninger Museum, Netherlands (1993–1994); Musée des Confluences, Lyon, France (2001–2007); Great Egyptian Museum, Cairo, Egypt (2002–2003); and the Opera House, Gunagzhon, China (2003).[7]

This remarkably cryptic sketch (Figure 8.6) was part of the process of design for the BMW Welt, Munich, Germany. The building sited near the BMW headquarters was programmed to be a center for brand experience and vehicle delivery. Under a sculptural roof, the large hall acts as a multiuse market. At the center of the building is placed the 'Premiere' vehicle delivery area surrounded by suspended customer lounges that look out onto the event space and provide views to the BMW Headquarters.

The long, undulating, and heavy felt pen marks outline the form of the building. Very seldom lifted off of the paper, this line composes the whole shape with efficiency and perception. The continuous line demarcates the space without reference points. The image gives few hints of a ground line or datum from which to understand the orientation. The identification at the lower right is the best clue to 'reading' the relationships between the forms.

As an early design sketch, the floating shape could be describing both plan and section simultaneously. The gentle arc of the top piece, wavering underneath, could represent the roof supported by an hourglass structure and replicates an elevation view. The lower shape may reflect the plaza in front of the building acting as a plan.

This sketch was probably a personal thought since it makes no attempt to be explanatory. Although evoking the conceptual concerns for the BMW showroom, it is the type of sketch looking for relationships rather than communication to the clients. A similar version has been posted on the COOP HIMMELB(L)AU website which may indicate that after the project reached a more final stage the firm felt this sketch was the most representative diagram of the project. As a diagram it may hold the essence of the building as it was conceived, pure its ideal and prior to the gravity necessary for construction.

FIGURE 8.7

Correa, Charles (1930)
Housing sketch, 1999

An architect, planner, activist, and theoretician, Charles Correa 'has done pioneering work on urban issues and low-cost shelter in the Third World.'[8] 'He was Chief Architect for "Navi Mumbai," the new city of 2 million people, across the harbor from Bombay, and in 1985 Prime Minister Rajiv Gandhi appointed him Chairman of the National Commission on Urbanism.'

Correa studied architecture at the University of Michigan and at the Massachusetts Institute of Technology. He has maintained a private practice in Bombay since 1958. Continually interested in education, he has taught at universities in India and abroad, including Harvard University, University of Pennsylvania and Cambridge University; he currently holds the position of Farwell Bemis Professor at the Massachusetts Institute of Technology. His biography lists that he has received numerous honors and awards, including an Honorary Doctorate from the University of Michigan (1980), the RIBA (Royal Institute of British Architects) Gold Medal (1984), and the Praemium Imperiale of Japan (1994).

The work from Correa's architectural practice is varied with such projects as the Mahatma Gandhi Memorial at the Sabarmati Ashram, the Jawahar Kala Kendra in Jaipur, and the State Assembly for Madhya Pradesh. He has also designed numerous housing projects for Delhi, Bombay, Ahmedabad, and Bangalore.

Correa says his sketch (Figure 8.7) 'is about housing – an area sadly neglected by architects today, but one of vital importance to us in India. It illustrates some of the key issues (and compulsive imagery!) that have been seminal to my own work.' He explains how the sketch explores issues such as open courtyards that act as additional rooms in a warm climate, and points out that the 'casual and rhythmic layering' of domestic architecture is very flexible. Correa views this building as revealing the movement of the human occupants within it.

The minimal sketch is rendered with a blunt pencil on a fairly rough surface; this can be seen in the thick lines that leave white texture. The pencil mark is not dense because the graphite skips over the valleys in the paper. The relatively slow lines describe the edges of the forms. Surprisingly controlled, the sketch seems to be comprised of very few marks. It appears Correa rarely lifted the pencil off the paper; he had a strong concept in mind before he began. The diagrammatic qualities of the image seem to represent his thinking quite succinctly. Since he was concerned with the 'malleable,' or flexible, use of the building, his sketch (as an analogy) may have acted as a blank slate, allowing the humans to participate with the architecture. The minimal technique may reinforce this notion.

This beautiful sketch is fascinating. Those with little artistic skill or dexterity have historically envied the image-making abilities of artists and architects; most specifically, the ability to draw a free-hand representation that matches the intended image. Without guidelines and with a precision hand, the sketch was drawn from either observation or a very clear image in the mind's eye. Correa's remarkably precise imagination springs from his enormous experience and talent. Seeing the outline of the design was enough for Correa to place himself in the sketch and imagine the look and function of the building. His ability to view the potential of an idea with a simple sketch is a remarkable skill; it requires much practice as well as a thoughtful relationship with his sketching instruments.

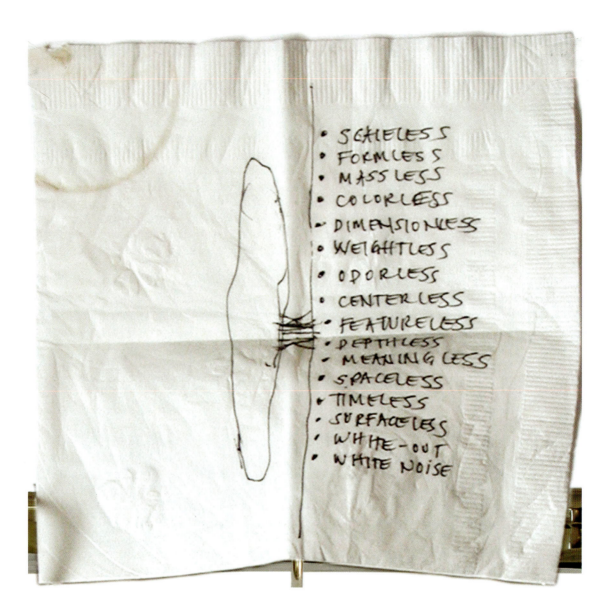

FIGURE 8.8

Diller, Elizabeth (1954)

Blur process sketch, December 28, 1998, Blur Building, Swiss Expo 2002, 7.5 × 7.5 in.,
Ink on napkin

Elizabeth Diller has constantly questioned the state of architecture. First collaborating with Ricardo Scofidio, their interdisciplinary studio now includes Charles Renfro and bears the name Diller + Scofidio + Renfro (D + S + R). Their work merges architecture, the visual arts, and the performing arts, which take the form of architectural projects, temporary and permanent site-specific art works, multimedia theater, electronic media, and print.

'Diller was born in Lodz, Poland, in 1954. She attended The Cooper Union School of Art and received a Bachelor of Architecture in 1979 from The Cooper Union School of Architecture.'[9] The studio is currently designing the public spaces of Lincoln Center in New York and two architectural projects as the result of international competitions. Other completed projects, of various scales, include: X,Y, a permanent installation for a pachinko parlor in Kobe, Japan; Travelogues, a permanent installation at the new JFK International Arrivals Terminal in New York; and two dance collaborations with the Lyon Ballet Opera and Charleroi Danses. They have been honored with numerous awards such as the MacArthur Foundation Award and the Arnold W. Brunner Memorial Prize in Architecture from the American Academy of Arts and Letters.

The page opposite (Figure 8.8) is a conceptual sketch by Diller for Blur Building. 'Blur Building is an exhibition pavilion for the Swiss Expo 2002 on Lake Nuechatal in the town of Yverdon-les-bain. [It] is an architecture of atmosphere.' The building is made of a lightweight tensegrity structure and water. 'Water is pumped from the lake, filtered, and shot as a fine mist through a dense array of high-pressure mist nozzles. The resulting fog mass produced is a dynamic interplay of natural and manmade forces. … Upon entering the fog mass, visual and acoustic references are erased, leaving only an optical 'white-out' and the 'white-noise' of the pulsing nozzles. … Unlike entering a building, Blur is a habitable medium – one that is spaceless, formless, featureless, depthless, scaleless, massless, surfaceless, and dimensionless.'

The sketch taped into a three-ring binder is a combination of diagram and written text. It has been sketched on a paper napkin with ink. The paper napkin suggests a discussion over a meal, where two or more people were brainstorming and reached for the most convenient writing surface. With this sketch they are showing the architecture of atmosphere, listing all of the qualities of architecture that can be 'blurred' with this project. To the left is a simple yet poignant diagram of the ephemeral cloud. A vertical line divides the words from the diagram and also acts as a ground line for the fog mass. The 'less' points have been bulleted to separate their importance as conceptual ideas. The strong theoretical nature of this project shows in how the words and the cloud are given equal space on the napkin.

The lines forming the mist sketch are bold and constructed of nearly single line weight. They overlap where they join to close the shape and at the points where the pen caught on the soft paper of the napkin. With a few vertical lines to represent the structure and water source, the succinct description was complete. The diagrammatic qualities of this sketch show the pointed thinking of Diller and her colleagues. The idea was so 'dimensionless' that its physical manifestation may not have been necessary. As a conversation the diagram assisted to understand the words and the form (or formlessness). One might speculate that the paper napkin was retained more for the words than the cloud.

FIGURE 8.9

Gehry, Frank (1929)

Process elevation sketches, October 1991, Guggenheim Museum Bilbao, Spain, 12.3 × 9.2 in.

Frank Gehry, famous for the dynamic forms of his signature buildings, is probably the most known and respected architect currently practicing in the United States. Gehry was born in Toronto in 1929 and moved with his family to Los Angeles in 1947. He studied at the University of Southern California and Harvard University before entering practice in 1962. His office, Gehry Partners, LLP, is a full service firm with broad international experience in museum, theater, performance, academic, and commercial projects. A few of his most celebrated include: Guggenheim Museum Bilbao in Bilbao, Spain; Experience Music Project in Seattle, Washington; Nationale-Nederlanden Building in Prague, Czech Republic; Walt Disney Concert Hall in Los Angles, California; and the Vitra International Headquarters in Basel, Switzerland.

Gehry and his architectural work have won awards from international foundations. He won the Pritzker Prize in 1989, the Arnold W. Brunner Memorial Prize in Architecture from the American Academy of Arts and Letters, and the American Institute of Architects Gold Medal in 1999. Gehry commonly uses sketches for first conceptual ideas and throughout his design process. He also depends on physical models in all scales and 'CATIA, a highly sophisticated 3-dimensional computer modeling program originally created for use by the aerospace industry, to thoroughly document designs and to rationalize the bidding, fabrication, and construction process.'[10] This program allows him to accurately model and fabricate the expressive and irregular shapes distinctive of his architecture.

The sketches that Gehry uses to begin his process are fluid and expressive. These sketches have been included in numerous publications and exhibitions of his work. Although they are private notations, he is not averse to making public his design process. Many of these first expressions of the building represent the search for form and volumes as can be viewed in this sketch for the Guggenheim Museum, Bilbao (Figure 8.9).

On the page are three freehand sketches rendered in ink on white paper. They appear to be elevation views since the volumes extend horizontally. Most likely, Gehry was studying the same elevation because each image displays a similar horizontal wing to the left with a more articulated shape to the center and right. He was holding the pen lightly as the ink line moved smoothly across the page. In some areas, it appears that the lines are continuous; Gehry seldom picks the pen up off the surface of the paper. Similar to a technique from fine art, *gesture* drawing attempts to capture the essence of the human form with the buildup of lines describing the interior muscles, not necessarily the exterior edges. This comparison is fitting, since Gehry's architecture contains a tremendous amount of internal energy.

The roof and center shapes seem to be alternatives, with three different approaches. The sketch to the right exhibits triangular elements on the roof, while the top sketch shows arced pieces and a stepped façade. The center feature shows aggressive diagonal lines on top of what appears to be openings. The fast strokes may mean that he was unhappy with the solution and considered eliminating it as a possibility. They could also suggest that he was shading a part of the façade, to view it more three-dimensionally. The wavy roof-lines show a fluidity that might represent a conceptual theme. Having a conceptual idea in mind, he was allowing his thoughts to flow, evaluating possible forms as he worked on each sketch. The exuberance of his style and the quick way he explores form are indicators of his fresh and expressive architecture.

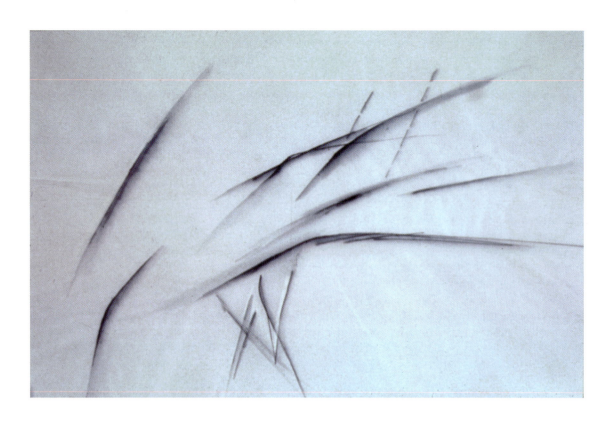

FIGURE 8.10

Hadid, Zaha (1950)

Preliminary sketch, 1991, Vitra Fire Station, Weil Am Rheim, Germany,
11.7 × 16.5 in., Acrylic and ink on tracing paper

Zaha Hadid continually stretches the boundaries of architecture and urban design. Dividing her concentration between practice, teaching, and research, 'her work experiments with new spatial concepts intensifying existing urban landscapes in the pursuit of a visionary aesthetic that encompasses all fields of design.' The 2004 Pritzker Prize winner, Hadid's design is both innovative and provocative.[11] As published in the jurors' comments, the architectural critic Ada Louise Huxtable writes: 'Hadid's fragmented geometry and fluid mobility do more than create an abstract, dynamic beauty; this is a body of work that explores and expresses the world we live in.'[12]

Born in Baghdad, Iraq, Hadid began her architecture studies at the Architectural Association in London and was awarded the Diploma Prize in 1977. Starting her practice in the Office for Metropolitan Architecture, she taught at the Architectural Association until 1987. She has been teaching at various schools in Germany, Austria, and the United States.

Articulating her theories on architecture, Hadid has won numerous competitions, including: The Peak, Hong Kong (1983); Cardiff Bay Opera House, Wales (1994); Bergisel Ski-Jump, Innsbruck (1999); Maritime Ferry Terminal, Salerno (2000); and BMW Central Plant Building, Leipzig (2002). Her work has been widely published in periodicals and monographs. She has received numerous awards, such as the Honorable Member of the American Academy of Arts and Letters (2000); Honorary Fellowship of the American Institute of Architects (2000); and the Commander of the British Empire (2002).

Hadid consistently uses drawings and paintings as exploration in her design process. These often abstract slices and shards represent her approach to architecture. The images become the impetus for conceptual stages. This sketched image (Figure 8.10) demonstrates a beginning for the Vitra Fire Station in Weil am Rhein, Germany. The commission was to build a fire station, and the program extended to include the boundary walls of the site, a bicycle shed, and an exercise pavilion. The building was developed to define the landscaped zone of the linear site. This resulted in a long narrow building alongside the street. The structure has been cut and **bent** to portray a 'collision of directions.' 'The space-defining and screening functions of the building were the point of departure for the development of the architectural concept: a linear, layered series of walls. The programme of the firestation inhabits the spaces between these **walls**, which **puncture**, **tilt** and **break** according to the functional requirements.'

The sketch, although minimal, reflects these concepts. The page shows several angled lines, primarily extending from the lower left to the upper right. Most appear to be rendered with ink or watercolor and a brush. This gives a hazy, indefinite shadow to the lines, softening them and accentuating the differences in thickness. Many of the lines are straight, although several have distinct kinks in them to evoke the change in directions Hadid describes in her concept statement. The marks have been layered nearly parallel to suggest motion, creating a tension in the spaces between.

This sketch is a beautiful and succinct diagram of Hadid's thinking. The images, although brief and abstract, present the clear concept of the walls that 'puncture, tilt, and break.' It is preliminary, preparatory, and describes an outline of her design process.

FIGURE 8.11

Hara, Hiroshi (1936)
Mid-Air City sketch, 1989, Umeda Sky Building, Kita-ku, Osaka, Japan, 1993, 3.6 × 2.1 in., Air brush, colored pencil

An innovative architect, Hiroshi Hara is known for his fanciful and emotive buildings. He often uses building materials to achieve unique effects, such as the cloud-like walls of the Tasaki Museum of Art. Hara was born in Kawasaki in 1936. He attended the University of Tokyo for his BA and MA studies, receiving a Ph.D. in 1964. He immediately began teaching at the University of Tokyo, where he continues today as a Professor Emeritus. He has collaborated as a designer since 1970, with such projects as Tasaki Museum of Art in Nagano (1986); Iida City Museum, Nagano (1988); and the Kyoto Station Building (1997). Since 1999, Hara has headed the firm that bears his name, Hiroshi Hara + Atelier. Several of his most recent works include: Hiroshima Municipal Building (2000); Komaba Campus, Meguro-ku (2001); and the Sapporo Dome (2001). Hara has been the recipient of numerous awards for architectural design, including competition project awards.[13]

One of Hara's most published buildings is the Umeda Sky Building in Osaka. This beautiful glass and steel high-rise building was built in 1993. It was conceived as two paired towers, connected by glass escalators with a balcony stretched between them. The platform in the sky has a circular cutout crossed with thin 'catwalk' passages. The flush glass curtain wall is reflective and appears blue.

This sketch (Figure 8.11) appears to be an early 'ideogram,' in that it shows a large complex of tall buildings connected by ramps, walkways, and escalators. The fantasy image reveals platforms of potentially occupied space (implied by small windows), dotted with several large oculi opening a view to the sky. The horizontal slabs are vaguely sketched in pencil over fluffy clouds and the light framing seemingly floats above a large, historic building. Without articulated structural support, the walkways and cutouts integrate with the clouds to cover the city. The ring of high-rise buildings lends some support to the framework, but maintains a certain amount of transparency since the buildings are abstractly defined.

The smooth underside of the frames morph into clouds on their upper sides. Their light color assists in their cloud-like nature and weightlessness. The sketch's ambiguous forms and tenuous connections provide a surreal impression, as if Hara is designing an ideal future at the same time he is designing for Osaka.

Eerie light, emitting from behind the dark historic building, creates an atmospheric quality of an active and glowing city. Its industrial look and exposed structure mix the technical with the ephemeral. Hara's sketch describes the idea of the Umeda building, rather than the reality of its final construction. The image is both an illusion (speculating on a possible future) and an allusion (referring to conceptual notions of urbanism).

In comparison to the sketch, the building, as constructed, retains the thin skywalks and an oculus but only part of the sketch's vast urbanism. The two towers resemble the sketch's towers, achieving a certain transparency. The sky-platform effectively evokes the tenuous qualities of residing in the sky (the theme of the sketch). The steel and glass add to the illusion and dramatic impression.

FIGURE 8.12

Hecker, Zvi (1931)

Spiral sketch, 1986, Spiral Apartment House, Ramat-Gan, Israel, 21 × 29 cm,
Black ink on white paper

An architect with an international practice, Zvi Hecker approaches architecture from strong conceptual symbolism. Using the shape of a 'sunflower' as impetus for such projects as the Jewish Primary School in Berlin (1991–1995) and the Sunflower of Ramat Hasharon in Tel-Aviv (1986–1995), he creates distinctly emotive buildings. Other of his renowned projects include the Palmach Museum of History in Tel-Aviv, the Holocaust Memorial in Berlin, and the Jewish Cultural Center in Duisburg.

Hecker was born in Poland and lived in Samarkand and Krakow until he emigrated to Israel in 1950. His architectural education began at the Krakow Polytechnic (1949–1950), and he graduated from the Israeli Institute of Technology in Haifa with a degree in engineering and architecture (1955). In addition to his training in architecture, he studied painting at the Avni Academy of Art in Tel-Aviv (1955–1957). While working with Eldar Sharon and Alfred Neumann, Hecker began his private practice now known as Zvi Hecker | Architect | Berlin, with offices in Tel-Aviv and Amsterdam. In addition to his active practice, he has held positions of visiting professor at schools in Canada, Israel, Austria and the United States.[14]

The stimulus for this sketch (Figure 8.12) came from the program for the Spiral Apartment House in Ramat Gan. Hecker's beautiful and astonishing construction is formed with masonry and tile, exhibiting a porous weave of fragmented spiral columns defining inhabitable space. He writes about the concept of the spiral as it pertains to this building and the sketch. 'The Spiral's incompleteness is also its poetry, because poetry is the most precise expression of our need for precision. Expressive as it is, the Spiral can't be fully understood. It speaks to many languages at once and at the same time. It speaks Arabic about human condition. It argues in Hebrew in the sheer necessity to bring the muscles and materials together, but it is quite fluent in Russian when construction becomes architecture. Its Italian is very Baroque, as spoken in Piedmont by Guarino Guarini. The Spiral is a tower of Babel in miniature.'[15] Hecker is describing the fluidity of a spiral and his reasons for using it as impetus for this building. Its inspiring nature carries many facets and allusions that can be translated into architecture.

By Hecker's own admission (recognized after its completion), the sketch resembles the complex layering of spaces in Piranesi's *carceri*. With similar hatched lines, the sketch contains the fragmented and ambiguous spatial illusion as Piranesi's etchings. The very dense page overlaps cylindrical shapes. Blending pieces of architectural form, such as windows and stairs, with abstract contours, he suggests an impression of movement and transition. This collage of architectural notations was not meant to produce a faithful view of the proposed building but rather an allusion. This sketch is both an *illusion* and an *allusion*. Both words with roots in play, the sketch is a fabricated (thus not realistic) view of the building at the same time being a reference to an abstract idea.

The fragmented pieces have been rendered to help Hecker visualize the concept in three dimensions. Constantly moving between positive and negative space, the sketch also transitions between elevation and plan, seen markedly in the stairs to the left. The connected, but still disjointed, pieces fill the entire page with nervous activity.

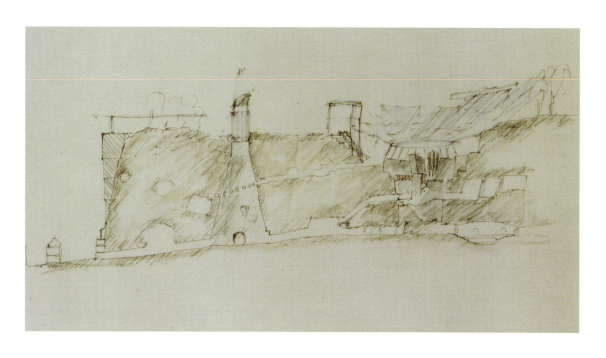

FIGURE 8.13

Hollein, Hans (1934)

Museum in der Rock of the Mönchsberg Competition 1989, 1st prize, which became,
the Guggenheim Museum Salzburg 1990, 1989, Feasibility study and 2001 updating of project as
Art Center Monchsberg, 75.5 × 55.5 cm, Pencil, crayon on transparent paper

The Pritzker Prize-winning architect Hans Hollein is also an artist and educator. His postmodern building, the Museum of Modern Art in Frankfurt, launched his international reputation.

Born in Vienna, Hollein's first architectural education was from the Academy of Fine Arts. Receiving the Harkness Fellowship, he traveled to the United States, where he began his graduate studies at the Illinois Institute of Technology in Chicago and graduated from the University of California at Berkeley in 1960. Acquiring apprenticeship in Sweden and the United States, he began his private practice in 1964.

Hollein has been continually involved in architectural education. He taught at the Academy of Fine Arts in Düsseldorf from 1967 to 1976. Since then he has been a professor at the University of Applied Arts in Vienna. He has taught as a visiting professor in such American universities as Washington University and Yale University.

Hollein has completed many buildings including the Municipal Museum Abteiberg in Monchengladbach near Düsseldorf (1983–1991); Haas House, Vienna (1985–1990); the Austrian Embassy, Berlin (1997–2001); and Interbank, Lima (1996–2001). In addition to the Pritzker Prize in 1985, he was awarded the Grand Austrian State Prize in 1983 and the Chicago Architecture Award in 1990.

The sketch illustrated here (Figure 8.13) is an early study for the Guggenheim Museum in Salzburg. The project was initially designed in response to an architecture competition for a museum in the rock, and was envisioned to connect the lower level of the Old Town with the plateau on top of the Mönchsberg. The depression in the surface emits light into the lower public spaces, while the exhibit rooms are artificially illuminated. In an area of Austria accustomed to mining, the tunneling permits an unusual combination of rooms. As Hollein writes: 'In contrast to conventional additive-tectonic forms of construction, subtractive "building" into the rock allows more freedom, a plastic, more complex spatial conception and expansion – a genuine three-dimensionality.'

The sketch exhibits these excavated paths which connect the skylit spaces and the entrance. Rendered with pencil and crayon, the rock has been loosely poché to emphasize the outline of the voids/passages. This describes the essence of the project, as Hollein writes: 'The sketches show exactly the total design of this project, which is also one of the project of creating space by subtraction.'[16] The freeform sketching technique of the underground spaces are in contrast to the more carefully constructed lines of the architecture exposed to the exterior. Recognizing the freedom of boring into the rock, the excavations were less confined and could be represented with more abstraction. Two variations of the light shaft indicate that this sketch was preliminary. Hollein used colored crayons to emphasize several of these details; the blue of the skylight and red for the opening in the mountain's depression.

The best method to visualize this building was through section sketches and drawings. Sections more efficiently express the subtractive qualities of this design, showing the cuts into the rock and the fit of the structure into the depression, called the 'sunk.' The section allowed Hollein to understand the whole project, conceiving from the inside-out and viewing the distances between the spaces which normally are studied in plan.

FIGURE 8.14

Krier, Rob (1938)

Spatial sequences sketch, 1978, Prager-Platz, Berlin, Germany, 26 × 30 cm, Oil chalk with pencil on canvas

Rob Krier is an architect, sculptor, and urban theorist with a broad range of talents. Krier was born in Grevenmacher, Luxembourg. He studied architecture at the Technical University of Munich, Germany. Upon finishing, he entered into collaboration with O. M. Ungers and Frei Otto in Germany. Krier has long been associated with academia, teaching at schools in Germany, France, and Austria. Krier has also continued to practice with offices in Vienna, Montpellier, and most recently in Berlin, in partnership with Christoph Kohl.[17]

Krier's recent projects in collaboration with Kohl have revolved around their interests in New Urbanism. Several of their recent urban projects include: Batavia Haven, Lelystad, Netherlands (a waterfront development); Brandevoort, Helmond, Netherlands (an urban development plan); and Citadel Broekpolder, Beverwijk/Heemskerk, Netherlands (a community masterplan). Supporting this interest in city spaces, Krier has authored books on urban theory and architectural composition, a few being *Town Spaces: Contemporary Interpretation in Traditional Urbanism* and *Urban Space*.

This page (Figure 8.14) contains sketches exploring the Prager-Platz project in Berlin. From 1978, this series represents Krier's method of visual analysis through the use of sketches. Eight of the nine sketches illuminate visions of a historic town center in both plan and perspective. The center sketch conveys the overall oval theme and the other images are detail perspectives, evaluating more specific public and private spaces intended for this proposal.

Krier describes the rationale behind his thinking while working on this project:

> 'The traces of the war that are here to be seen from the starting point for the project begun in 1978. We proposed an extensive reconstruction of the original oval ground plan. The points where the streets meet the square were to be architecturally accentuated. The best flats were to be situated at these corners. In the interior of the block, we planned to put an adult education facility, a kindergarten, a library, and restaurants, as well as a large swimming pool. The designs for the individual buildings were to be created in collaboration with other architects. Cupolas, vaults, and gables of glass supply above-average natural lighting to the primary spaces. Public spaces generally make a transition from solid wall to void through semi-solid colonnades and galleries. According to our design philosophy, street façades are treated as continuous surfaces, intended to conserve the historic urban fabric.'

As Krier has intended the buildings to be constructed in collaboration with other architects, these sketches may be suggestions for the 'flavor' of the space or designs for the public spaces in the new construction.

The page, densely covered with sketches, reveals Krier's enjoyment in thinking with the pencil. The vignettes fill the page without spacing between the separate scenes. They have been rendered in hues of blue, pink, yellow, brown, and orange colored pencils. Although blue has been chosen for water and the skylights, Krier has playfully rendered a pink plaza and bright yellow walls.

The series appears to be a method for Krier to visualize a walk through the spaces. Since the project was designed to have continuous street façades, the design could be best understood through snapshots of the internal 'rooms.' Whether these sketches were meant to represent specific buildings may be irrelevant. Since perspectives (besides models) are the most effective way to view interior space, these sketches bring the observer inside and successfully seduce an overall impression conveying the 'feeling' of the buildings.

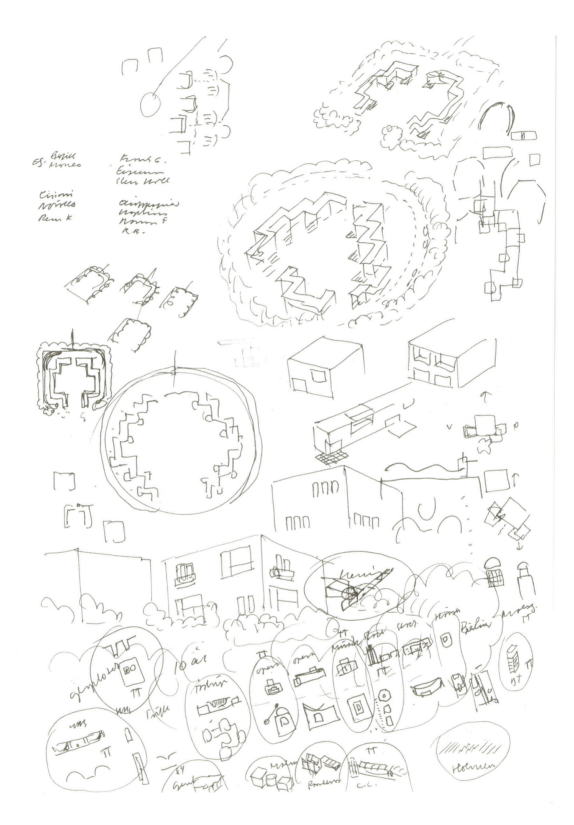

FIGURE 8.15

238

Larsen, Henning (1925)

Sketch featuring many of the studio's most important buildings, Various projects,
21 × 29.7 cm, Fountain pen on paper

Henning Larsen has built remarkable architecture in Denmark and around the world. Particularly adept with steel, glass, and stone, his structures exhibit clean lines and a sensitive balance between solidity and transparency. Born in Jutland, Denmark, he attended architecture school at the Royal Academy of Fine Arts in Copenhagen, the Architectural Association in London, and Massachusetts Institute of Technology in Boston. In 1952, he began apprenticeships in the United States and Denmark. In 1959, he founded his architectural practice Henning Larsen Tegnestue A/S.

A dedicated educator, Larsen has taught as a visiting professor at Yale and Princeton Universities in the United States and the School of Architecture, Aarhus, Denmark. Long associated with the Royal Academy of Fine Arts, Copenhagen, he was a Professor of Architecture (1968–1995). His architecture has been recognized with such honors as the C.F. Hansen Award (1985); the Aga Khan Architectural Award (1989); the Kasper Salin Award (1997); the Margot and Thorvald Dreyer Foundation's architectural award (1999); the Stockholm Award (2001); and the Rostocker Architekturpreis (2004), in addition to being the founder of the periodical *SKALA*.[18]

This sketch by Larsen (Figure 8.15) conveys a thought process that relies on the analysis of past projects to influence the design of a building complex. Rendered with similar line weight and crowded on the page, the images consist of plans, perspectives, and diagrams. On the upper portion of this page are several plans and axonometric-like studies exploring a series of connected buildings. These buildings are zigzagged around a central open space and surrounded with a border of foliage. Larsen appears to be visually testing alternatives for this complex, some within a circular boundary, others in a square. In his description of this project, Larsen indicated that the sketch includes images of numerous of his extant structures. Although not all-inclusive, the projects illustrated are as follows: Gentofte Central Library (1970–1979); Copenhagen Business School (1980–1989); Churchill College (1980–1989); Enghøj Church of Randers (1991); Ny Carlsberg Glyptotek (1991); BT-House (1992); Concert Hall at Copenhagen Harbor Waterfront (1993); Hørsholm Parish Community Centre (1993); and Opera in Copenhagen (2000). An interesting archive of his former projects, Larsen may have been sifting through the organization of each of these buildings as precedent. The small diagrams act as a 'visual dictionary' of possible (and successful) organizational solutions. They may also represent for Larsen the relationship between the project and its *parti*.

Larsen depends on his sketches for design inspiration. On the website arcspace he is quoted describing his relationship with sketches. 'I can be inspired by a sudden image. My mind works like mad. The light strikes off some curbstones, it looks lovely. It's a detail. One never stops discovering new facets of something: contrasts, dimensions. It's all processed by the mind, you can't set it out like a column of figures, but still it falls into place. You can worry and worry over a problem without finding an answer, then in the morning when you wake up, there it is. Suddenly it's all so obvious. That's how to do it. That's how it will look. There are all sorts of problems I can't sort out. When that happens I sketch it all out on a piece of paper, solely in order to remind myself of the essentials.'

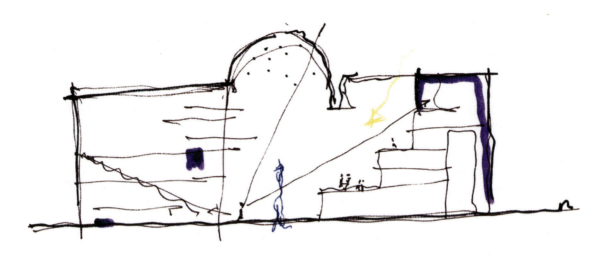

FIGURE 8.16

Legorreta, Ricardo (1931)

Section sketch, UCSF Mission Bay Campus Community Center, San Francisco,
California, Felt marker on paper

Ricardo Legorreta is a contemporary Mexican architect whose work reflects the bold geometric forms of the international style, introducing elements of regionalism with his sensitive use of color and natural light in a fresh approach to architecture.

Legorreta was born in Mexico City and studied architecture at the Universidad Nacional Autonoma de México, graduating in 1952. He began an apprenticeship with the architect Jose Villagran Garcia in 1948 and became a partner in 1955. After freelancing for several years, he opened his own firm in 1963 entitled Legorreta + Legorreta. An educator, he has taught at schools of architecture in such countries as Japan, Argentina, Colombia, Guatemala, England, France, Israel, and the United States, to name a few. His incredible talent has been recognized with honors and awards including: two Silver Medals in the First Biennial of Mexican Architecture (1990); two Gold Medals in the Second Mexican Biennial of Architecture (1992); UIA Gold Medal, given in Beijing (1999); and the American Institute of Architects Gold Medal (2000).[19]

Legorreta completed buildings of various types and scales, they include: IBM Offices, Mexico City; Museum of Contemporary Art, Monterrey, Mexico; Children's Discovery Museum, San Jose, California; Cathedral in Managua, Nicaragua; San Antonio Library, Texas; and the Chapultepec Zoo, Mexico City.

This concise image (Figure 8.16) is a sketch for the University of California, San Francisco Mission Bay Campus Community Center. The building was created to bring the campus community together with a gymnasium, swimming pools, food services, auditorium, and retail space. Built in 2000, the structure is organized around a central atrium that 'will serve as an orienting point, assembling the different spaces and helping the users to establish a visual connection within the building.'

Rendered in ink with yellow and violet felt tip pen, this sketch is a study for the 400 seat auditorium. The space has been articulated with a flat roof and a vaulted skylight. The sketch appears to be an early exploration since the final solution does not show this type of roof. The interior features blocks of tiered seating on both sides. The right side of the sketch shows the auditorium in elevation, viewing the front of the barriers. Legorreta has included people for scale; the seated audience have been suggested with brief dots for heads. On the right is a passageway for 'backstage' or exit/entrance accessibility. On the left side of the sketch is a section representing the rise of the stairs. The stair's location has been guided by a sloped line overlaid with a wavy line to replicate steps. The far edges of the seating boxes are minimally indicated as horizontal marks. In the center of the sketch stands both a tall central feature and a scale figure on the stage. Lines have been drawn from the figure's head to the top tier of the seating and the vaulted ceiling. These arrows suggest Legorreta's concern for acoustics and sight lines within the space. A pale yellow arrow waves down from the ceiling, possibly indicating the admittance of sunlight.

The lines of the sketch are minimal and considered. It appears the single line thickness for exterior walls was reinforced with a heavier pen. Drawn relatively slowly, the lines undulate slightly with the movement of the instrument. They suggest Legorreta was holding the various pens quite loosely, concentrating on the accuracy of their location. Dots in the dome/vault may indicate texture or a perforation of the ceiling.

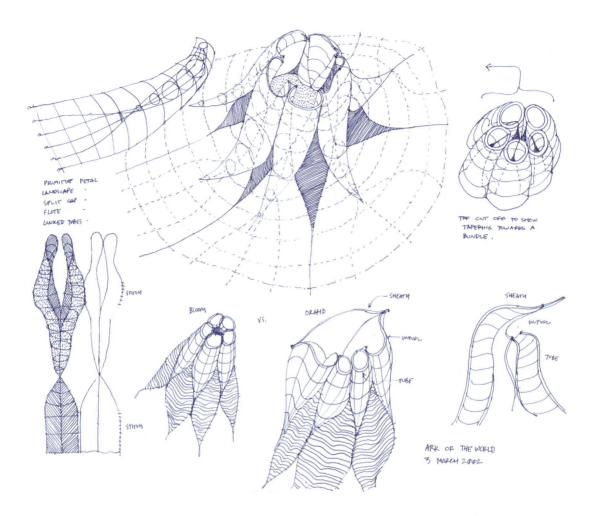

PRIMITIVE PETAL
LANDSCAPE
SPLIT GAP
FLUTE
LINKED TUBES

TOP CUT OFF TO SHOW
TAPERING TOWARDS A
BUNDLE.

STITCH

STITCH

BLOOM   VS.   ORCHID   SHEATH   SHEATH
                                          UNFURL   UNFURL
                                                              TUBE
                                          TUBE

ARK OF THE WORLD
3 MARCH 2002

FIGURE 8.17

Lynn, Greg (1964)

Preliminary exploratory museum sketches, March 3, 2002, Ark of the World Museum and Interpretive Center, San Juan, Costa Rica, 11 × 14 in., Ink on Bristol paper

'The studio of Greg Lynn FORM has been at the cutting edge of design in the field of architecture when it comes to the use of computer-aided design.' This statement from Lynn's publicity materials is important when considering the vast number of his publications, exhibitions, and lectures. Experimenting with advanced technology for design and fabrication, he has been innovative with 'smooth, shiny, undulating, unarticulated, and seamless' digital forms for his design process.[20]

Lynn graduated from Miami University of Ohio in 1986 with Baccalaureate degrees in Philosophy and Environmental Design. He attended Princeton University for his Professional degree, Master of Architecture. He worked briefly in the office of Antoine Predock Architect in 1987 before his employment with Eisenman Architects from 1987 to 1991. With his own practice, Lynn began working on competitions and theoretical projects. Although continuously involved with competitions, in recent years he has also collaborated on several built works, including the Korean Presbyterian Church of New York (1999); Cincinnati County Day School (2001); and Ark of the World Museum and Interpretive Center, San Juan, Costa Rica (1999).

Considering his theoretical approach, Lynn has taught at Universities in Europe and the United States. Much of his time is spent with exhibitions of his work and writing. His most recent books are *Predator*, published by the Wexner Center, and *Embryological House*, published by Princeton Architectural Press.

In some of his writings, Lynn has speculated on the sketch, especially concerning how he uses the digital medium to sketch. He discusses three forms of sketches. First, the sketch as expression, where the image envisions the future architecture and communicates design intent. The second is the diagram, which can be 'used for disciplining complexity into legible spatial simplicity.' The third sketch he titles the *plexus*, and is depicted as 'a centralized organization defined by a cloud or collection of points' that can be 'a network of curved vectors that imply a relative center without an exact point of origin or radius.' Lynn recognizes that the computer sketch has tremendous precision, but instead of finding limitation in this medium, he employs its properties to experiment with digital fabrication and calculus-based form.

This freehand image (Figure 8.17) appears to be from a computer-generated exploration of tubular form. The geometries of the shapes, although repetitive, are each slightly irregular. On the page Lynn has identified the various bundles of shapes in organic terms: bloom, orchid, and petal. Strikingly, these forms appear to be sketched with construction in mind. Although perspectives dashed lines within their shapes show the form in its entirety. This use of see-through glasses to view what is behind suggests this sketch is not about viewing the finished composition, but rather inspecting the joining of the shapes. Although a common drawing convention, the dotted line technique helps to clarify the relationships between the pieces and adds to the three-dimensional impression.

Rendered in blue ink, the sketch is remarkably precise – very necessary when viewing such complex combinations. Often, drawing can be a factor in understanding, and although rendered easily with a computer program, the hand sketches may have allowed him a chance to analyze during the action of sketching.

FIGURE 8.18

Miralles, Enric (1955–2000)

Preliminary plan sketch, 1992–1995, Mollet del Valles, Park and Civic Center, Barcelona, Spain, Graffiti and crayon on paper

The Spanish architect Enric Miralles, in his short life, influenced the urban fabric of his home city, Barcelona. His architecture utilized a layered mosaic of materials to create playful façades.

Miralles began his architectural career when he graduated from the Escuela Técnica Superior de Arquitectura de Barcelona. He first worked with the architects Helio Piñon and Alberto Viaplana (1973–1985), and opened a firm with Carme Pinós in 1984. In 1993, he joined with Benedetta Tagliabue to form the practice EMBT Arquitectes Associats SL.[21] Their urban spaces, Plaça dels Paisos Catalans and the Park in Besós in Barcelona, use color-ful active screens to enliven these public parks. Kinetic in nature, these sculptural constructions also act as shading devices for a perpetually sunny city. Other projects from the office of Enric Miralles and Benedetta Tagliabue collaborative include: the Scottish Parliament Building on the Royal Mile in Edinburgh's Old Town (1998); Construction of the Reader's Circle Headquarters in Madrid (1991); Utrecht Civic Center (1995); first prize for IUV Headquarters, Venice (1999); and the Mollet del Valles Park and Civic Center in Barcelona, Spain (2000). The Parliament Building grows out of the site resembling a collection of upturned boats and seashore imagery. The design employs a leaf theme (based on a flower motif by Charles Rennie Mackintosh) accented by a steel and glass roof with laminated oak beams. Miralles was a visiting professor at universities in the United States, Britain, Italy and Austria. He directed postgraduate studies at the Städelschule in Frankfurt, Harvard University, and the Architectural University in Barcelona (Zabalbeascoa and Marcos, 1999).

This is a sketch for the Mollet del Valles Park and Civic Center (Figure 8.18). Colorful and expressive, this image uses crayon to form crucial relationships between concepts or representational spaces. The sketch portrays primary colors as indicators. Bold patches of orange and yellow fill in circles on the left. Green and blue linear strokes extend upward and out to the right and left of the central forms. Seemingly random shapes in the form of lozenges and arcs work their way across the page to provide interludes between the areas of color. A very quick sketch, the vibrant strokes zigzag tightly to fill in shapes or loosely form the linear extensions. The poché spaces are conveyed with straight and parallel lines contrasted by the sparsely nervous lines that cover a larger area. This diagonal movement indicates the way the squiggled lines, not lifting the crayon off the paper, ultimately create areas of potential form.

The pressure on the sketching tool varies across the page; sometimes light, at other points strong and forceful. Appearing as plan or elevation relationships, the sketch reflects conceptual intentions. When Miralles and Tagliabue wrote about this project they were also describing the ephemeral and exploratory nature of the sketch. 'The main interest of this project is, maybe, not directly in it, but in the "themes" it contains; the suspension of the building, of graffiti becoming architecture, of the colors of a painting becoming places, of the suspended spirit of the users, of unexpected connection. ... We like to think that this project could be a project for the "near future," being a more subtle conception of architecture. Architecture of the future will be lighter, especially in its concept.' The sketch helps to define the idea of the future project.

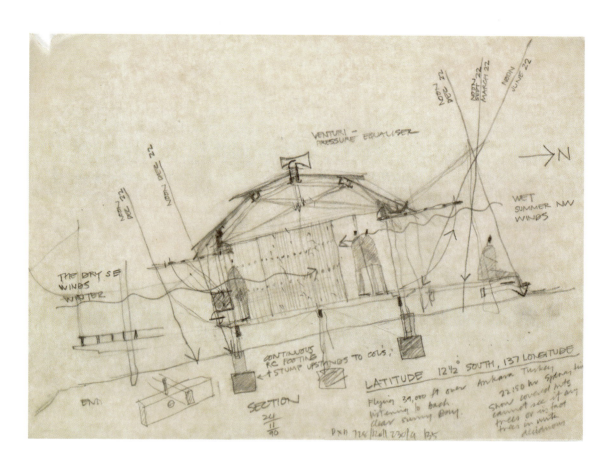

FIGURE 8.19

Murcutt, Glenn (1936)

Sketch plan, 1992, Glenn Murcutt Collection: Marika Banduk [Alderton] House, Yirrikala
(PXD 728/Roll 230/A 135), 26 × 37 cm, Pencil sketch on butter (trace) paper

Glenn Murcutt has a private practice, designing mostly houses that are environmentally sensitive. His architecture expects buildings to respond to their climate and landscape. Awarded the Pritzker Prize in Architecture in 2002, Murcutt works alone, concentrating on small projects where he has greater control of the outcome.

During a family trip, Murcutt was born in London. The family returned to Australia in 1941, where he has lived since. He studied architecture at the University of New South Wales, graduating in 1961. After travels to Europe, he served an apprenticeship with the architectural firm of Anchor, Mortlock, Murray & Wooley until 1969. Strongly influenced by Mies van der Rohe, Murcutt has also studied the vernacular architecture and culture of the indigenous people of Australia. His carefully detailed buildings limit the environmental impact on their sites, 'touching the earth lightly.'[22] A few examples of his published work include: Marika – Alderton House – Yirrkala Community, Eastern Arnheim Land, North Territory; Laurie Short House, Terrey Hills, Sydney; and projects in New South Wales: Magney House, Bingie Bingie; Minerals and Mining Museum, Broken Hill; and Bowral House, Southern Highlands.

This sketch (Figure 8.19) describes a section study for the small Marika Banduk (Alderton) House.[23] Rendered in pencil on 'butter paper' (yellow tracing paper), Murcutt envisions the complex integration of structure, environmental controls, and interior space for humans. The techniques show a slow and contemplative hand; expressing the winds as wavy lines becomes an analogy for the movement of air and the movement of the pencil. The deliberate lines study the intensity of the sun and the structure of the roof. The roof has been structured with beams, showing the space between the roofing material and the bracing. The floor, in section, indicates the joists and foundations. Two footings have been 'called out' and a third was added later. This sketch reveals how the building will sit lightly, lifted off the ground.

Other environmental issues are considered throughout the page. Winds from the southeast and northwest have been designated as wavy lines and arrows. Sun angles have been approximated for several times of the year (December 22, March 22, June 22) to help Murcutt design the widths of the overhangs. He was visually testing the amount of shade that would protect the interior of the house. Conscious of the sun's azimuth and altitude, he has noted the 'Latitude 12½° South, 137 Longitude' as a reminder.

The sketch primarily shows the relationship between interior space and the porch. By drawing one figure sitting on the porch, Murcutt reinforces the inside/outside continuance. The figures remind him of the inhabitants, the feeling of the space and the conditions of climate control.

The sketch represents a device to remind Murcutt of pertinent information, to evaluate the information visually, and record the thought process of design. There is reason to believe that the page was sketched while he was traveling. On the lower right, notes describe his location and musings about his state of mind. He writes: 'Flying 39,000 ft. over Ankara Turkey; listening to Bach; clear sunny day; 22:50 hr Sydney time.' The sketch can take him to the plains of Australia as a substitute medium and be a companion for thoughts wherever he travels.

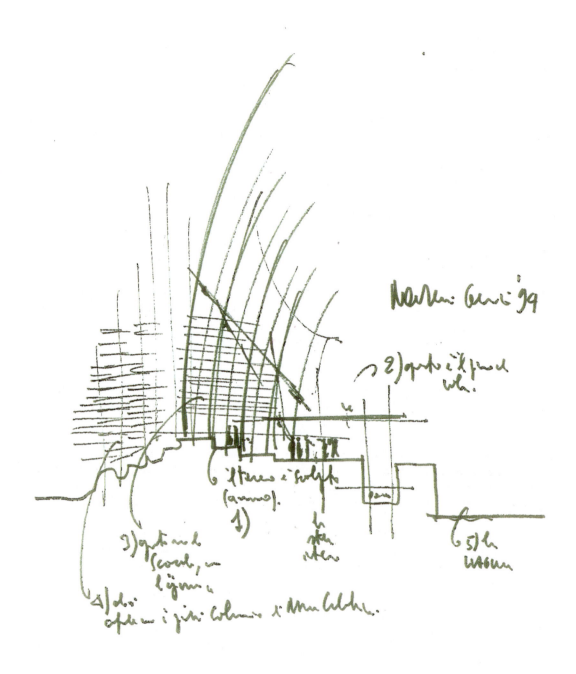

FIGURE 8.20

Piano, Renzo (1937)

Elevation sketch, 1991, Cultural Center Jean-Marie Tjibaou, Nouméa, New Caledonia, 8.3 × 11.7 in., Felt pen on paper

Ever since his partnership with Richard Rogers and the unveiling of the celebrated Centre Pompidou in Paris (1977), Renzo Piano has been a major figure in contemporary architecture. Born in Genoa, Italy, in 1937, he graduated from the school of architecture of the Milan Polytechnic. While a student, he worked under the design guidance of Franco Albini. Between 1965 and 1970, he met and began a friendship with Jean Prouvé, who had a deep influence on his professional life.

In 1971, with Rogers, he founded the Piano & Rogers agency and in 1977 joined with the engineer Peter Rice in the firm of l'Atelier Piano & Rice. Recently, Piano founded Renzo Piano Workshop with offices in Paris and Genoa. A few of his best known projects include: office building for Olivetti, Naples (1984); Menil Collection Museum, Houston (1986); S. Nicola Football Stadium, Bari (1990); Kensai International Airport Terminal, Osaka (1994); the Debis Building (Headquarters of Daimler Benz), Berlin (1997); Lodi Bank Headquarters, Lodi (1998); and the Aurora Place, high-rise offices and apartment blocks, Sydney (2000).[24]

The winner of the 1998 Pritzker Prize, Piano has received many awards and honors from foundations around the world. He has been widely published in numerous catalogues, articles, and books about his work including the *Renzo Piano Building Workshop, Complete Works*, Phaidon Press in 1997. One of his most celebrated recent projects is the Cultural Center Jean-Marie Tjibaou, Nouméa, New Caledonia, completed in 1998.

This sketch (Figure 8.20) is an exploration for the Center. Piano has used a narrow, green felt pen to render a section cut through one of the exhibit spaces. The ground plane has been sketched more slowly, showing a heavier, controlled line. Wavy to the left and straighter to the right, it expresses his understanding of the natural site as it transforms into the building. The instrument has given him a bold mark that can be somewhat varied, thick or thin. The trees behind the building and the lattice of the back wall have been treated with similar horizontal strokes showing his concern for integration of the site. The lines of the building and the section cut are substantially heavier than the marks he used for proportioning and dimensioning. These lines are firm and decisive, with little hesitation except for the roof of the pavilion. Here Piano appears to be studying the beginning and ending of the roof and its angle.

This sketch also represents the concept of profile.[25] A profile is an outline of an object but it can also reveal the relationship between inside and outside. This relationship allows architects to comprehend how the building meets the sky and how it meets the ground, and the solid/void relationships between the two. Piano's section sketch began a dialogue about how far the humans needed to step up into this building and what that meant for the experience of the space. He has included scale figures to further understand the height of the roof and the volume of the space.

The tall, fast strokes may represent Piano's thinking on the contextual aspects of the project. Since they may have been less defined as architectural elements, he could sketch them in tall, fast gestures. In the project as built, they became structural elements that define space.

FIGURE 8.21

Roche, Kevin (1922)

View of Central Administration Building, Headquarters of Banco Santander, outside Madrid, Spain

The Pritzker Prize jury was insightful when they cited Kevin Roche's architectural design work as innovative. Employing new technologies combined with sensitive design solutions, his architecture constantly questions in a way that is inventive. Roche considers the design of each project on all scales, from the site and interiors, to the details. His elegant solutions have made him one of the most celebrated architects in the United States.

Born in Dublin, Ireland, Roche emigrated to the United States in 1948 and began graduate work at the Illinois Institute of Technology, Chicago. Completing his studies, he joined the firm of Eero Saarinen becoming the principal associate in design (1954–1961). After Saarinen's death in 1961, Roche and colleague John Dinkeloo completed the large number of projects in progress, including the TWA Terminal at John F. Kennedy Airport in New York and Dulles International Airport in Washington, D.C. In 1966 they formed the architectural firm of Kevin Roche John Dinkeloo and Associates.[26]

Besides being honored with the Pritzker Prize in 1982, Roche has been recognized with the Académie d'Architecture Grand Gold Medal (1977); the American Academy and Institute of Arts and Letters Gold 'Medal' Award for Architecture (1990); and both the American Institute of Architecture Gold Medal Award and Twenty-five Year Award (1993, 1995), to name a few of his awards. A selection of projects designed by Roche include: the Metropolitan Museum of Art, New York; the Oakland Museum, California; the Jewish Museum, New York; Bouygues World Headquarters, Paris, France; Shiodome Office Development Complex, Tokyo, Japan; and the Massachusetts Institute of Technology, Zesiger Sports and Fitness Center, Cambridge, Massachusetts.

In addition to all the media architects use to visualize design proposals, Roche writes that he finds 'sketches very helpful in exploring ideas particularly in concert with study models.' Similar to techniques employed by Saarinen's office, Roche studies the spatial qualities of his designs with many types of models, large models, full-scale mock-ups, and three-dimensional details.

This sketch (Figure 8.21) is an early study for the financial complex of Banco Santander outside Madrid, Spain. The complex of buildings has been arranged around a transparent circular structure. Horizontal layers of glass are framed by slender masses which create a contrast between the solid and transparent.

The sketch is small and bold. The few lines give a total impression without corrections or erasures. Roche appears to have outlined the forms in perspective, then to provide volume applied firm parallel lines on shadowed surfaces. The crisp corners of the boxes have been rendered before the pencil became dull, then using a blunt pencil, a few strokes articulate the rectangular planes. This change of texture acts to clearly differentiate the materials.

As a comprehensive view of the building, the sketch conveys a similar amount of detail over the whole image. Wavy lines, where the solid rectangles meet the glass cylinder, suggest the crenulated connection between the layers and the frame. Sketching too fast to define the stepped connection, the continuous line undulates seemingly independent of the horizon lines. This almost organic connection breaks the strong vertical and horizontal elements and reinforces the speed of Roche's thought process.

The sketch proved to be such a true and concise expression that the corporation, Banco Santander, chose to use it as a representative image for the project. It sums up the essence, relationships, and appearance of the building.

67/118   Micro Sofia 95

FIGURE 8.22

Safdie, Moshe (1938)

Exploration Place sketch, Exploration Place Science Museum, Wichita, Kansas

Beginning his architectural career with the celebrated master plan for the 1967 World Exhibition and Habitat '67, Moshe Safdie is an international figure in contemporary architecture, completing projects such as museums, airports, educational institutions, federal courthouses, performing arts centers, and libraries.

Moshe Safdie was born in Haifa, Israel. After moving to Canada with his family, he studied architecture at McGill University. Upon graduating in 1961, he apprenticed with Louis I. Kahn in Philadelphia. He then moved to Montreal, where he became involved with the World Exhibition. In 1970, he established a Jerusalem branch office participating in the rebuilding of that city. There he was responsible for major segments of the restoration of the Old City and the reconstruction of the new center, along with projects such as the Yad Vashem Holocaust Museum and the Rabin Memorial Center.

Safdie has taught at Yale, McGill, and Ben Gurion universities and was Director of the Urban Design Program and the Ian Woodner Professor of Architecture and Urban Design at the Harvard Graduate School of Design. He maintains offices in Boston, Jerusalem, and Toronto. A few of his most renown projects include: Quebec Museum of Civilization, Vancouver Library Square, Telfair Museum of Art in Savannah, Khalsa Heritage Memorial Complex, United States Institute of Peace Headquarters in Washington, D.C., and the National Campus for the Archaeology of Israel in Jerusalem. Safdie has published many books and been the recipient of numerous awards including the Gold Medal of the Royal Architectural Institute of Canada.[27]

This sketch (Figure 8.22) represents an early conceptual design for the Exploration Place Science Center and Children's Museum in Wichita, Kansas. The project is a one hundred square foot building of galleries, theaters, and exhibit space. It is located in downtown Wichita where the Arkansas and Little Arkansas rivers meet. Constructed of toroid geometries that form a series of concave roofs, the exhibition building becomes an 'island' extending into the river and, in contrast, the 'land' building has been inserted deep into the earth.

The sketch shows a series of unarticulated geometric shapes perched on a dark body of wavy lines. Safdie writes that this sketch 'was done at the earliest design phases in which I had concluded that the museum should, in part, be an island within the river, expressive of the component parts of the individual galleries that make up the museum.' The image appears to capture Safdie's first thoughts. Unsure of the shape the future structure would take, the sketch uses light lines to give the gesture of what the building will be. Because of the abstract form, he filled the shapes with color to articulate volumes, most likely to begin to view the combination of parts. The façades have not yet been given windows or materiality, but instead convey the shadows of planes. At this point the pieces could not be viewed as a building, but a suggestion that assisted Safdie in exploring the next iteration.

Rendered with ink and either chalk or crayon, in values of blue and tan, the lines are expressive and brief; few strokes of the pen outline a possible building. The river in the foreground is the most worked feature, showing waves and areas of deep blue. Sensitive to the site, Safdie has chosen to view the building from the river. This emphasizes the strong relationship the building has with its site, and is most likely part of the impetus for the design conception.

FIGURE 8.23

Siza Vieira, Álvaro Joaquim Melo (1933)

Process sketch, Galician Center for Contemporary Art, Santiago de Compostela, Spain

The recipient of numerous awards, including the 1992 Pritzker Prize, this architect is known to the world as Álvaro Siza. His architecture appears to reflect the white boxes of modernism, but upon further inspection, one can view how his buildings inspire through the conscious interplay of form and shadow.

Siza was born in Matosinhos, near Porto, Portugal. He studied at the School of Architecture, University of Porto (1949–1955). Beginning a practice while still in school, he completed his first project in 1954. Many of his early buildings were designed in collaboration with the architect Fernando Távora (1955–1958). Siza's practice, over the last fifty years, has specialized primarily in domestic projects, schools, and exhibition spaces. A few of these buildings include the Bouça Housing Project (1973–1977); a high school, Setúbal (1986–1994); Meteorological Centre in the Olympic Village, Barcelona (1989–1992); Museum of the Serralves Foundation, Porto (1991–1999); and the Portuguese Pavilion for Expo 98, Lisbon (1997–1998). With honors too numerous to fully list, the Portuguese Architects Association gave him the National Prize of Architecture in 1993. Siza has also been awarded with the Praemium Imperiale by the Japan Art Association (1998), Premio Internazionale di Architettura Sacra by *Fondazione Frate Sole* in Pavia (2000), and the International Medal of Arts by Consejera de las Artes in Madrid (2002).[28]

This sketch for the Centro Galego Arte Contemporanea (CGAC – Galician Centre for Contemporary Art) reflects Siza's concern for the exterior massing and façade articulation of this building. He writes that the project represents a study of volumes, materials and language. In this project he is concerned with the small site, and the various scales and significance of the surrounding structures. The program that designated exhibition space, auditorium, and cafeteria and service areas is shown in the separation of volumes by the various functional spaces.

Having viewed several of Siza's design sketches, this sketch (Figure 8.23) conveys his typical process where he stacks numerous perspectives on one sheet. Several of the views show the building from a distance emphasizing how the building sits on the terrain. The variations on a theme overlap where a new thought possessed him, ignoring the image beneath. Not necessarily the result of scarce availability of paper, the dense proximity of the sketches probably allowed Siza to constantly reference either the overall form of the building or the earlier alternative solutions.

The sketches appear to be thoughtful studies rather than first abstract impressions. This shows in the techniques of texture (drawing the separate pieces of granite on the façade) and light accentuating the surface materials. The low perspective angle of the sketch on the upper left demonstrates the monumentality of the bold forms. This study sketch appears to have been concerned with the joining of the volumes and the understanding of solid/void relationships, not necessarily the first organizational diagrams. Each sketch has been thoroughly articulated as if he needed to participate with its construction. This intense ability to see as part of a design process can be connected to understanding as Siza writes: 'There are two different words in Portuguese that mean "to look" and "to see and understand" (*olhar* and *ver*). The tool of an architect is to be able to see.'[29] Less about an immediate impression the sketches contain a certain pondering that reveals their volumetric interaction.

FIGURE 8.24

Soleri, Paolo (1919)

Drawing of an early concept of Arcosanti, April 1971, (from the Paolo Soleri sketchbook #7, page 333), Arcosanti Foundation, Mayer, Arizona

An urban planning theoretician and visionary architect, Paolo Soleri is best known for his work on the Arcosanti, the prototype futurist city being constructed in Arizona. Based on the concept of 'Arcology,' his theory 'advocates cities designed to maximize the interaction and accessibility associated with an urban environment; minimize the use of energy, raw materials, and land, reducing waste and environmental pollution; and allow interaction with the surrounding natural environment.'[30] Born in Italy in 1919, Soleri was educated at the Ecole d'Art Industriel in Grenoble, France. He also attended the Torino Liceo Artistico, Academia Albertina and graduated with a Ph.D. from the Torino Politechnico in 1946. He has been conferred with many honors and awards including the Golden Lion Award, La Biennale di Venezia, and most recently the Commendatore della Repubblica Italiana. He has also received numerous grants and fellowships for research and development by such foundations as the Guggenheim and the National Endowment for the Arts. Soleri has published his provoking sketches in several books.

Soleri writes in his 1971 publication, *The Sketchbooks of Paolo Soleri*, that his sketchbooks

> 'are actually a visual archive of my daily work.'[31] These books are approximately 400 pages each and rendered 'with large ballpoint pens or laundry markers; occasionally pencils or wax crayons are used.'

Soleri writes about the design process evident in the use of his sketchbooks:

> 'A natural question arises: Has the procedure of a "bookkeeping" of the mind influenced the thinking and living process? Probably yes. There is an underlying structure to every life, a structure that can be driven deep into the recesses of the self but also one that can be brought to the surface, or better, can be brought "visually" into the process of life by various devices. The sketchbooks are one of these devices. ... I do not know if I can explain why I work in series. That is to say, every time I develop an idea, I then proceed to conceive a series of variations on the theme. ... Another explanation is that there is no such thing as the complete, final, or perfect response to any challenge, even when the challenge is specific and detailed. As soon as the first idea works itself onto paper, all its scarcely known relatives with different degrees of legitimacy are in close pursuit. So there they come, sketchy and naked, to be picked up again later for reassessment and characterization.'

Soleri has been constantly sketching his theoretical visions for cities. His books of sketches feature interconnected structures within large building complexes. This sketch (Figure 8.24) appears to be part of the structure for Arcosanti, and it is typical of the massive structures that are the foundations of the arcology for his city. The sketch has been rendered freehand with a nearly perfect semicircular dome as the dominant feature. The lines indicate a slow, thoughtful approach. Slightly wavering, they seem to achieve proportion and the relationships of forms to give a general impression of the structure and space. Although sketched carefully to show shadow and detail, many of the forms are misshapen to reveal less concern with the mechanics of the sketch, as some are reworked to find the optimum shape. Sketched in ink, a medium that discourages changes, there are very few 'mistakes.' One might conclude that this was not the first thought, but a sketch that evolved during the making.

NOTES

1. Biographical information provided by Agrest and Gandelsonas Architects.
2. Biography of Tadao Ando and information on the Church of the Light provided by Tadao Ando Architect & Associates.
3. Biographical materials and information on the Cymbalista Synagogue and Jewish Heritage Centre supplied by Mario Botta Architetto.
4. Schizzi di studio, in Botta, M. (1991). *Mario Botta – Schizzi di studio per l'edificio in Via Nizzola a Bellinzona. Spazio XXI.* Arti grafiche A. Salvioni. Sent by Mario Botta Architetto, translated and paraphrased by me.
5. Biography and descriptions of the Tenerife project has been quoted and paraphrased from a publicity statement sent by Calatrava's office.
6. Biography and information on the Nanhai Hotel provided by the office of Chen Shi Min.
7. Biographical and project information provided by COOP HIMMELB(L)AU.
8. Biography of Charles Correa from information provided by his architectural firm.
9. Quotes and paraphrased biographical material provided by Diller + Scofidio + Renfro.
10. Quote and above information from publicity materials provided by Gehry Partners, LLP.
11. Quotes, paraphrased biography, and information on the Vitra Fire Station taken from materials provided by Zaha Hadid Architects.
12. Juror's comments posted on the Pritzker Prize website.
13. Biography of Hiroshi Hara in publicity materials provided by Hiroshi Hara + Atelier.
14. Biography of Zvi Hecker provided by Zvi Hecker | Architect | Berlin.
15. Quote from information provided by Zvi Hecker.
16. Biography of Hans Hollein on the Pritzker Prize website. Information provided by the firm Hans Hollein, Architekt concerning the design for the Guggenheim Museum in Salzburg; articles 'A Guggenheim Museum for Salzburg' by Wieland Schmied, and 'The Museum in the Rock' by Hans Hollein from the publication *The Guggenheim Museum Salzburg* by the Solomon R. Guggenheim Foundation, Zentrum für Kunst und Medientechnologie, Karlsruhe, and Residenz Verlag.
17. Quote and biographical materials provided by Rob Krier. Also information about their current projects from the Rob Krier Christoph Kohl website.
18. Biography provided by Henning Larsen Tegnestue A/S.
19. Information on Ricardo Legorreta, his biography and facts about the UCSF Mission Bay Campus Community Center from publicity provided by Legorreta + Legorreta and his roster of projects from the firm's website.
20. Facts about Greg Lynn's work and quotes by him from publicity and articles sent to me by Greg Lynn FORM.
21. Information on the firm EMBT Arquitectes Associats SL and this sketch from the arcspace website.
22. Biography of Glenn Murcutt on the Pritzker Prize website.
23. Thanks to the Glenn Murcutt Collection, Mitchell Library, State Library of New South Wales for providing this sketch. Copyright permission secured from Glenn Murcutt.
24. Biography and information on Renzo Piano's projects, awards and publications provided by the Renzo Piano Workshop.
25. Seminar with Marco Frascari discussing issues of *cutting, breaking and peeling.* Georgia Institue of Technology, Atlanta, Georgia.
26. Biography provided by the office of Kevin Roche John Dinkeloo and Associates. Additional information was collected from the Pritzker Prize publicity materials.
27. Biography, quotes concerning the sketch by Moshe Safdie, and information on the Exploration Place Science Center and Children's Museum provided by Moshe Safdie and Associates, Inc. Architects and Planners.
28. Biography provided by Alvaro Siza 2 – Arquitecto, LDA.
29. arcspace.com.

30. Arcosanti Foundation publicity materials.
31. Quotes and paraphrased text from the preface of Paolo Soleri's 1971 book, published by the MIT Press, provided by the Cosanti Foundation, 2004.

BIBLIOGRAPHY

Botta, M. (1984). Introduction by Norberg-Schulz, C., text by Zardini, M., edited by Futagawa, Y. (1984). *The Architecture of Mario Botta*. Rizzoli.

Chen, S.M. (1998). *Chen Shi Min: Selected and Current Works*. Images Publishing Group.

De Biasi, P-M. (1996). What is a Literary Draft? Toward a Functional Typology of Genetic Documentation. *Yale French Studies* 89, 26–36.

Eco, U. (1976). *A Theory of Semiotics*. Indiana University Press.

Forster, K.W., Arnold, H.S. and Dal Co, F. (1998). *Frank O. Gehry: The Complete Works*. Monacelli Press.

Gibson, J.J. edited by Reed, E. and Jones, R. (1982). *Reasons for Realism: Selected Essays of James J. Gibson*. Lawrence Erlbaum Associates.

Hans, J.S. (1980). Hermeneutics, Play, Deconstruction. *Philosophy Today*. Winter 1980, 299–317.

Hans, J.S. (1981). *The Play of the World*. The University of Massachusetts Press.

Harpham, G.G. (1982). *On the Grotesque: Strategies of Contradiction in Art and Literature*. Princeton University Press.

Jenny, L. (1996). Genetic Criticism and its Myths. *Yale French Studies*, 89, 9–25.

Kearney, R. (1988). The Wake of the Imagination: Toward a Postmodern Culture. University of Minnesta Press.

Krier, R. (2003). *Town Spaces: Contemporary Interpretations in Traditional Urbanism*. Birkhauser.

Kris, E. and Kurz, O. (1979). *Legend, Myth, and Magic in the Image of the Artist*. Yale University Press.

Robinson-Valery, J. (1996). The Rough and the Polished. *Yale French Studies*, 89, 59–66.

Wollheim, R. (1974). *On Art and the Mind*. Harvard University Press.

Zabalbeascoa, A. and Marcos, J.R. eds (1999). *Miralles Tagliabue: Time Architecture*. Gingko Press.

INDEX